D0924626

PAX ROMANA

by: *jonathan*HICKMAN

IMAGE COMICS, INC.

Robert Kirkman - *chief operating officer* • **Erik Larsen** - *chief financial officer*
Todd McFarlane - *president* • **Marc Silvestri** - *chief executive officer* • **Jim Valentino** - *vice-president*

Eric Stephenson - *publisher* • **Todd Martinez** - *sales & licensing coordinator* • **Jennifer de Guzman** - *pr & marketing director*
Branwyn Bigglestone - *accounts manager* • **Emily Miller** - *accounting assistant*
Jamie Parreno - *marketing assistant* • **Jenna Savage** - *administrative assistant* • **Sarah deLaine** - *events coordinator*
Kevin Yuen - *digital rights coordinator* • **Jonathan Chan** - *production manager* • **Drew Gill** - *art director*
Monica Garcia - *production artist* • **Vincent Kukua** - *production artist* • **Jana Cook** - *production artist*

www.imagecomics.com
International Rights inquiries contact: **foreignlicensing@imagecomics.com**

PAX ROMANA
ISBN: 978-1-58240-873-6
Third Printing

Published by Image Comics, Inc. Office of publication: 2001 Center St., 6th Floor, Berkeley, CA 94704. Copyright © 2013 Jonathan Hickman. Originally published in single magazine form as PAX ROMANA #1-4. All rights reserved. PAX ROMANA (including all prominent characters featured herein), its logo and all character likenesses are trademarks of Jonathan Hickman, unless otherwise noted. Image Comics® and its logos are registered trademarks and copyrights of Image Comics, Inc. All rights reserved. No part of this publication may be reproduced or transmitted, in any form or by any means (except for short excerpts for review purposes) without the express written permission of Image Comics, Inc. All names, characters, events and locales in this publication are entirely fictional. Any resemblance to actual persons (living or dead), events or places, without satiric intent, is coincidental.

Printed in the U.S.A.
For information regarding the CPSIA on this printed material call: 203-595-3636 and provide reference # RICH – 467679

FOR
THE LITTLE KING
AND THE OLD WORM

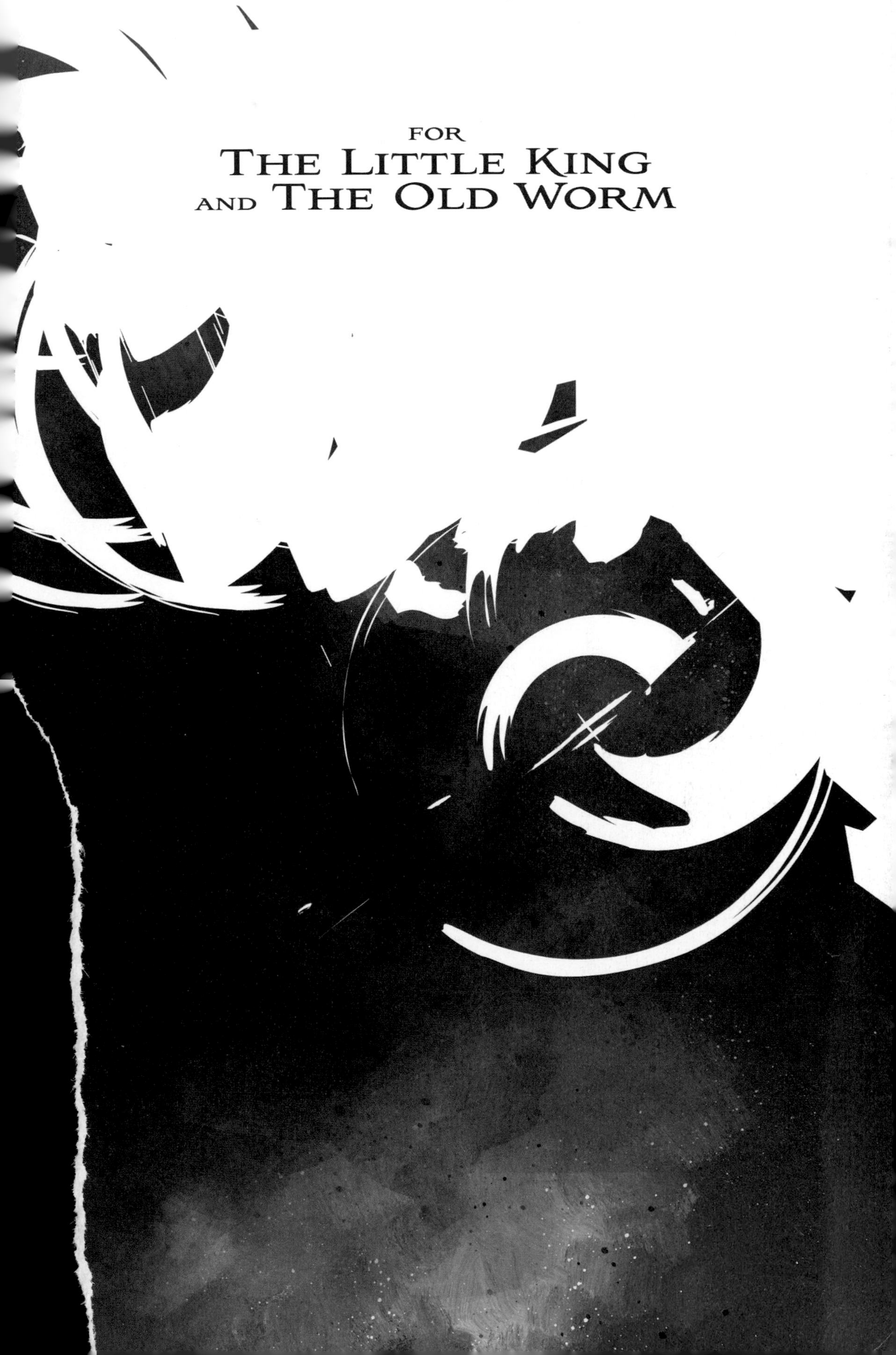

foreWORD

Hyperbole first:

Jonathan Hickman is The *Next Big Thing.*

The next *Warren Ellis.* The next *Frank Miller.* The next *Alan Moore.*

I'm calling it now.

This is why:

The vast majority of new comic book creators make their debut with a variation on a well-established, spandex theme. Superhero comics continue to dominate the sales charts, so on your first outing, you turn to another permutation of capes and cowls, cops and crime, because it's flashy, and marketable, and you might be able to wring a moderate paycheck out of it.

It's also easy. And familiar. And *safe.*

With his first comic, **THE NIGHTLY NEWS**, Jonathan Hickman made something startlingly original and un-commercial, something with a look and tone that was wholly his own. NIGHTLY was stylish, fearless, thought-provoking, meticulously researched and annotated, wildly entertaining, and different.

It was also about blowing journalists' heads off.

Of course, the lazy comparisons to Paddy Chayefsky's *Network* were inescapable. I made them, too.

See, I live in LA, an endlessly smoggy sales floor where every nascent creative idea is ultimately described as a hybrid of other pre-existing works.

"It's a *Dark Knight Returns* approach to *Spider-Man.*"

"It's *Jaws* crossed with *Old Yeller.*"

"It's *High School Musical* meets *Mean Streets.*"

But if Jonathan Hickman's debut bore a faint, thematic resemblance to *Network*, then his follow-up, **PAX ROMANA** defies comparison to any pre-existing content. The comic you're reading right now isn't some easy amalgam. It's a time-travelling, alternate history of the Western World, the tale of a group of mercenaries on an extra-temporal crusade, delivered in the form of an intricate and violent bedtime story told to a child-king. Any attempt to make a cheap, 30-second sales pitch for **PAX ROMANA** is instantly thwarted by its depth and complexity.

It's also a tremendously enjoyable and unpredictable page-turner, and you'll feel smarter for having read it. *I promise.*

More importantly, PAX firmly establishes the "Hickman style": That unique design aesthetic (all that white!). The distinctive color-palette. The detailed graphs, and grids, and footnotes. The challenging, audacious content. And the total inability to phone anything in.

PAX ROMANA proves that NIGHTLY wasn't a marvelous fluke. There's a guiding design principle here -- a visual and narrative signature that's splashed across all of Hickman's work, and it's unlike anything else in comics today. There's something wonderfully rewarding about reading each of Hickman's meticulous footnotes -- you can't help but admire the sheer magnitude of thought -- and wit -- that clearly went into each page of PAX. For God's sake, this comic book serves up entire pages of text -- the transcripts of bureaucratic meetings held in the year 2053 -- and it's still riveting.

So back to that "*Next Big Thing*" part:

With PAX, Hickman has cemented his position as a crea who defies easy comparison. And for those who point to top of this page, where I gleefully anointed Mr. Hick with that most L.A. of superlatives, "The Next Big T and grouped him with other visionaries like Moore, and Ellis, I'd add that the primary thing he has in co with those giants is a wholly singular voice, one th clearly influence comics in the years to come. In fac fairly confident that the term "Hickmanesque" v applied to the inevitable stream of writers and artist embrace elements of his unique style in the next dec

That's right. Poor Hickman, relentlessly original, is ab become part of that hybrid pitch formula when the generation of comics creators come calling. Cong tions, Hickman. Your name is about to become a de

"It's like *PAX ROMANA* crossed with *ROOTS.*"

"It's a Hickmanesque take on *Silence of the Lambs.*"

"Imagine Jonathan Hickman's version of *The Muppe*

So, if you're looking for splashy pages of busty wo bikinis battling ninjas, you're reading the wrong f---in

If you're looking for the future of comics, *welcome ab*

BLAIR BU
Los Angele

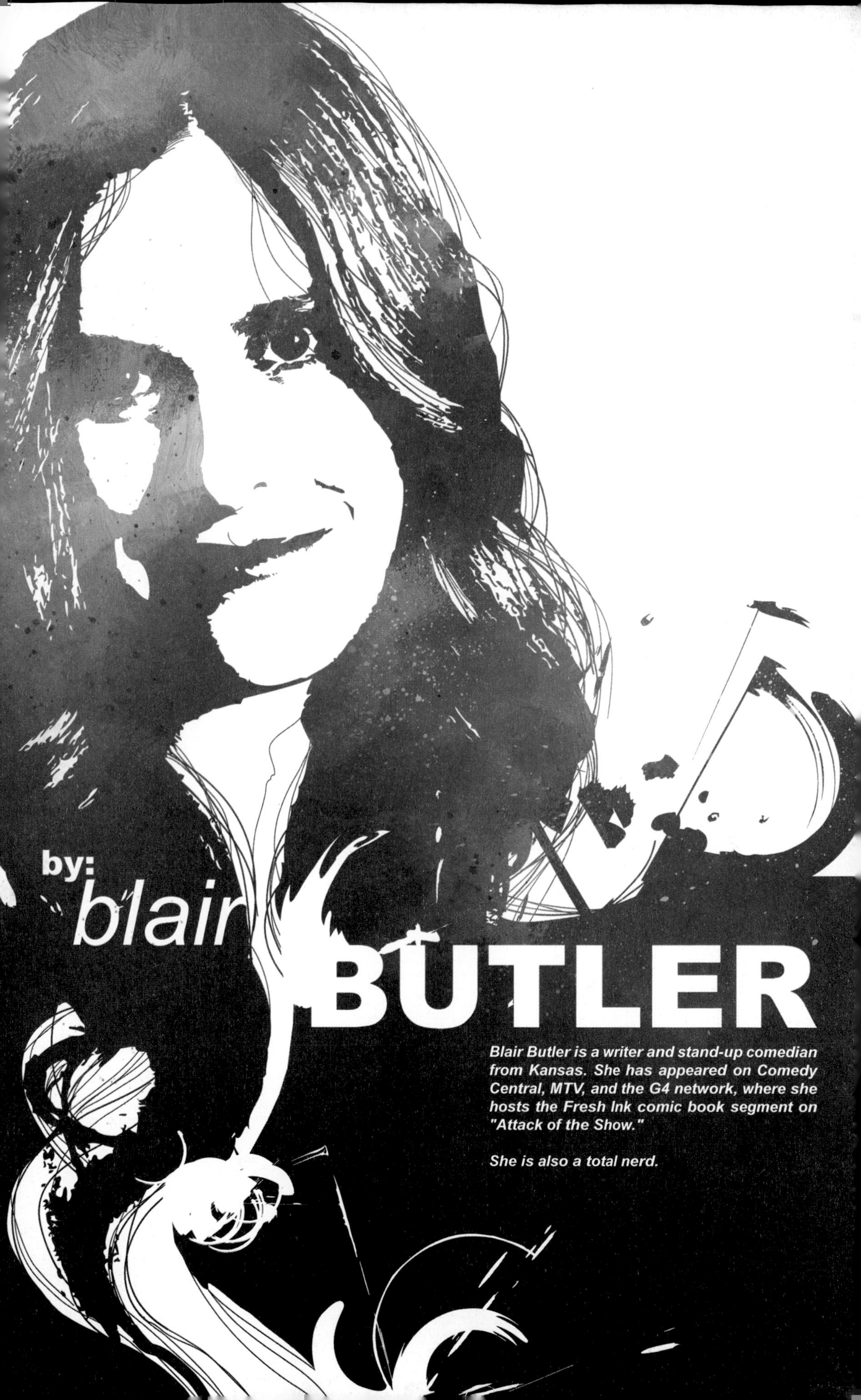

by: blair BUTLER

Blair Butler is a writer and stand-up comedian from Kansas. She has appeared on Comedy Central, MTV, and the G4 network, where she hosts the Fresh Ink comic book segment on "Attack of the Show."

She is also a total nerd.

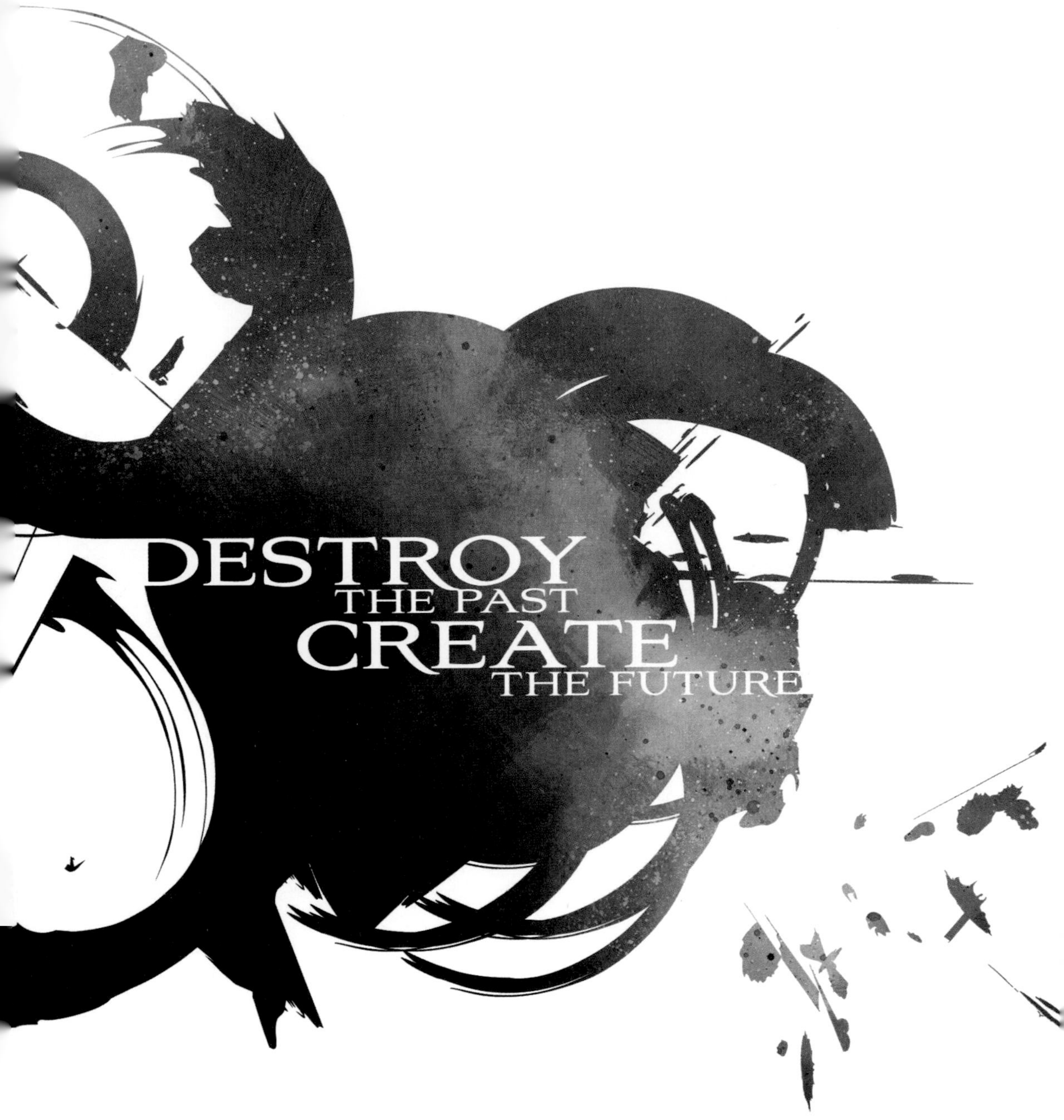
DESTROY
THE PAST
CREATE
THE FUTURE

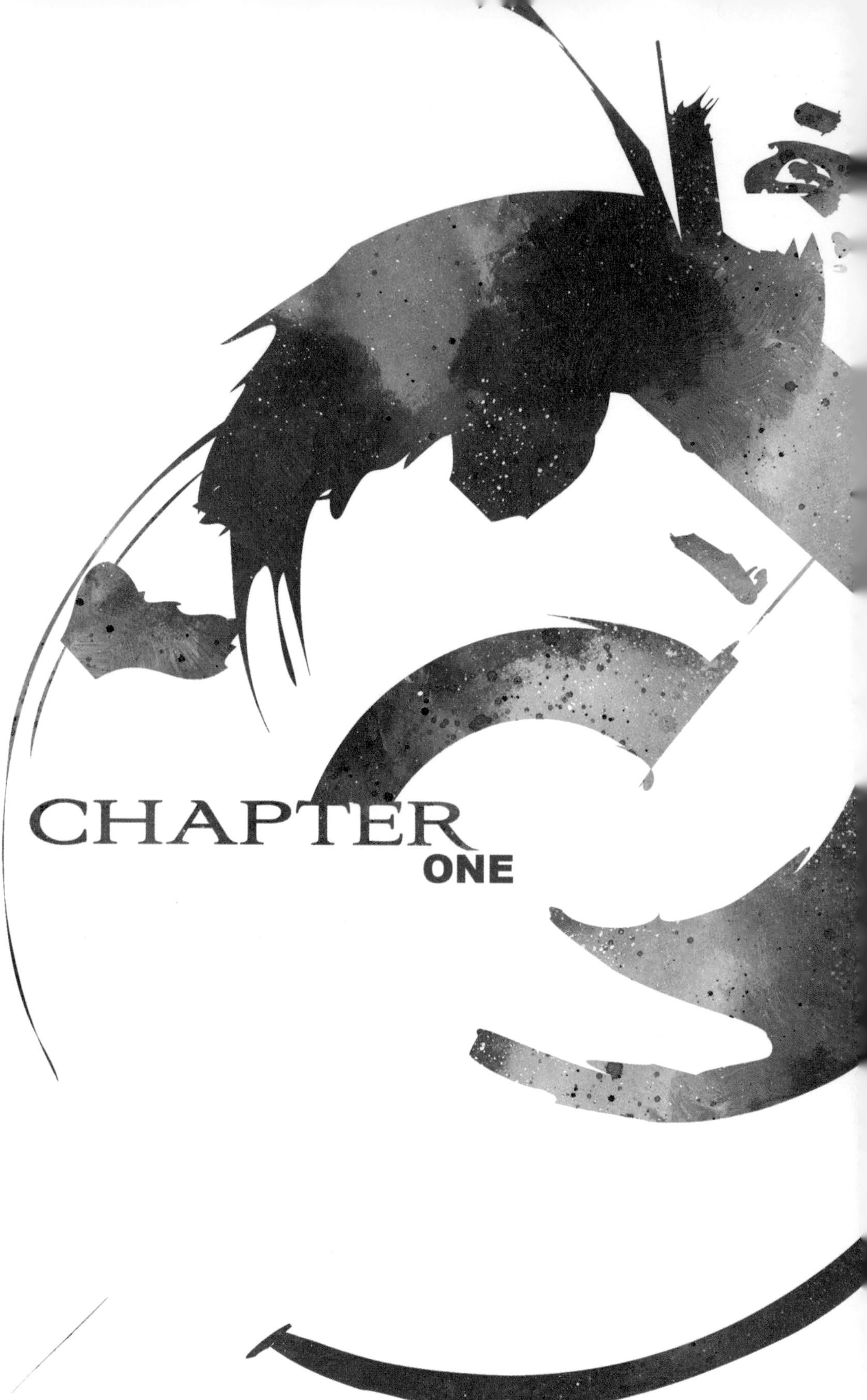

CHAPTER ONE

e megacity Constantinople
st-aurora, before the synthetic rains…

visitor from the Vatican --
at of the Unified Church of
Holy Roman Empire.

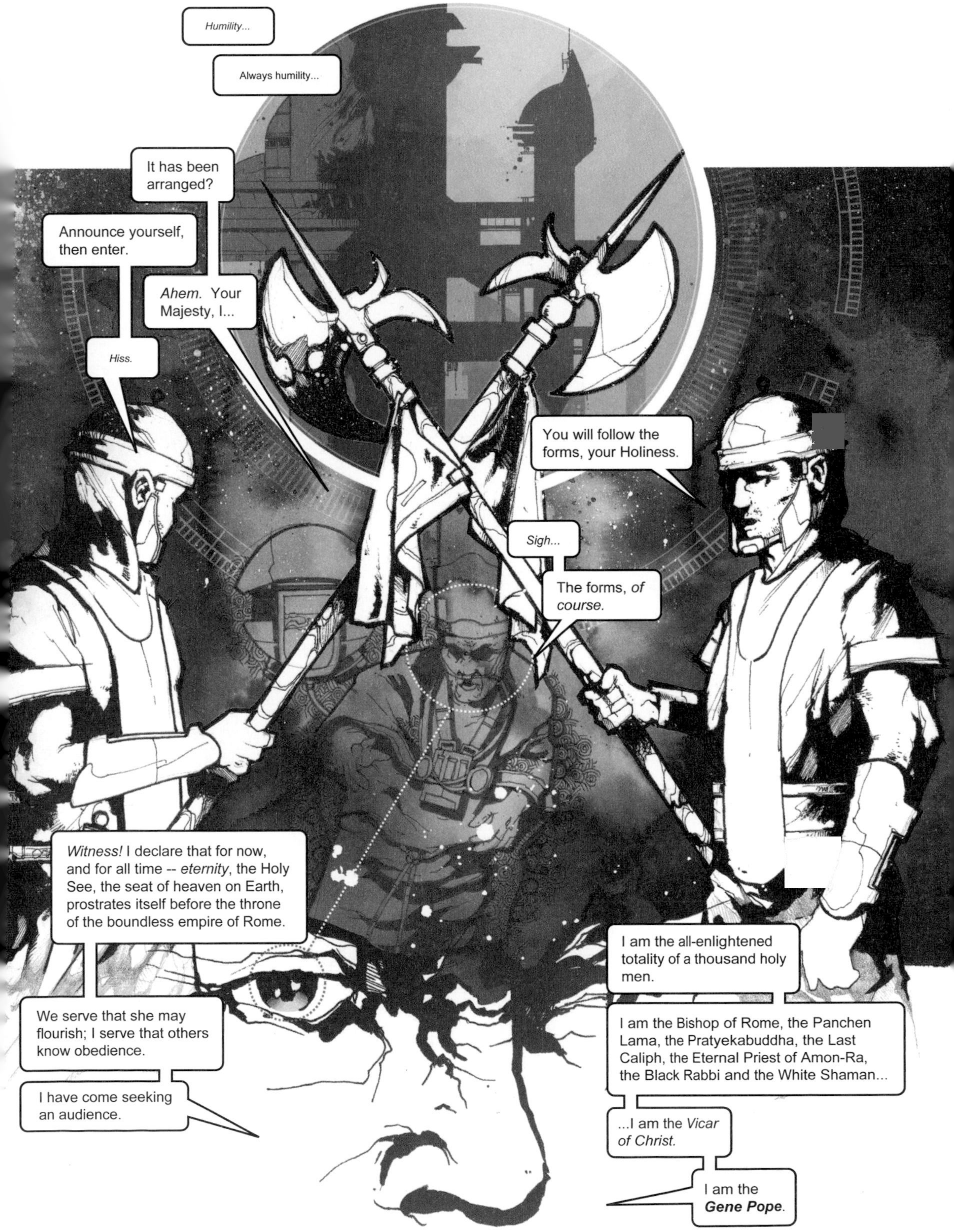

Humility...
Always humility...
It has been arranged?
Announce yourself, then enter.
Ahem. Your Majesty, I...
Hiss.
You will follow the forms, your Holiness.
Sigh...
The forms, *of course.*
Witness! I declare that for now, and for all time -- *eternity*, the Holy See, the seat of heaven on Earth, prostrates itself before the throne of the boundless empire of Rome.
We serve that she may flourish; I serve that others know obedience.
I have come seeking an audience.
I am the all-enlightened totality of a thousand holy men.
I am the Bishop of Rome, the Panchen Lama, the Pratyekabuddha, the Last Caliph, the Eternal Priest of Amon-Ra, the Black Rabbi and the White Shaman...
...I am the *Vicar of Christ.*
I am the ***Gene Pope***.

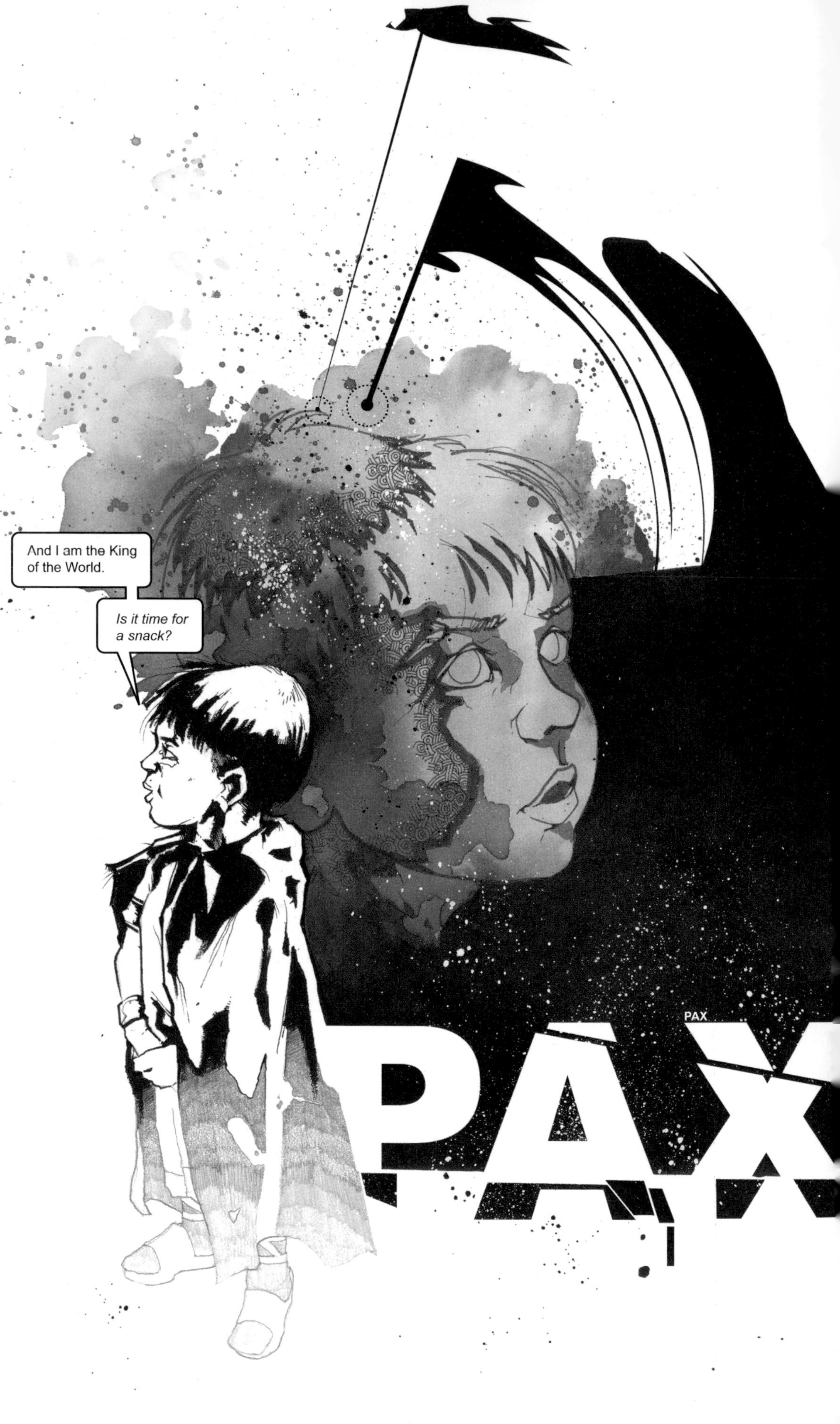
And I am the King of the World.
Is it time for a snack?
PAX
PAX

ROMANA

The Hidden Records

There will be talk of confusion in regards to our purpose. Let that end now!

The choice was ours, and as such, we claim all responsibility. What we did was not for personal glory, honor or some simplistic belief that we are right while so many others are wrong. What we did was for humanity itself.

There are those that believe that all human behavior can be labeled or described (by psychological and anthropological study based on biology and chemistry which themselves are subject to the primordial laws of nature) as primate in nature. We disagree.

We believe that not only is man not limited as such, but his very humanity is marked by his ability to overcome that nature – to go beyond his social and genetic boundaries and realize the vision of a new society.

And if, in the short term, the cost to achieve that is blood, so be it. We will do whatever it takes to destroy the past and create a greater future.

October 29th, 312 AD

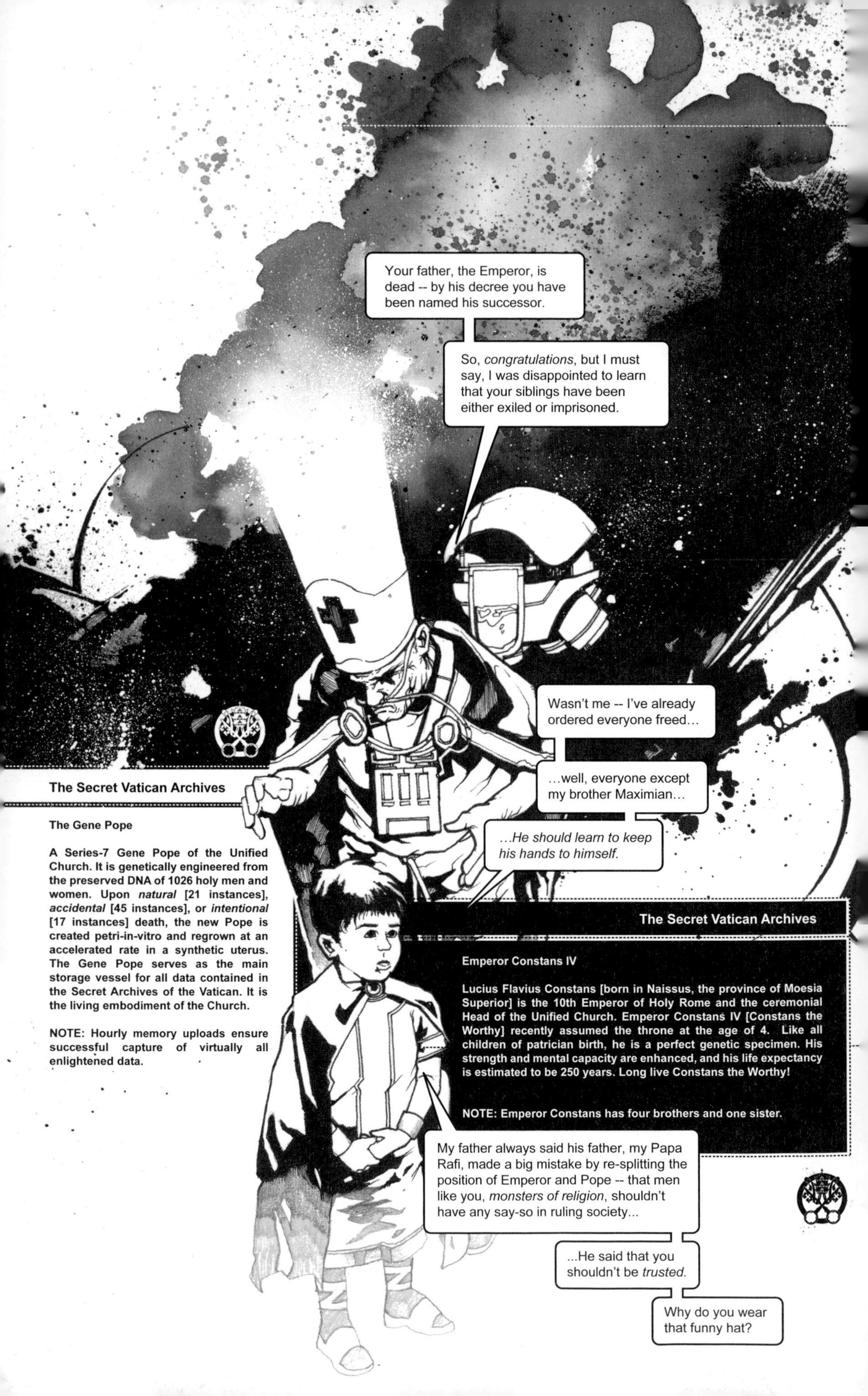

Your father, the Emperor, is dead -- by his decree you have been named his successor.
So, *congratulations*, but I must say, I was disappointed to learn that your siblings have been either exiled or imprisoned.
Wasn't me -- I've already ordered everyone freed…
…well, everyone except my brother Maximian…
…He should learn to keep his hands to himself.
My father always said his father, my Papa Rafi, made a big mistake by re-splitting the position of Emperor and Pope -- that men like you, *monsters of religion*, shouldn't have any say-so in ruling society...
...He said that you shouldn't be *trusted.*
Why do you wear that funny hat?

The Secret Vatican Archives

The Gene Pope

A Series-7 Gene Pope of the Unified Church. It is genetically engineered from the preserved DNA of 1026 holy men and women. Upon *natural* [21 instances], *accidental* [45 instances], or *intentional* [17 instances] death, the new Pope is created petri-in-vitro and regrown at an accelerated rate in a synthetic uterus. The Gene Pope serves as the main storage vessel for all data contained in the Secret Archives of the Vatican. It is the living embodiment of the Church.

NOTE: Hourly memory uploads ensure successful capture of virtually all enlightened data.

The Secret Vatican Archives

Emperor Constans IV

Lucius Flavius Constans [born in Naissus, the province of Moesia Superior] is the 10th Emperor of Holy Rome and the ceremonial Head of the Unified Church. Emperor Constans IV [Constans the Worthy] recently assumed the throne at the age of 4. Like all children of patrician birth, he is a perfect genetic specimen. His strength and mental capacity are enhanced, and his life expectancy is estimated to be 250 years. Long live Constans the Worthy!

NOTE: Emperor Constans has four brothers and one sister.

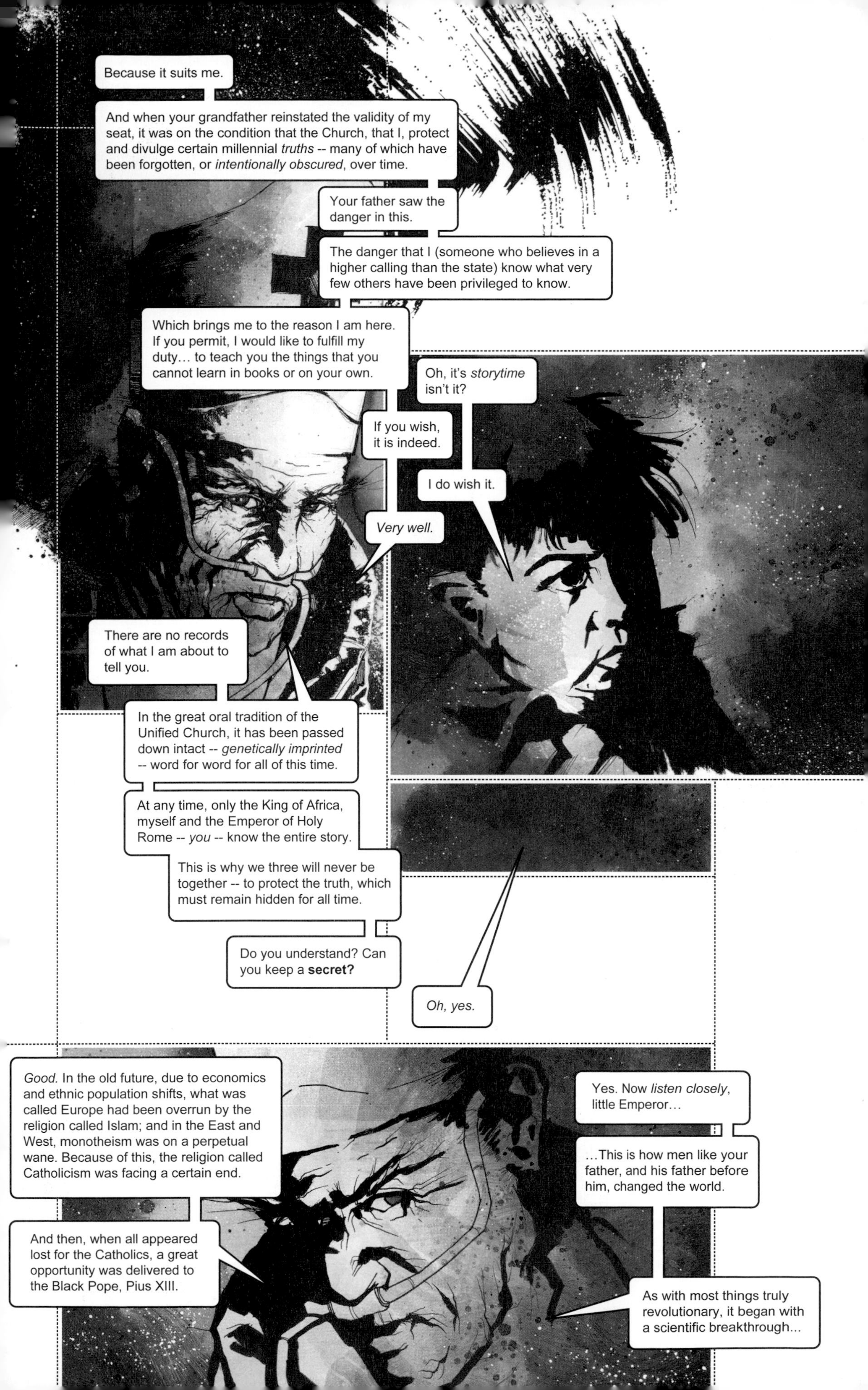
Because it suits me.
And when your grandfather reinstated the validity of my seat, it was on the condition that the Church, that I, protect and divulge certain millennial *truths* -- many of which have been forgotten, or *intentionally obscured*, over time.
Your father saw the danger in this.
The danger that I (someone who believes in a higher calling than the state) know what very few others have been privileged to know.
Which brings me to the reason I am here. If you permit, I would like to fulfill my duty… to teach you the things that you cannot learn in books or on your own.
Oh, it's *storytime* isn't it?
If you wish, it is indeed.
I do wish it.
Very well.
There are no records of what I am about to tell you.
In the great oral tradition of the Unified Church, it has been passed down intact -- *genetically imprinted* -- word for word for all of this time.
At any time, only the King of Africa, myself and the Emperor of Holy Rome -- *you* -- know the entire story.
This is why we three will never be together -- to protect the truth, which must remain hidden for all time.
Do you understand? Can you keep a **secret?**
Oh, yes.
Good. In the old future, due to economics and ethnic population shifts, what was called Europe had been overrun by the religion called Islam; and in the East and West, monotheism was on a perpetual wane. Because of this, the religion called Catholicism was facing a certain end.
And then, when all appeared lost for the Catholics, a great opportunity was delivered to the Black Pope, Pius XIII.
Yes. Now *listen closely*, little Emperor…
…This is how men like your father, and his father before him, changed the world.
As with most things truly revolutionary, it began with a scientific breakthrough...

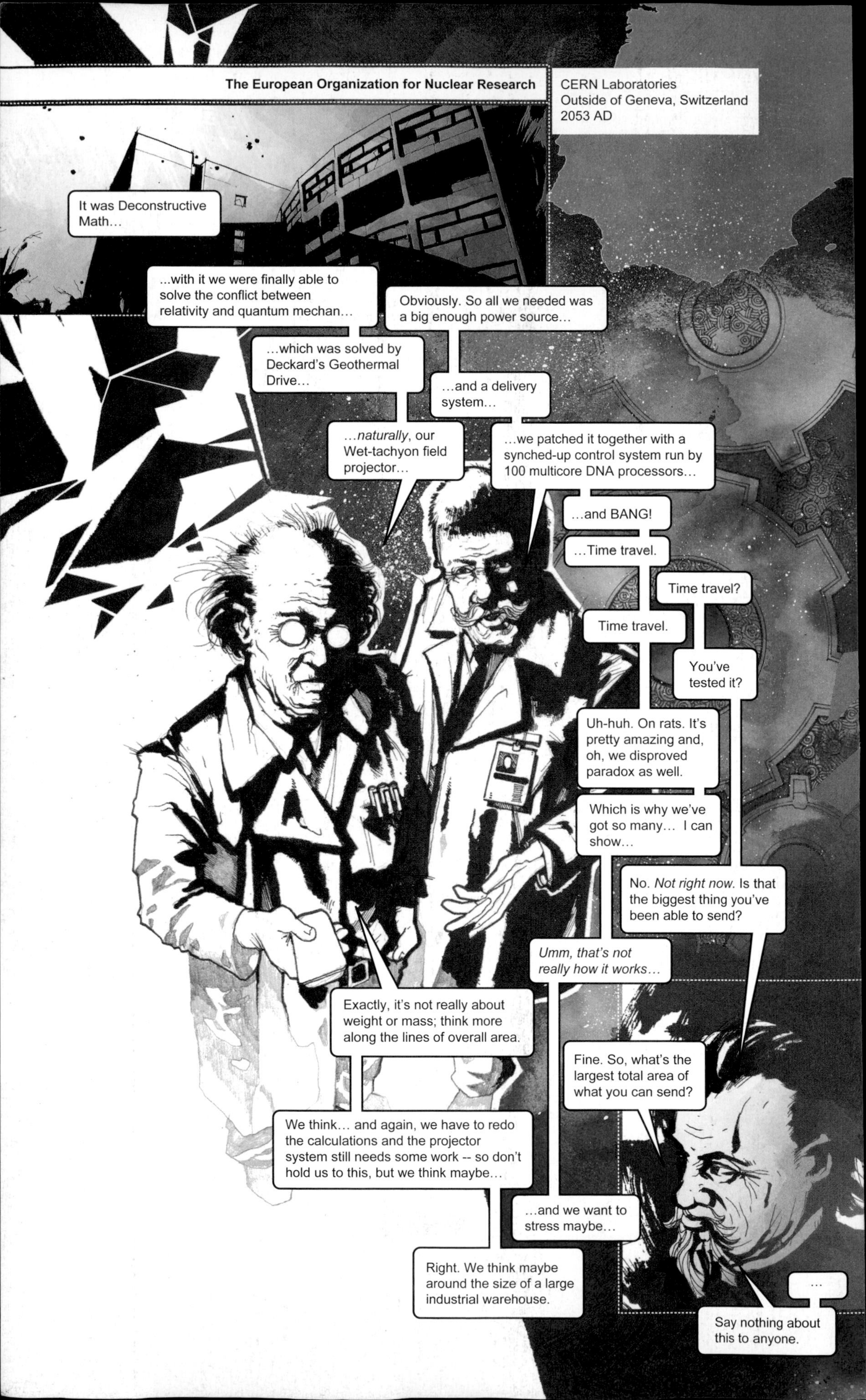
The European Organization for Nuclear Research
CERN Laboratories Outside of Geneva, Switzerland 2053 AD
It was Deconstructive Math…
...with it we were finally able to solve the conflict between relativity and quantum mechan…
…which was solved by Deckard's Geothermal Drive…
Obviously. So all we needed was a big enough power source…
…and a delivery system…
…*naturally*, our Wet-tachyon field projector…
…we patched it together with a synched-up control system run by 100 multicore DNA processors…
…and BANG!
…Time travel.
Time travel?
Time travel.
You've tested it?
Uh-huh. On rats. It's pretty amazing and, oh, we disproved paradox as well.
Which is why we've got so many… I can show…
No. *Not right now.* Is that the biggest thing you've been able to send?
Umm, that's not really how it works…
Exactly, it's not really about weight or mass; think more along the lines of overall area.
Fine. So, what's the largest total area of what you can send?
We think… and again, we have to redo the calculations and the projector system still needs some work -- so don't hold us to this, but we think maybe…
…and we want to stress maybe…
Right. We think maybe around the size of a large industrial warehouse.
…
Say nothing about this to anyone.

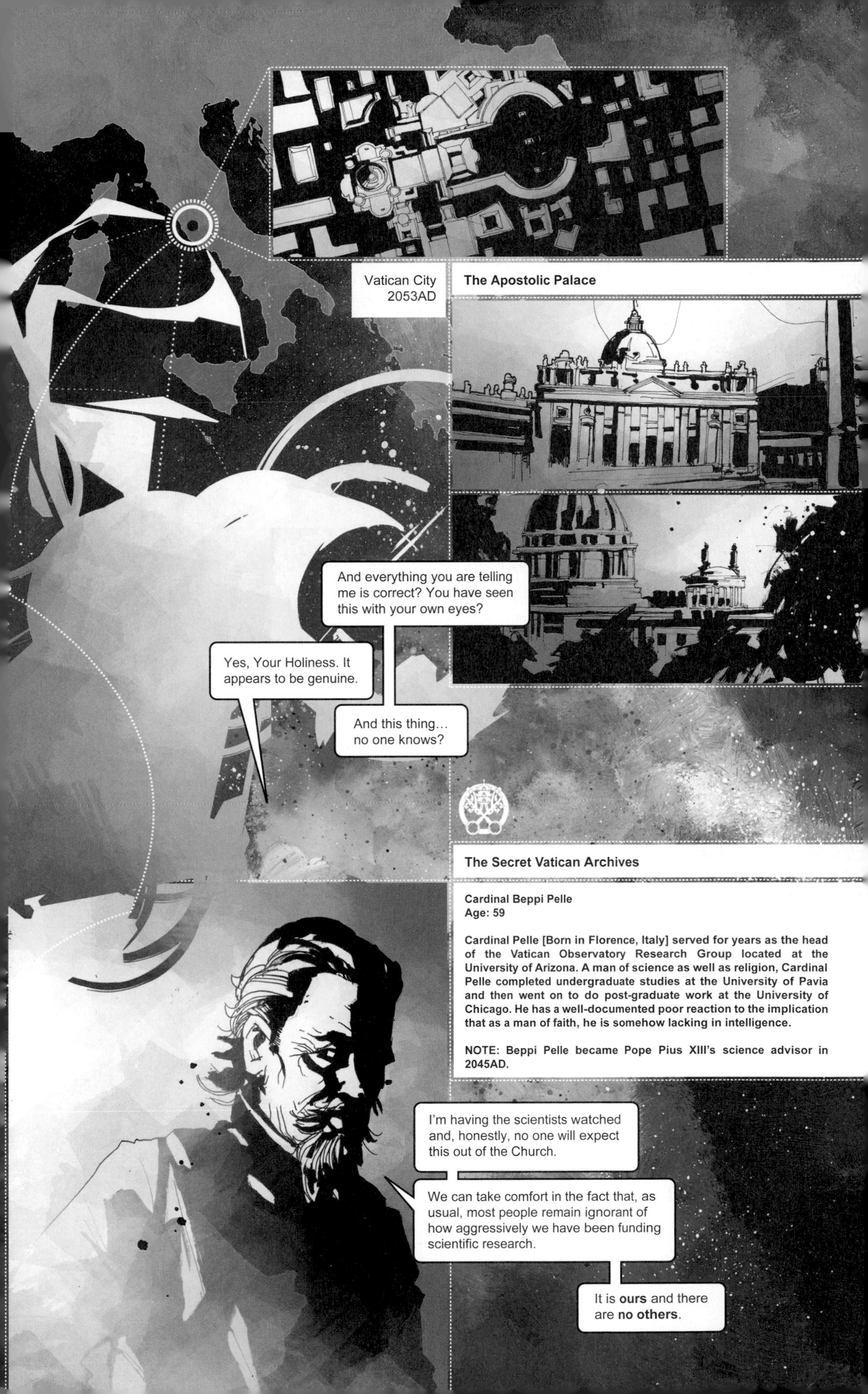
Vatican City 2053AD
The Apostolic Palace
And everything you are telling me is correct? You have seen this with your own eyes?
Yes, Your Holiness. It appears to be genuine.
And this thing… no one knows?
The Secret Vatican Archives
Cardinal Beppi Pelle
Age: 59
Cardinal Pelle [Born in Florence, Italy] served for years as the head of the Vatican Observatory Research Group located at the University of Arizona. A man of science as well as religion, Cardinal Pelle completed undergraduate studies at the University of Pavia and then went on to do post-graduate work at the University of Chicago. He has a well-documented poor reaction to the implication that as a man of faith, he is somehow lacking in intelligence.
NOTE: Beppi Pelle became Pope Pius XIII's science advisor in 2045AD.
I'm having the scientists watched and, honestly, no one will expect this out of the Church.
We can take comfort in the fact that, as usual, most people remain ignorant of how aggressively we have been funding scientific research.
It is **ours** and there are **no others**.

The Secret Vatican Archives

Pope Pius XIII
Age: 81

Paolo Maria Clemente DeCesare [called the Black Pope and born in Modena, Italy] was the second son of philosophy professor Angelo DeCesare and entered the clergy at the age of 24. When Pope Leo XIV suddenly died in 2032AD, Pius XIII was the moderate choice of three compromising factions at the Papal Conclave. A highly intelligent - but up to that point profoundly indifferent - religious historian, he was considered the safe, but somewhat progressive choice.

NOTE: The twenty-four years of his ascendancy are largely considered the second most tumultuous in the history of the Church.

I find the possibility of this remarkably disturbing.

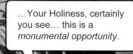

…Your Holiness, certainly you see… this is a *monumental opportunity*.

As you said before you began, Cardinal Pelle.

My initial reaction is to destroy this technology and have the scientists… *removed* from this kind of research. It is too dangerous and much too seductive.

We could make the world a better place.

Could we now?

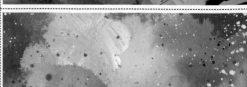

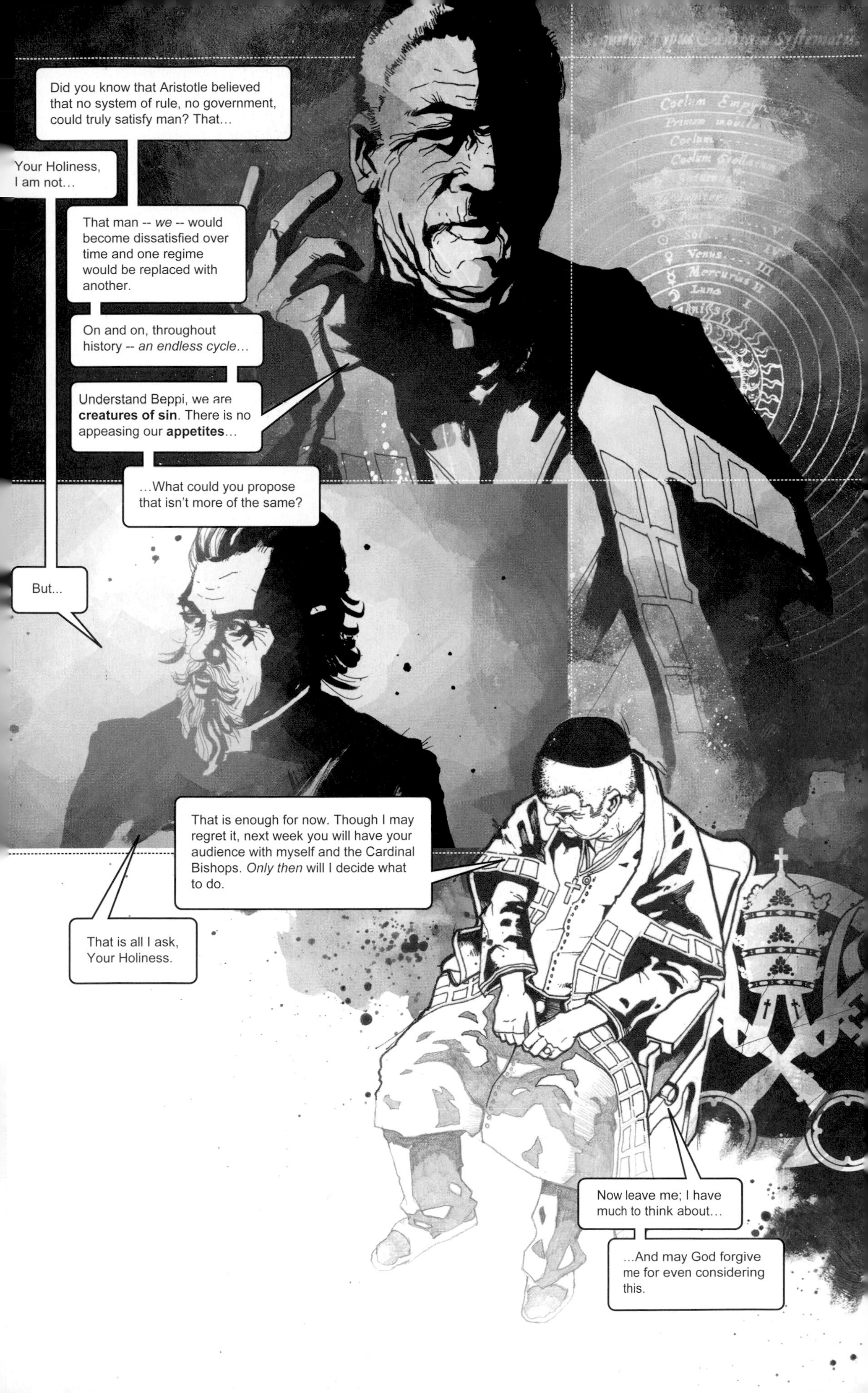

Did you know that Aristotle believed that no system of rule, no government, could truly satisfy man? That…
Your Holiness, I am not…
That man -- *we* -- would become dissatisfied over time and one regime would be replaced with another.
On and on, throughout history -- *an endless cycle*…
Understand Beppi, we are **creatures of sin**. There is no appeasing our **appetites**…
…What could you propose that isn't more of the same?
But...
That is enough for now. Though I may regret it, next week you will have your audience with myself and the Cardinal Bishops. *Only then* will I decide what to do.
That is all I ask, Your Holiness.
Now leave me; I have much to think about…
…And may God forgive me for even considering this.

From April 9th to April 11th, 2053AD, a series of meetings took place at the Vatican between Pope Pius XIII, Cardinal Pelle, and three Cardinals of the Order of Bishops. What began as a conversation about time travel ended with commitment to an extra-temporal crusade.

In attendance:

(PP) - Pope Pius XIII
(EF) - Cardinal Bishop Ennio Fregoso
(KM) - Cardinal Bishop Karl Meisner
(GD) - Cardinal Bishop Giovanni De Giorgi
(BP) - Cardinal Beppi Pelle

These are the relevant excerpts from that meeting in regards to:

The Primary Question

PP: You have all heard Cardinal Pelle's presentation and his, at this point unwarranted, assessment of the opportunities this technology provides the Church. The purpose of this meeting is to arrive at a definitive answer to the question: What should we do?

Is this providence, a gift from God himself, or yet another in the long line of arrogant, Babel-like displays of humanity?

GD: Your Holiness, if I may begin?

PP: Of course, and we are going to be here for quite some time, so while we are flirting with heresy, let's completely break with tradition and temporarily dispose of the honorifics, shall we?

GD: As you wish. I was simply going to say that it is imperative that this discussion not be held in a moral vacuum. We must recognize our current position and, if we remain on this course, the bleak outlook for the Church.

EF: Careful, Giovanni. How much of our current state of malaise is due to the failings of the Church? Is it not right to pay for our past sins?

BP: Do we ignore a greater good out of some pervasive fear of unworthiness? Is this not an opportunity to erase our previous transgressions?

KM: I could be convinced that it is, but might we do more harm than good? Can we guarantee success?

PP: These are exactly the questions we must answer.

Window of Opportunity

EF: Cardinal Pelle, have the scientists said whether there is a range, a limit, to how far we can travel back in time?

BP: They say there is a threshold, but that, in regards to human civilization, it is virtually irrelevant.

EF: So, if hypothetically we are considering this, to when should we go?

GD: The choices would be endless. We could return to before the Great Schism, to before the Crusades or the Reformation. We could return to see Christ on His cross, or to His birth or even before to…

PP: Enough of this! Returning to anytime before the resurrection is unacceptable. We are servants of Christ not collaborators. I will not entertain some grand fundamentalist scheme of an artificial Kingdom of Heaven.

KM: Yes. And it's also worth considering that our resources, while considerable in relation to what would be the contemporary, will be limited.

EF: Ah! We would need a support system to co-opt.

BP: Suggestions?

GD: The First Crusade? To go with Godfrey and end it all then and there?

KM: Vexillum sancti Petri, Giovanni? Up to our ankles in blood in the Al-Aqsa? I would think not. It must be a time before Muhammad and after the resurrection.

GD: Then it must be Rome.

PP: And if it is Rome, then it must be Constantine.

(From left to right: Cardinal Bishop Karl Meisner, Cardinal Bishop Ennio Fregoso, Cardinal Bishop Giovanni De Giorgi, Cardinal Beppi Pelle, Pope Pius XIII)

EF: The stance of the Church is clear on this. Pre-embryonic, prefabricated humans are an abomination -- soulless and unredeemable. Naturally conceived, post-birth enhancements are considered normal medical treatments and are looked on as no different than, say, vitamin supplements. As long as we maintain that distinction, there is no reason not to include, or even prefer, enhanced men and women.

PP: Yes, I approve of the idea behind having a concentrated singular message over what could be five generations of Romans.

EF: Which brings up another concern...

PP: Go ahead.

EF: We have to consider the impact of, *ahem*, cross-breeding with the indigenous population. We will be introducing life-extending genes into bloodlines that should have had none. How will we deal with this?

KM: It must be prevented. In fact, we should look seriously at sterilizing everyone going back. The long-term effects of two groups of people, one with extended life -- the other without, is the unavoidable subjugation of the lesser group.

BP: We've already discussed that this might not be a bad thing. And gelded crusaders, I think not.

PP: I will consider this, but we must not pass over more worthy candidates -- better, more righteous men, in lieu of some perfect-physicality bias.

Military Necessity

EF: And military? Should we even consider this?

BP: What's to consider? We have Swiss Guards outside the very doors to this room. Does that imply that we intend to murder? No. It says that we simply wish to protect ourselves.

KM: You're being foolish. The temptation will be to impose our will. You cannot deny that.

GD: It's worth pointing out, that in many instances, imposing our will might not be the wrong thing to do.

PP: Let's begin with the acceptable idea of a police force. And be assured, it is acceptable, as we would need to protect ourselves from the hoi polloi when we introduce revolutionary ideas like the Earth not being flat and it revolving around the sun. [Laughter]

Genetic Engineering

PP: For the record, on this, our third day on the subject, it seems that we are all, at least temporarily, in agreement to proceed with this idea. Are there any other points to be made?

GD: We have at length spoken about intellectual, moral and theological requirements of the men and women we would send back, what considerations have any of you given to the genetic question?

BP: Yes, should there be a requirement to limit selection to only those possessing enhanced physical attributes?

KM: We are talking about post-birth enhancements - we are certainly not considering the other, correct?

Who Leads

PP: And so we come to the question of who should lead this expedition?

KM: It must be a senior ecclesiastical authority.

GD: Yes, and we agreed on the importance of consistency of message, so it should be someone who has undergone enhancement treatments. This would obviously preclude any of us.

EF: So the question: Who is best suited for this? I would put forth Stuart Wells, Bishop of Conventry as a possible...

BP: [Interrupts] I have begun taking the treatments.

PP: You, Beppi? You want to do this?

BP: Your Holiness, if you would permit the indulgence -- I believe I was born for this. I know it.

PP: You should have been more...

GD: [Interrupts] He has my support.

KM: And mine as well.

PP: How about you, Ennio? Are you in on this manufactured little ambush?

EF: No, Your Holiness, I am not. In fact, I have always thought that Cardinal Pelle was too much of a politician... A bit indulgent... but in this, I believe he will serve us well. He is, after all, the most qualified.

PP: While I have not decided on what parameters this endeavor should be limited by, I have been convinced that it is worth doing -- to right ancient wrongs and enlighten the old world.

So very well, go, Cardinal Pelle, begin preparations for the great journey, and gather to you the very best of our believers.

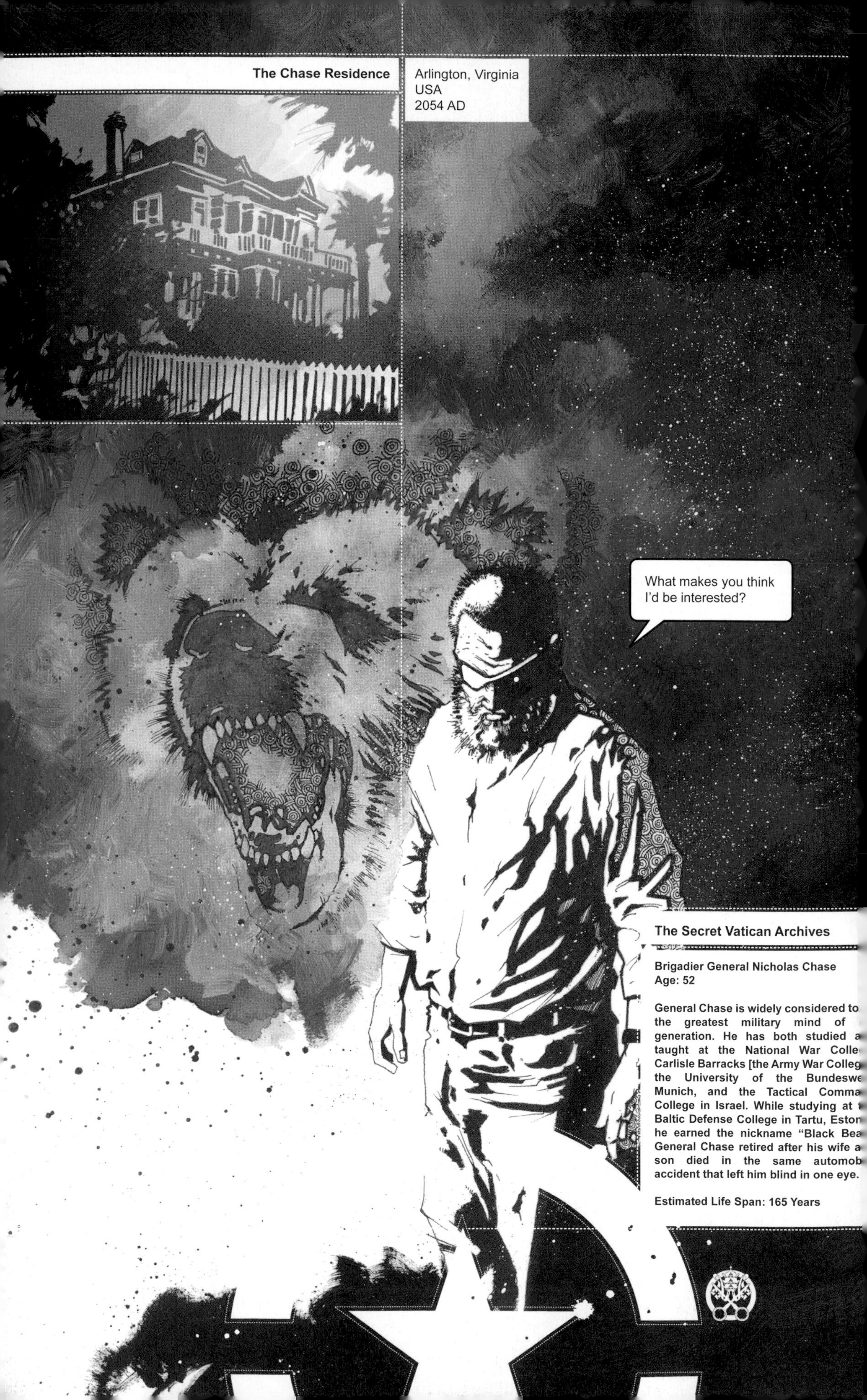
The Chase Residence
Arlington, Virginia
USA
2054 AD
What makes you think I'd be interested?
The Secret Vatican Archives
Brigadier General Nicholas Chase
Age: 52
General Chase is widely considered to the greatest military mind of generation. He has both studied a taught at the National War Colle Carlisle Barracks [the Army War Colleg the University of the Bundeswe Munich, and the Tactical Comma College in Israel. While studying at Baltic Defense College in Tartu, Eston he earned the nickname "Black Bea General Chase retired after his wife a son died in the same automob accident that left him blind in one eye.
Estimated Life Span: 165 Years

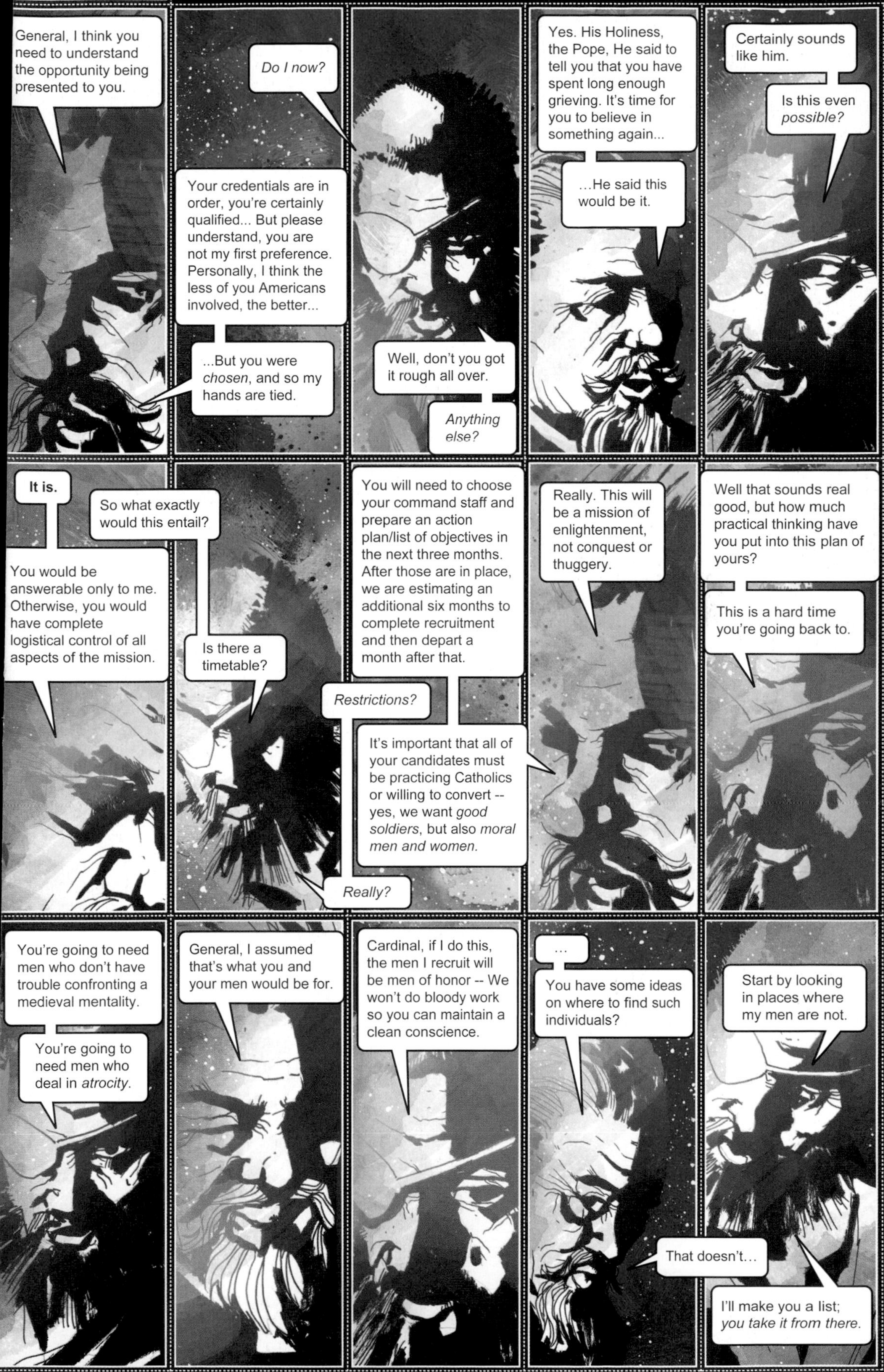
General, I think you need to understand the opportunity being presented to you.
Do I now?
Your credentials are in order, you're certainly qualified... But please understand, you are not my first preference. Personally, I think the less of you Americans involved, the better...
...But you were *chosen*, and so my hands are tied.
Well, don't you got it rough all over.
Anything else?
Yes. His Holiness, the Pope, He said to tell you that you have spent long enough grieving. It's time for you to believe in something again...
...He said this would be it.
Certainly sounds like him.
Is this even *possible?*
It is.
So what exactly would this entail?
You would be answerable only to me. Otherwise, you would have complete logistical control of all aspects of the mission.
Is there a timetable?
You will need to choose your command staff and prepare an action plan/list of objectives in the next three months. After those are in place, we are estimating an additional six months to complete recruitment and then depart a month after that.
Restrictions?
It's important that all of your candidates must be practicing Catholics or willing to convert -- yes, we want *good soldiers*, but also *moral men and women.*
Really?
Really. This will be a mission of enlightenment, not conquest or thuggery.
Well that sounds real good, but how much practical thinking have you put into this plan of yours?
This is a hard time you're going back to.
You're going to need men who don't have trouble confronting a medieval mentality.
You're going to need men who deal in *atrocity*.
General, I assumed that's what you and your men would be for.
Cardinal, if I do this, the men I recruit will be men of honor -- We won't do bloody work so you can maintain a clean conscience.
...
You have some ideas on where to find such individuals?
Start by looking in places where my men are not.
That doesn't...
I'll make you a list; *you take it from there.*

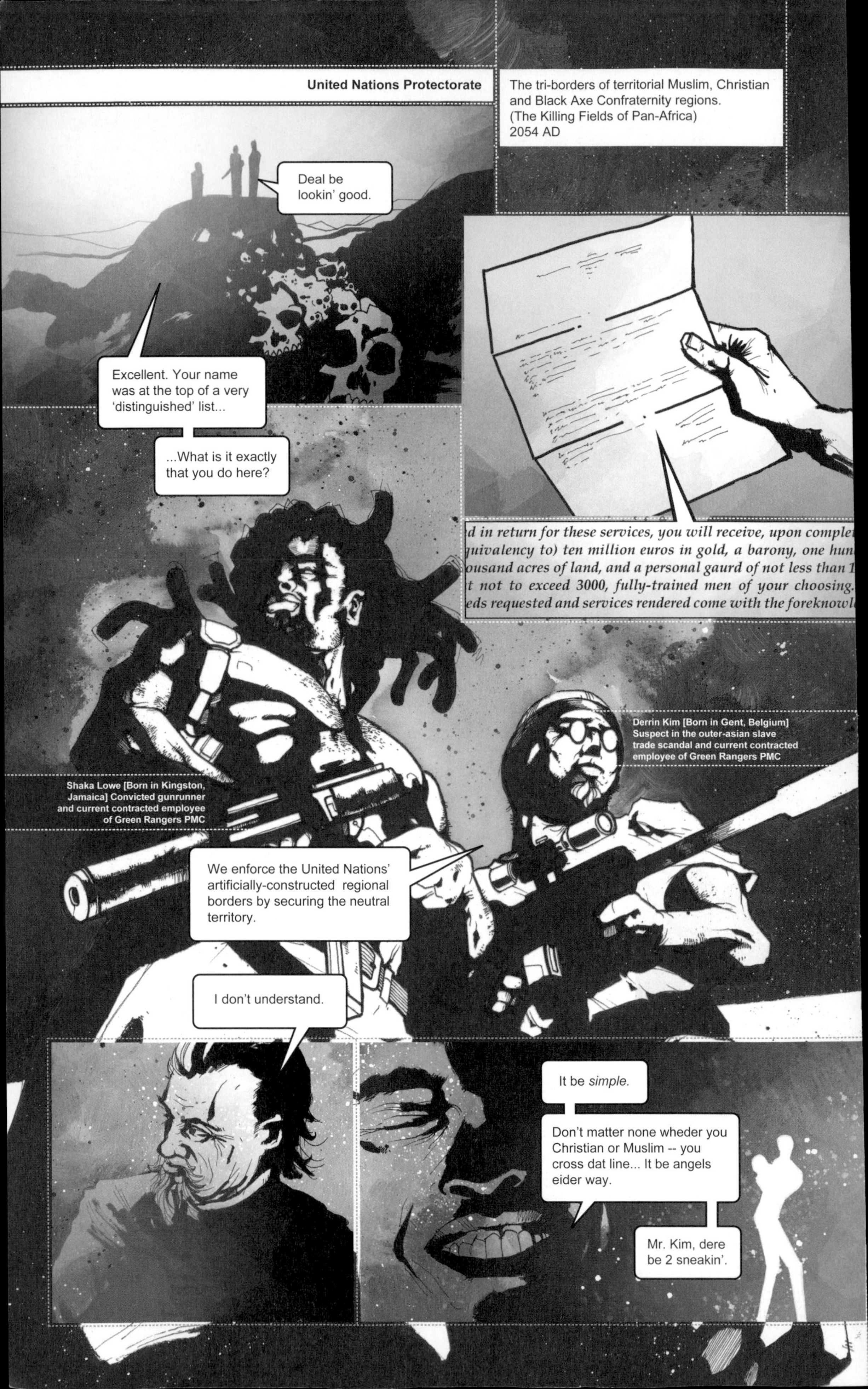
United Nations Protectorate
The tri-borders of territorial Muslim, Christian and Black Axe Confraternity regions. (The Killing Fields of Pan-Africa) 2054 AD
Deal be lookin' good.
d in return for these services, you will receive, upon complet quivalency to) ten million euros in gold, a barony, one hun ousand acres of land, and a personal gaurd of not less than 1 t not to exceed 3000, fully-trained men of your choosing. eds requested and services rendered come with the foreknowl
Excellent. Your name was at the top of a very 'distinguished' list...
...What is it exactly that you do here?
Derrin Kim [Born in Gent, Belgium] Suspect in the outer-asian slave trade scandal and current contracted employee of Green Rangers PMC
Shaka Lowe [Born in Kingston, Jamaica] Convicted gunrunner and current contracted employee of Green Rangers PMC
We enforce the United Nations' artificially-constructed regional borders by securing the neutral territory.
I don't understand.
It be *simple.*
Don't matter none wheder you Christian or Muslim -- you cross dat line... It be angels eider way.
Mr. Kim, dere be 2 sneakin'.

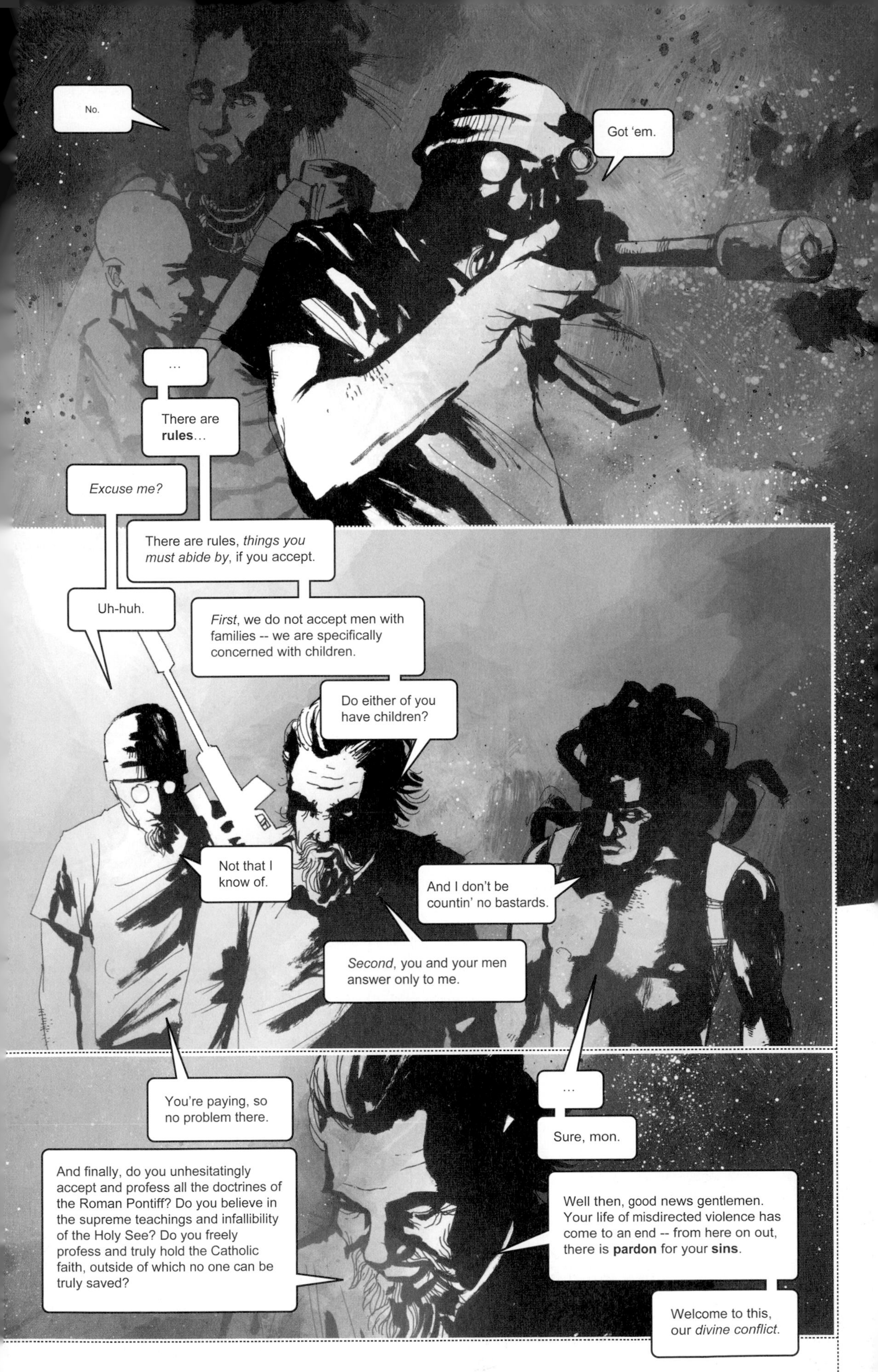
No.
Got 'em.
...
There are **rules**...
Excuse me?
There are rules, *things you must abide by*, if you accept.
Uh-huh.
First, we do not accept men with families -- we are specifically concerned with children.
Do either of you have children?
Not that I know of.
And I don't be countin' no bastards.
Second, you and your men answer only to me.
You're paying, so no problem there.
...
Sure, mon.
And finally, do you unhesitatingly accept and profess all the doctrines of the Roman Pontiff? Do you believe in the supreme teachings and infallibility of the Holy See? Do you freely profess and truly hold the Catholic faith, outside of which no one can be truly saved?
Well then, good news gentlemen. Your life of misdirected violence has come to an end -- from here on out, there is **pardon** for your **sins**.
Welcome to this, our *divine conflict*.

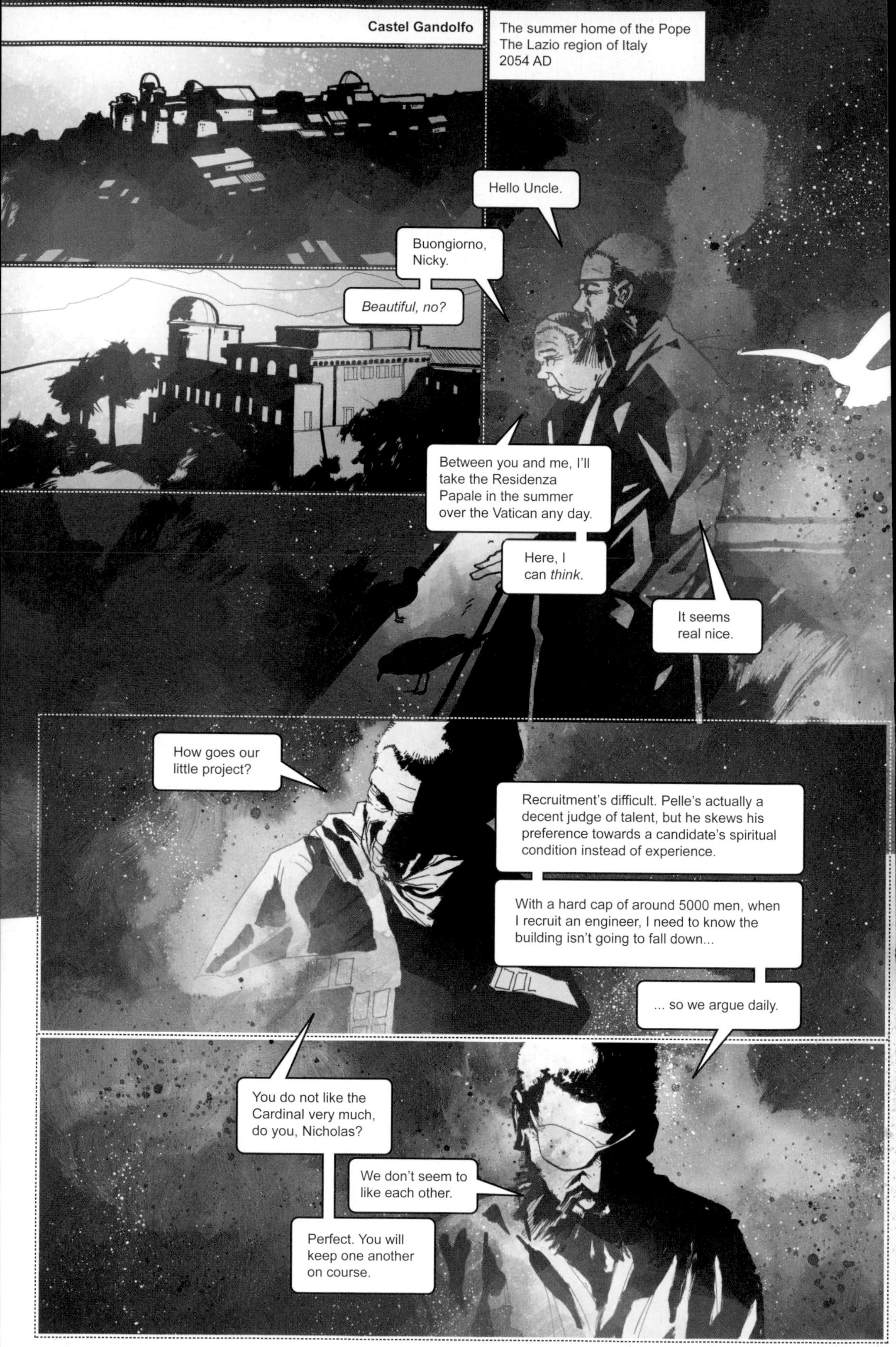
Castel Gandolfo
The summer home of the Pope
The Lazio region of Italy
2054 AD
Hello Uncle.
Buongiorno, Nicky.
Beautiful, no?
Between you and me, I'll take the Residenza Papale in the summer over the Vatican any day.
Here, I can *think*.
It seems real nice.
How goes our little project?
Recruitment's difficult. Pelle's actually a decent judge of talent, but he skews his preference towards a candidate's spiritual condition instead of experience.
With a hard cap of around 5000 men, when I recruit an engineer, I need to know the building isn't going to fall down...
... so we argue daily.
You do not like the Cardinal very much, do you, Nicholas?
We don't seem to like each other.
Perfect. You will keep one another on course.

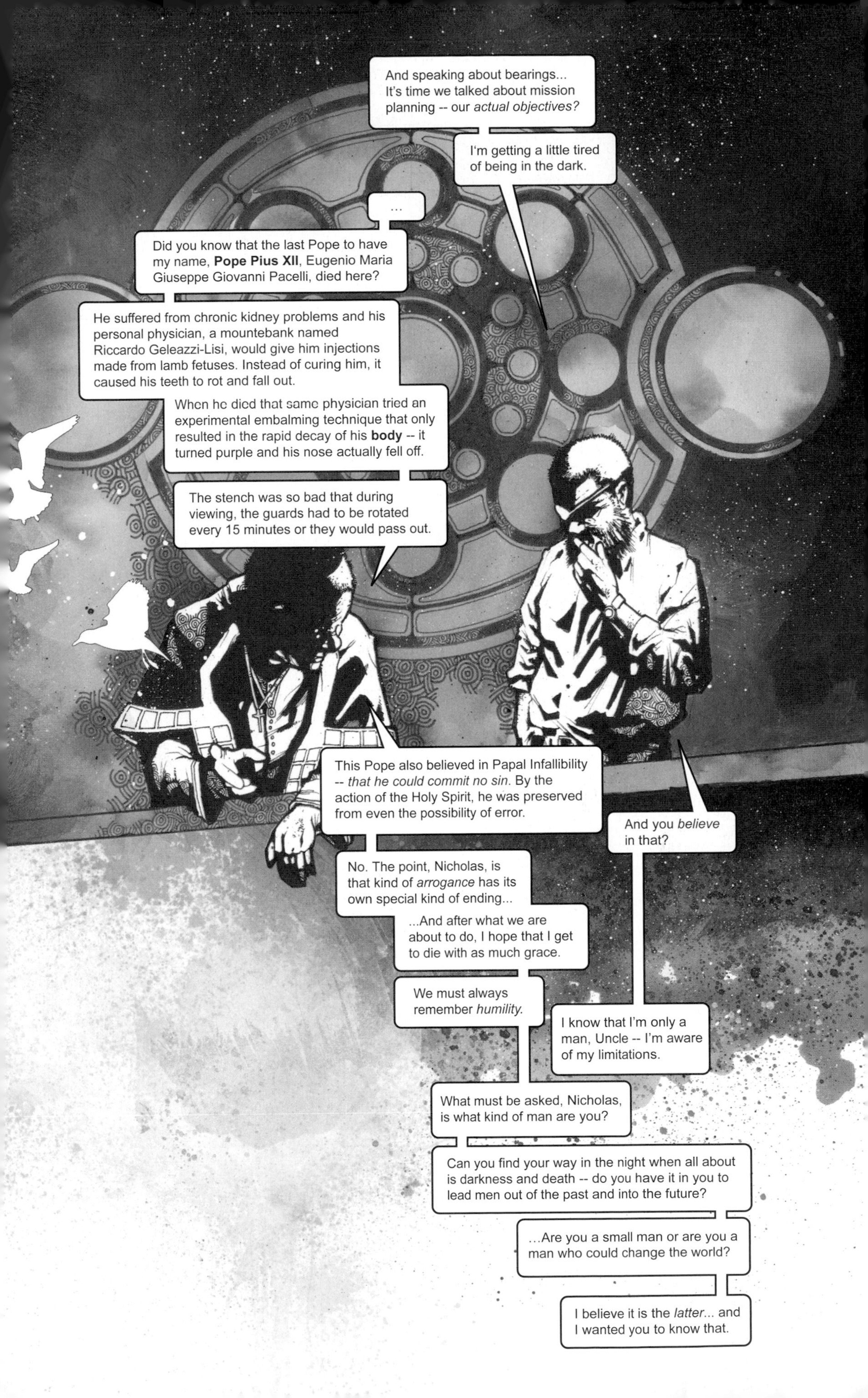
And speaking about bearings... It's time we talked about mission planning -- our *actual objectives?*
I'm getting a little tired of being in the dark.
...
Did you know that the last Pope to have my name, **Pope Pius XII**, Eugenio Maria Giuseppe Giovanni Pacelli, died here?
He suffered from chronic kidney problems and his personal physician, a mountebank named Riccardo Geleazzi-Lisi, would give him injections made from lamb fetuses. Instead of curing him, it caused his teeth to rot and fall out.
When he died that same physician tried an experimental embalming technique that only resulted in the rapid decay of his **body** -- it turned purple and his nose actually fell off.
The stench was so bad that during viewing, the guards had to be rotated every 15 minutes or they would pass out.
This Pope also believed in Papal Infallibility -- *that he could commit no sin*. By the action of the Holy Spirit, he was preserved from even the possibility of error.
And you *believe* in that?
No. The point, Nicholas, is that kind of *arrogance* has its own special kind of ending...
...And after what we are about to do, I hope that I get to die with as much grace.
We must always remember *humility.*
I know that I'm only a man, Uncle -- I'm aware of my limitations.
What must be asked, Nicholas, is what kind of man are you?
Can you find your way in the night when all about is darkness and death -- do you have it in you to lead men out of the past and into the future?
...Are you a small man or are you a man who could change the world?
I believe it is the *latter*... and I wanted you to know that.

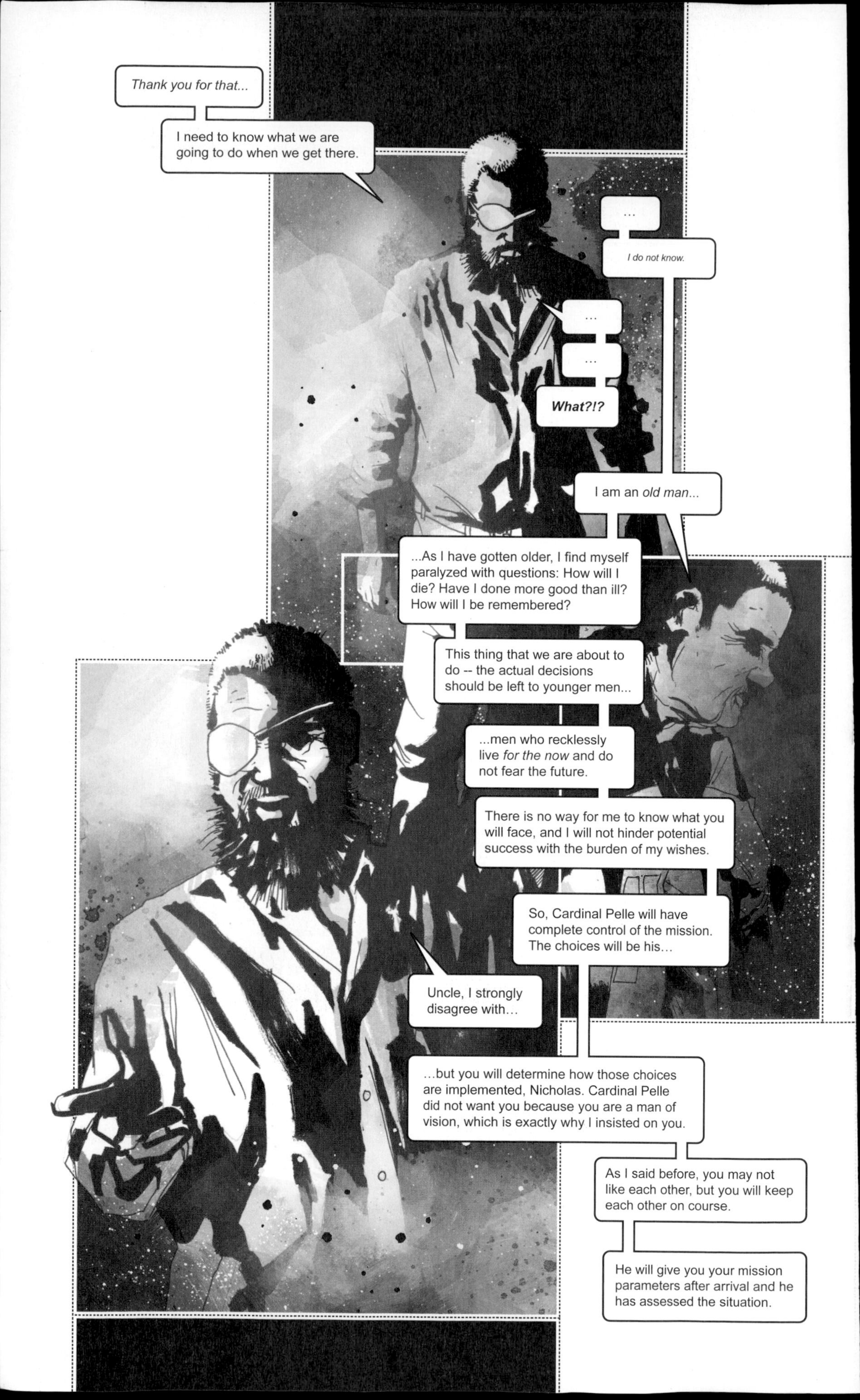
Thank you for that...
I need to know what we are going to do when we get there.
...
I do not know.
...
...
What?!?
I am an old man...
...As I have gotten older, I find myself paralyzed with questions: How will I die? Have I done more good than ill? How will I be remembered?
This thing that we are about to do -- the actual decisions should be left to younger men...
...men who recklessly live for the now and do not fear the future.
There is no way for me to know what you will face, and I will not hinder potential success with the burden of my wishes.
So, Cardinal Pelle will have complete control of the mission. The choices will be his...
Uncle, I strongly disagree with...
...but you will determine how those choices are implemented, Nicholas. Cardinal Pelle did not want you because you are a man of vision, which is exactly why I insisted on you.
As I said before, you may not like each other, but you will keep each other on course.
He will give you your mission parameters after arrival and he has assessed the situation.

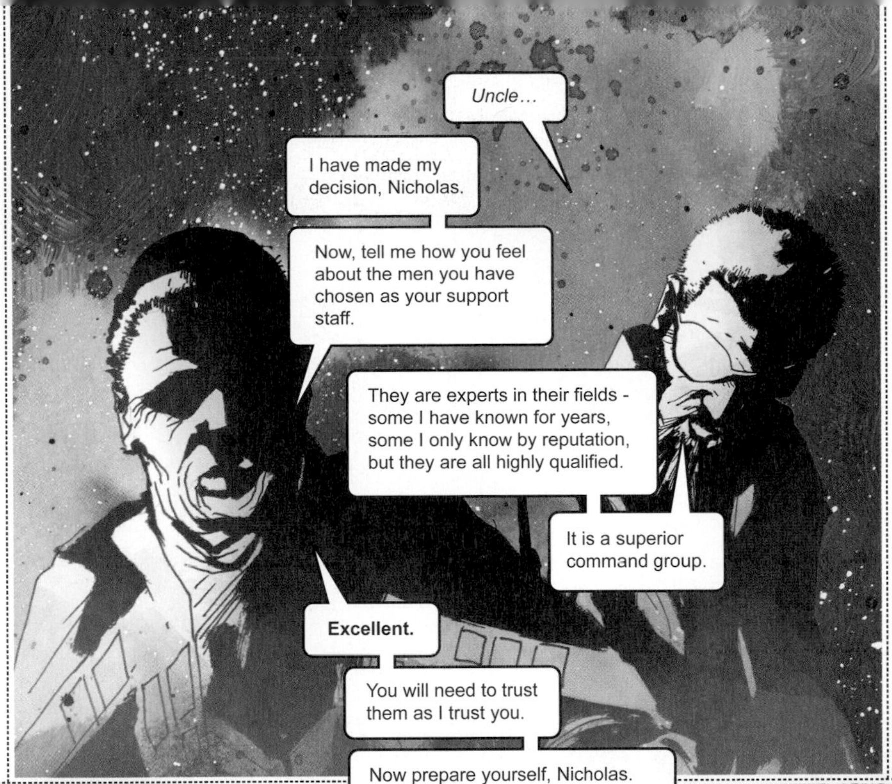
Uncle...
I have made my decision, Nicholas.
Now, tell me how you feel about the men you have chosen as your support staff.
They are experts in their fields - some I have known for years, some I only know by reputation, but they are all highly qualified.
It is a superior command group.
Excellent.
You will need to trust them as I trust you.
Now prepare yourself, Nicholas. It is time for you to make the world a better place.

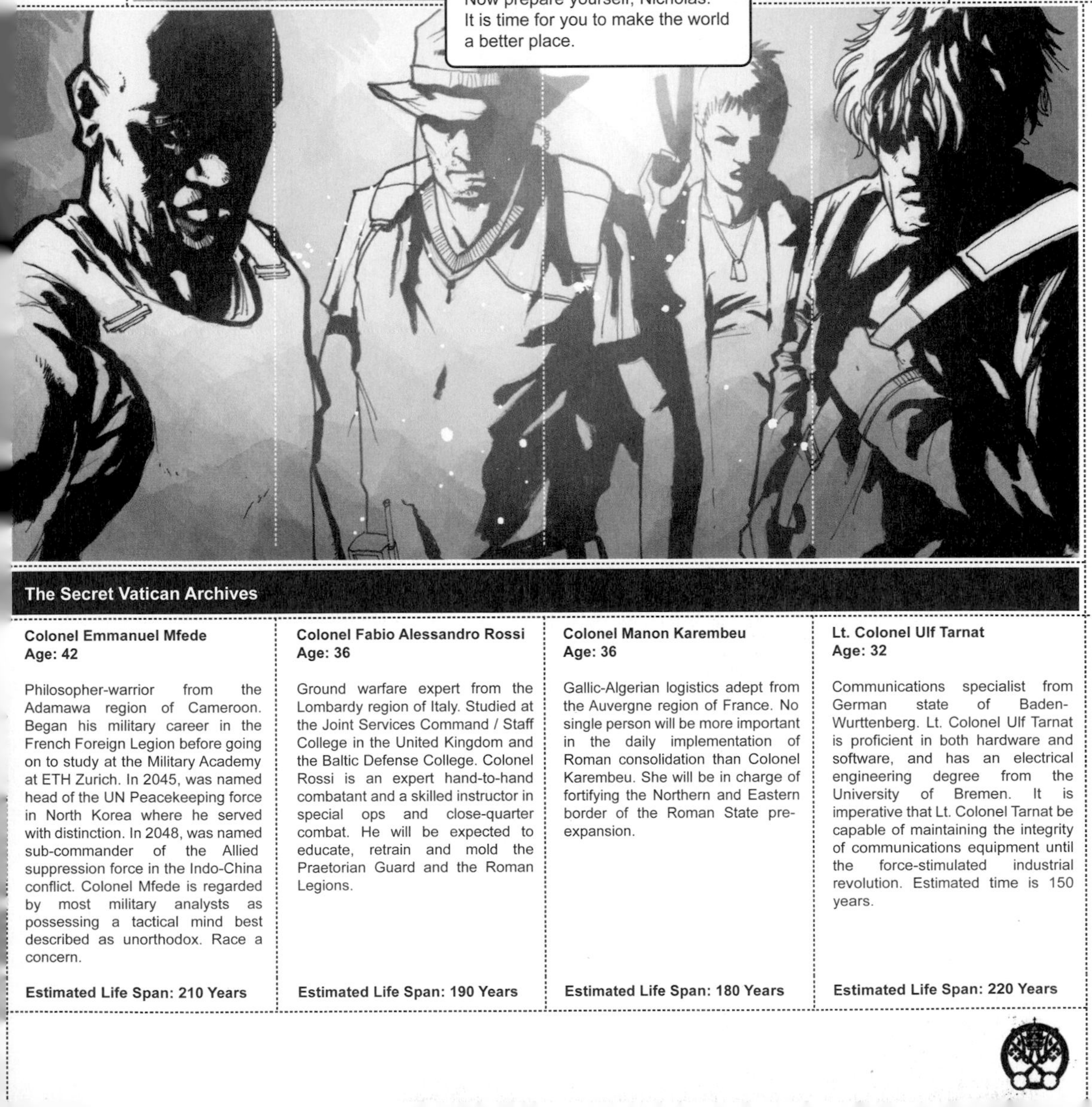

The Secret Vatican Archives

Colonel Emmanuel Mfede
Age: 42

Philosopher-warrior from the Adamawa region of Cameroon. Began his military career in the French Foreign Legion before going on to study at the Military Academy at ETH Zurich. In 2045, was named head of the UN Peacekeeping force in North Korea where he served with distinction. In 2048, was named sub-commander of the Allied suppression force in the Indo-China conflict. Colonel Mfede is regarded by most military analysts as possessing a tactical mind best described as unorthodox. Race a concern.

Estimated Life Span: 210 Years

Colonel Fabio Alessandro Rossi
Age: 36

Ground warfare expert from the Lombardy region of Italy. Studied at the Joint Services Command / Staff College in the United Kingdom and the Baltic Defense College. Colonel Rossi is an expert hand-to-hand combatant and a skilled instructor in special ops and close-quarter combat. He will be expected to educate, retrain and mold the Praetorian Guard and the Roman Legions.

Estimated Life Span: 190 Years

Colonel Manon Karembeu
Age: 36

Gallic-Algerian logistics adept from the Auvergne region of France. No single person will be more important in the daily implementation of Roman consolidation than Colonel Karembeu. She will be in charge of fortifying the Northern and Eastern border of the Roman State pre-expansion.

Estimated Life Span: 180 Years

Lt. Colonel Ulf Tarnat
Age: 32

Communications specialist from German state of Baden-Wurttenberg. Lt. Colonel Ulf Tarnat is proficient in both hardware and software, and has an electrical engineering degree from the University of Bremen. It is imperative that Lt. Colonel Tarnat be capable of maintaining the integrity of communications equipment until the force-stimulated industrial revolution. Estimated time is 150 years.

Estimated Life Span: 220 Years

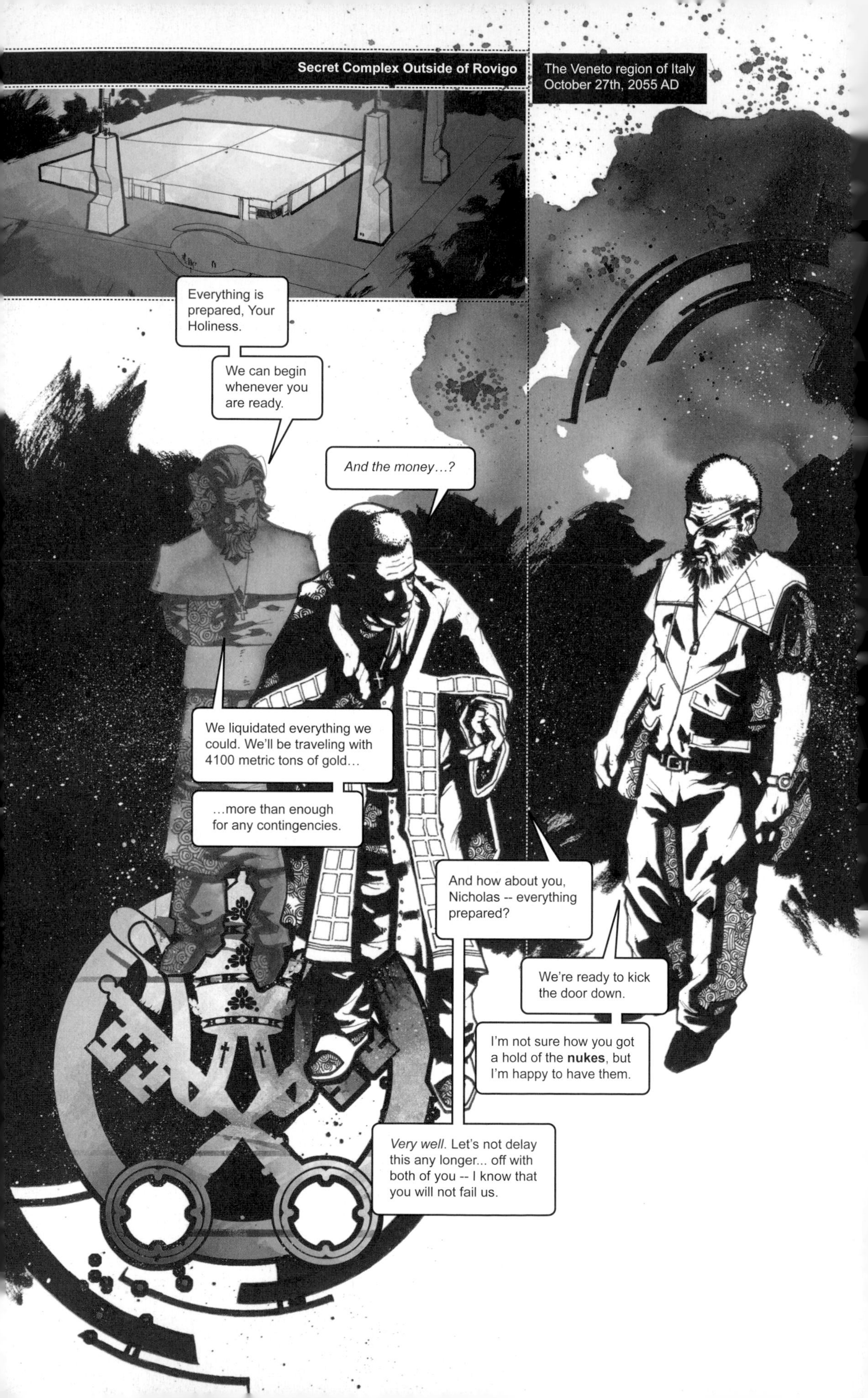
Secret Complex Outside of Rovigo
The Veneto region of Italy October 27th, 2055 AD
Everything is prepared, Your Holiness.
We can begin whenever you are ready.
And the money…?
We liquidated everything we could. We'll be traveling with 4100 metric tons of gold…
…more than enough for any contingencies.
And how about you, Nicholas -- everything prepared?
We're ready to kick the door down.
I'm not sure how you got a hold of the **nukes**, but I'm happy to have them.
Very well. Let's not delay this any longer... off with both of you -- I know that you will not fail us.

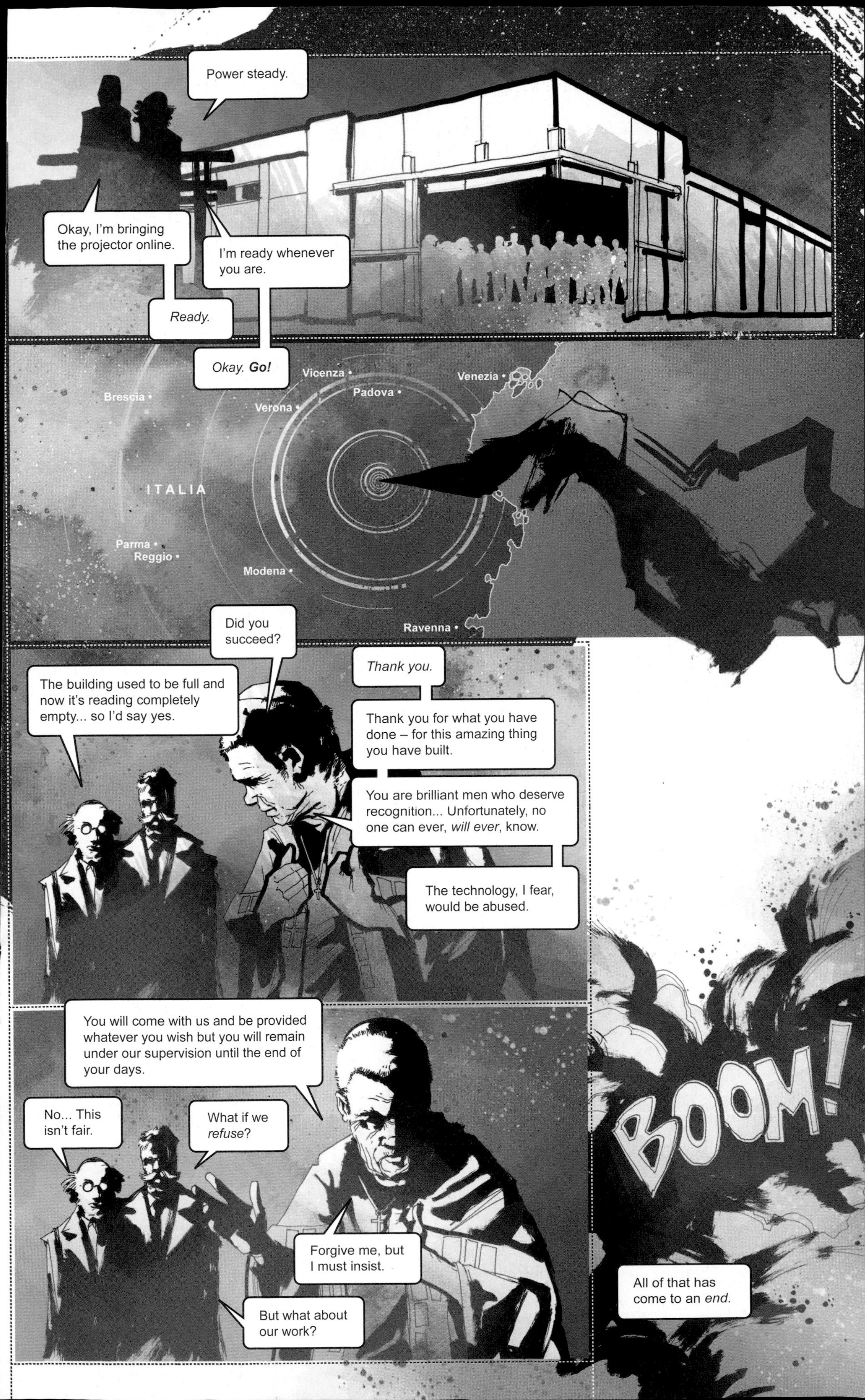

Power steady.
Okay, I'm bringing the projector online.
I'm ready whenever you are.
Ready.
Okay. **Go!**
Vicenza
Venezia
Brescia
Padova
Verona
ITALIA
Parma
Reggio
Modena
Ravenna
Did you succeed?
The building used to be full and now it's reading completely empty... so I'd say yes.
Thank you.
Thank you for what you have done – for this amazing thing you have built.
You are brilliant men who deserve recognition... Unfortunately, no one can ever, *will ever*, know.
The technology, I fear, would be abused.
You will come with us and be provided whatever you wish but you will remain under our supervision until the end of your days.
No... This isn't fair.
What if we *refuse*?
Forgive me, but I must insist.
But what about our work?
BOOM!
All of that has come to an *end*.

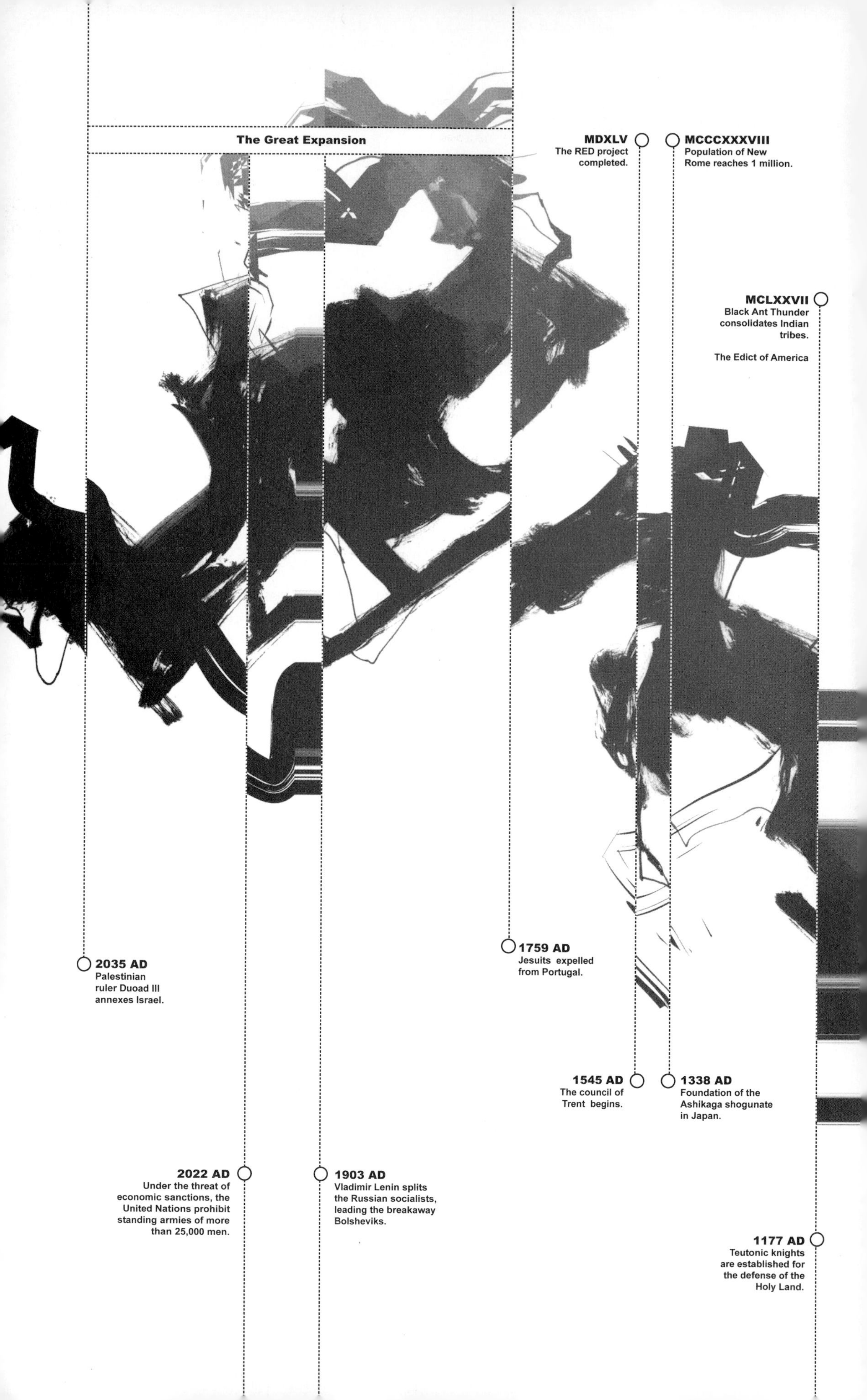

The Great Expansion
MDXLV
The RED project completed.
MCCCXXXVIII
Population of New Rome reaches 1 million.
MCLXXVII
Black Ant Thunder consolidates Indian tribes.
The Edict of America
2035 AD
Palestinian ruler Duoad III annexes Israel.
1759 AD
Jesuits expelled from Portugal.
1545 AD
The council of Trent begins.
1338 AD
Foundation of the Ashikaga shogunate in Japan.
2022 AD
Under the threat of economic sanctions, the United Nations prohibit standing armies of more than 25,000 men.
1903 AD
Vladimir Lenin splits the Russian socialists, leading the breakaway Bolsheviks.
1177 AD
Teutonic knights are established for the defense of the Holy Land.

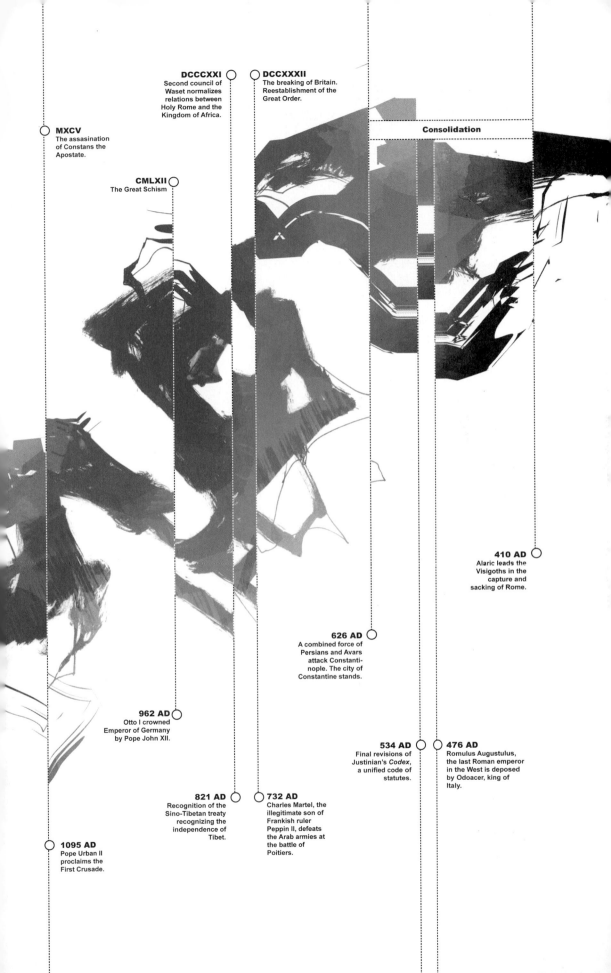

MXCV
The assasination
of Constans the
Apostate.

DCCCXXI
Second council of
Waset normalizes
relations between
Holy Rome and the
Kingdom of Africa.

DCCXXXII
The breaking of Britain.
Reestablishment of the
Great Order.

Consolidation

CMLXII
The Great Schism

410 AD
Alaric leads the
Visigoths in the
capture and
sacking of Rome.

626 AD
A combined force of
Persians and Avars
attack Constanti-
nople. The city of
Constantine stands.

962 AD
Otto I crowned
Emperor of Germany
by Pope John XII.

534 AD
Final revisions of
Justinian's *Codex*,
a unified code of
statutes.

476 AD
Romulus Augustulus,
the last Roman emperor
in the West is deposed
by Odoacer, king of
Italy.

821 AD
Recognition of the
Sino-Tibetan treaty
recognizing the
independence of
Tibet.

732 AD
Charles Martel, the
illegitimate son of
Frankish ruler
Peppin II, defeats
the Arab armies at
the battle of
Poitiers.

1095 AD
Pope Urban II
proclaims the
First Crusade.

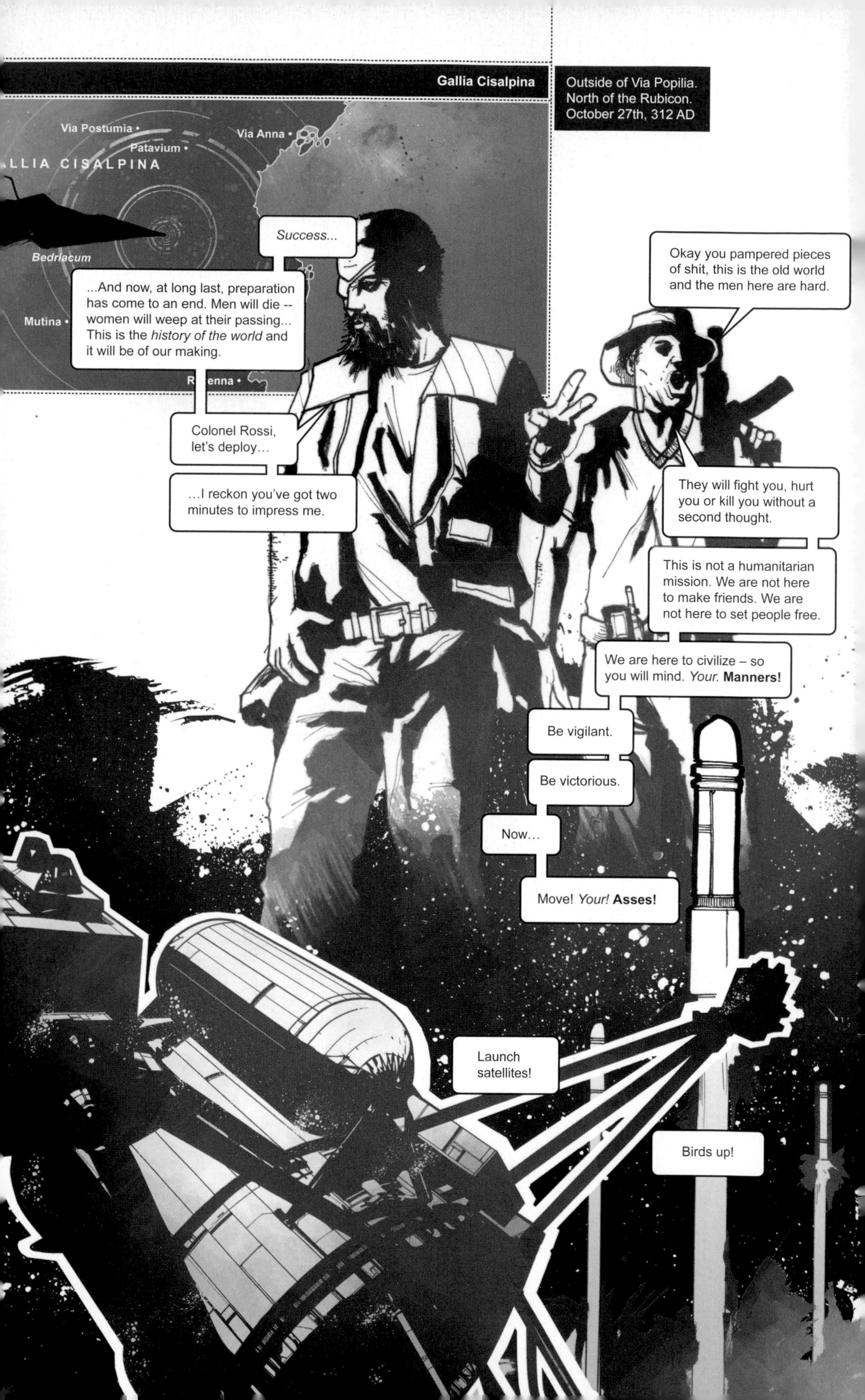
Gallia Cisalpina
Outside of Via Popilia.
North of the Rubicon.
October 27th, 312 AD
Via Postumia •
Via Anna •
Patavium •
LLIA CISALPINA
Bedriacum
Mutina •
Success...
...And now, at long last, preparation has come to an end. Men will die -- women will weep at their passing... This is the *history of the world* and it will be of our making.
Colonel Rossi, let's deploy…
…I reckon you've got two minutes to impress me.
Okay you pampered pieces of shit, this is the old world and the men here are hard.
They will fight you, hurt you or kill you without a second thought.
This is not a humanitarian mission. We are not here to make friends. We are not here to set people free.
We are here to civilize – so you will mind. *Your.* **Manners!**
Be vigilant.
Be victorious.
Now…
Move! *Your!* **Asses!**
Launch satellites!
Birds up!

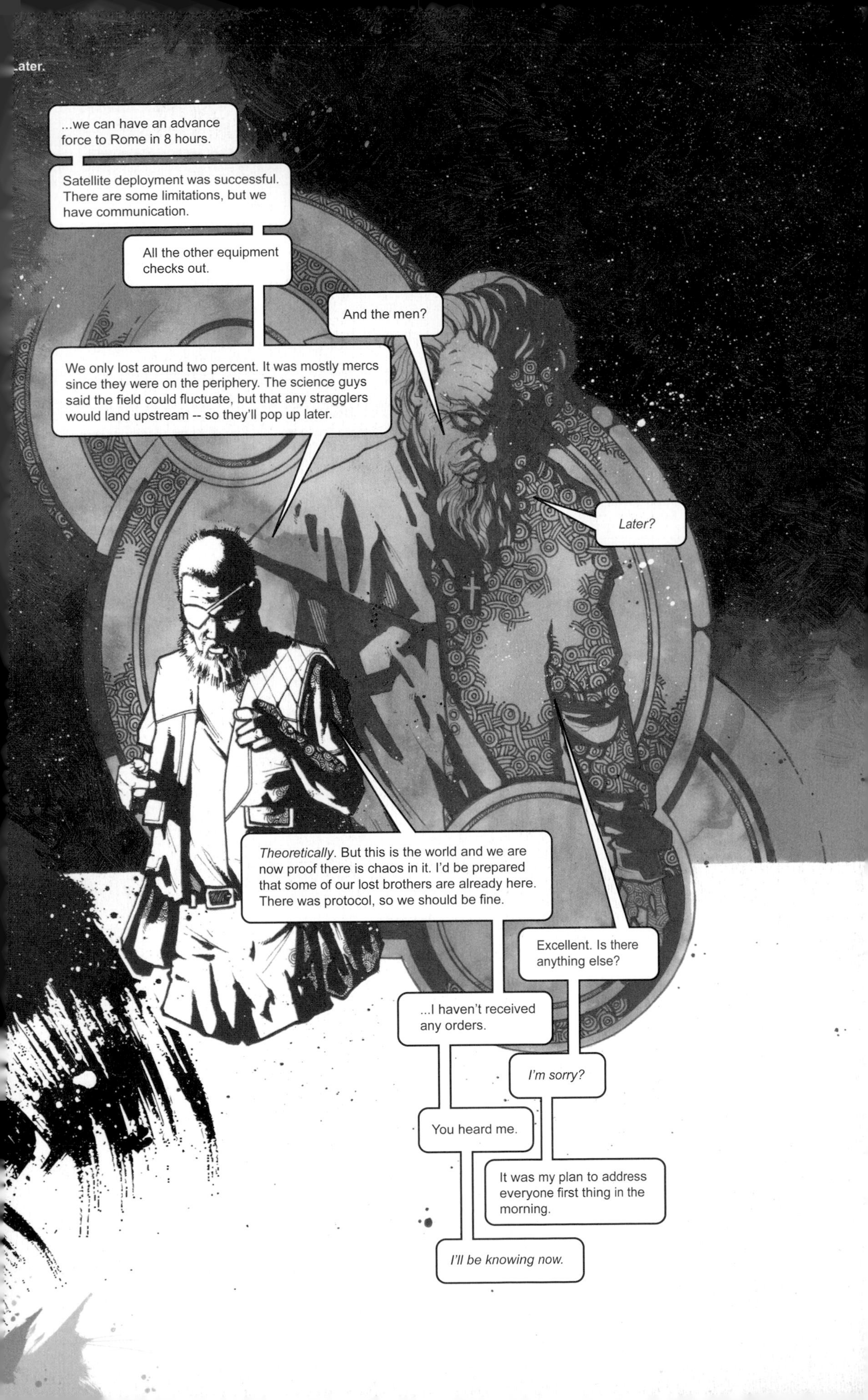
Later.
...we can have an advance force to Rome in 8 hours.
Satellite deployment was successful. There are some limitations, but we have communication.
All the other equipment checks out.
And the men?
We only lost around two percent. It was mostly mercs since they were on the periphery. The science guys said the field could fluctuate, but that any stragglers would land upstream -- so they'll pop up later.
Later?
Theoretically. But this is the world and we are now proof there is chaos in it. I'd be prepared that some of our lost brothers are already here. There was protocol, so we should be fine.
Excellent. Is there anything else?
...I haven't received any orders.
I'm sorry?
You heard me.
It was my plan to address everyone first thing in the morning.
I'll be knowing now.

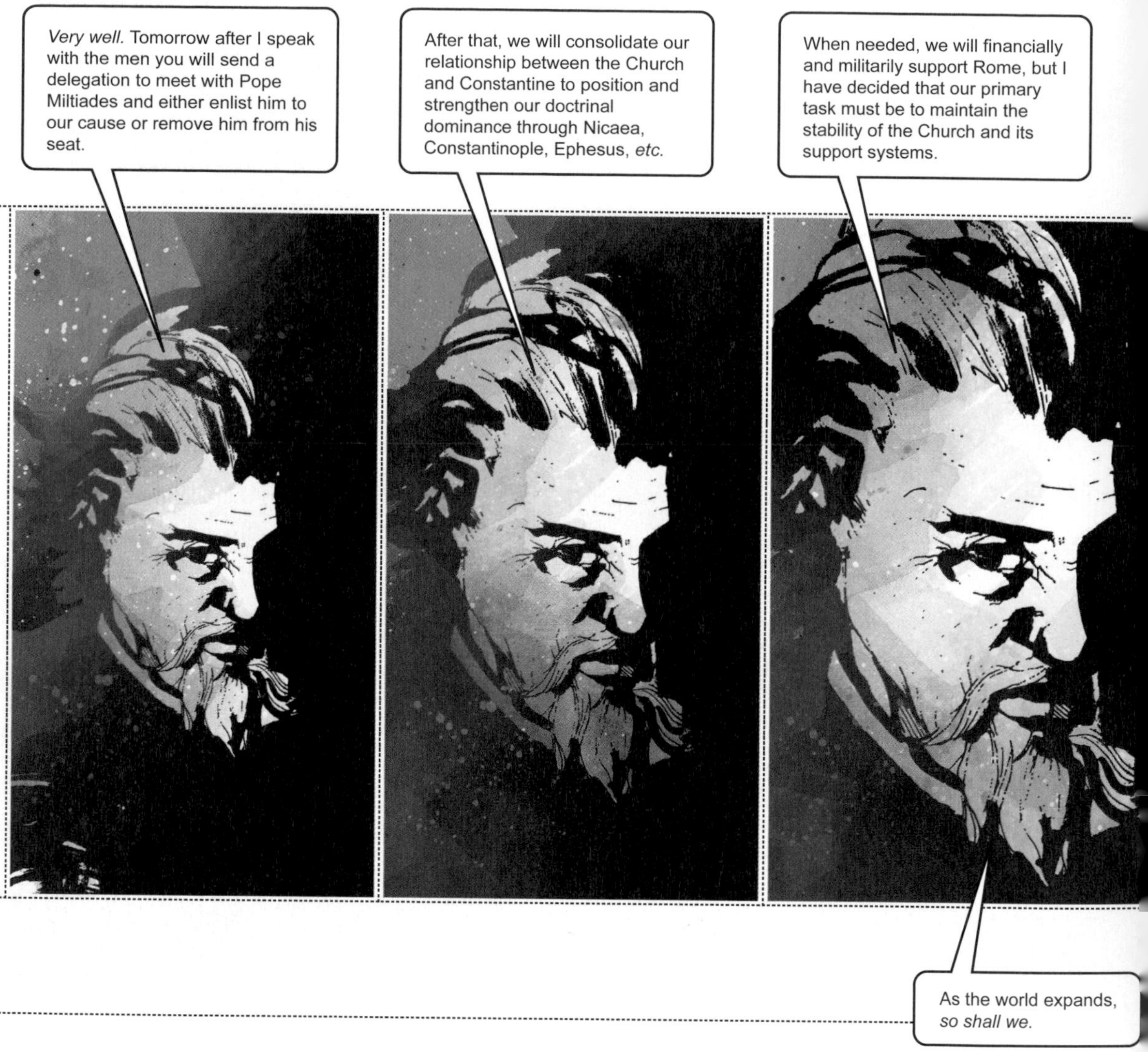
Very well. Tomorrow after I speak with the men you will send a delegation to meet with Pope Miltiades and either enlist him to our cause or remove him from his seat.
After that, we will consolidate our relationship between the Church and Constantine to position and strengthen our doctrinal dominance through Nicaea, Constantinople, Ephesus, *etc.*
When needed, we will financially and militarily support Rome, but I have decided that our primary task must be to maintain the stability of the Church and its support systems.
As the world expands, *so shall we.*

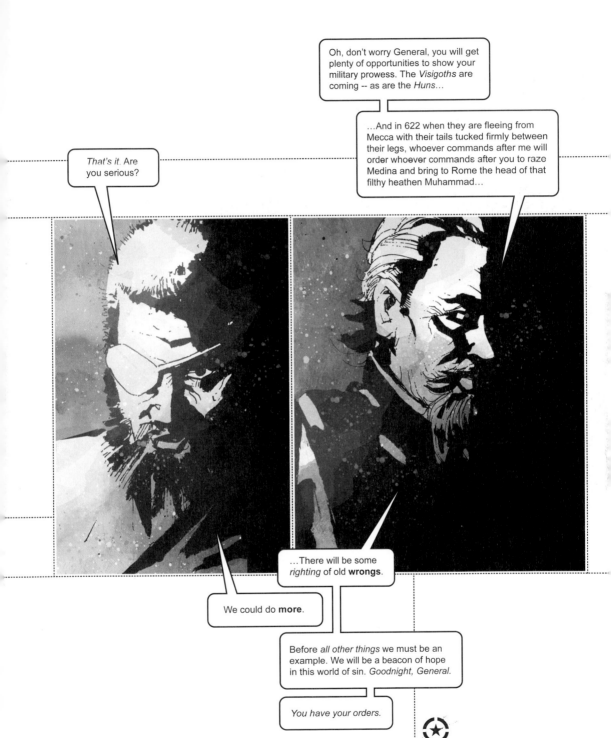

Oh, don't worry General, you will get plenty of opportunities to show your military prowess. The *Visigoths* are coming -- as are the *Huns*...

...And in 622 when they are fleeing from Mecca with their tails tucked firmly between their legs, whoever commands after me will order whoever commands after you to raze Medina and bring to Rome the head of that filthy heathen Muhammad...

That's it. Are you serious?

...There will be some *righting* of old **wrongs**.

We could do **more**.

Before *all other things* we must be an example. We will be a beacon of hope in this world of sin. *Goodnight, General.*

You have your orders.

The Hidden Records

It was not enough.

The next morning.

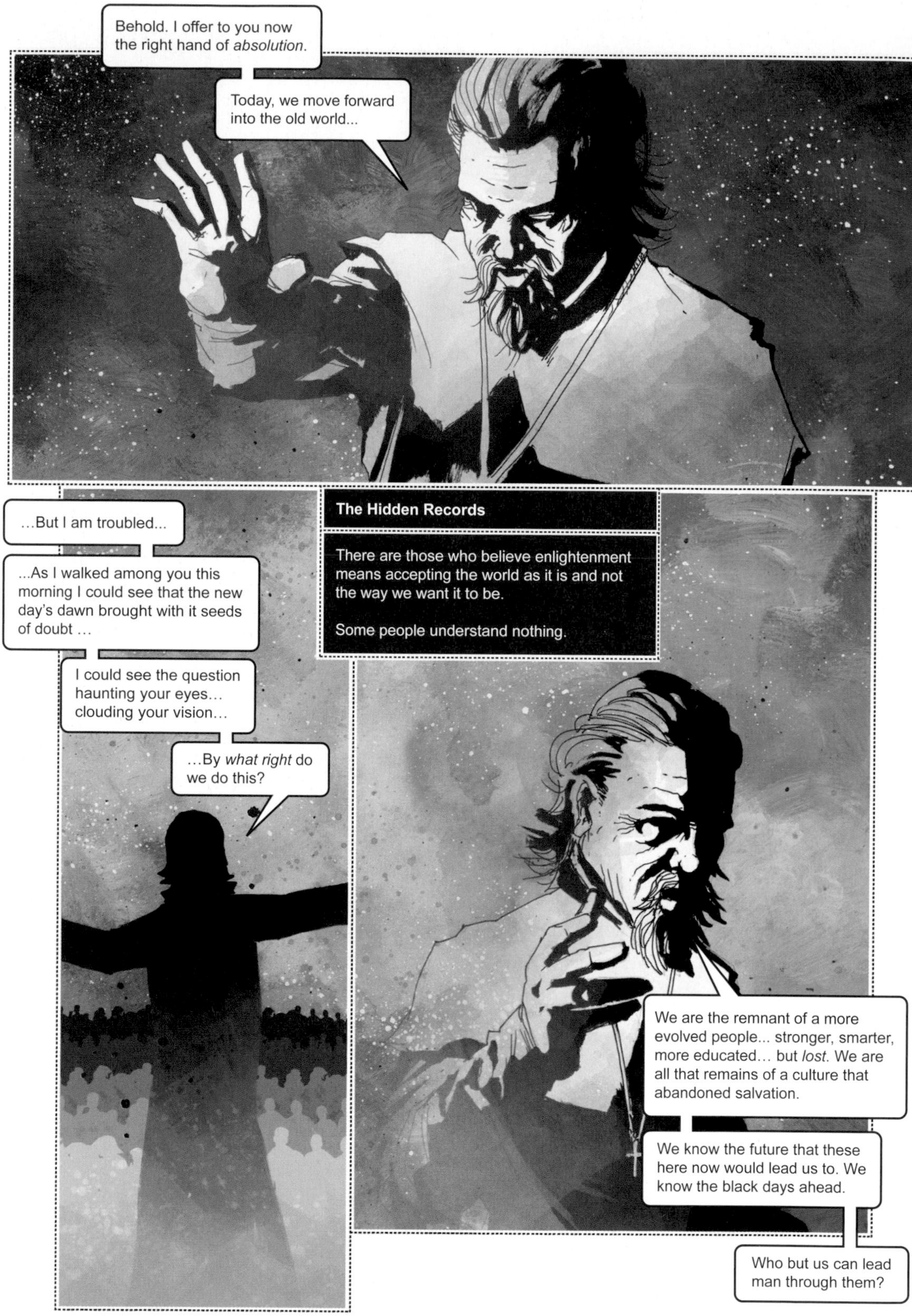

Behold. I offer to you now the right hand of *absolution*.
Today, we move forward into the old world...
...But I am troubled...
...As I walked among you this morning I could see that the new day's dawn brought with it seeds of doubt …
I could see the question haunting your eyes… clouding your vision…
...By *what right* do we do this?
The Hidden Records
There are those who believe enlightenment means accepting the world as it is and not the way we want it to be.
Some people understand nothing.
We are the remnant of a more evolved people... stronger, smarter, more educated… but *lost*. We are all that remains of a culture that abandoned salvation.
We know the future that these here now would lead us to. We know the black days ahead.
Who but us can lead man through them?

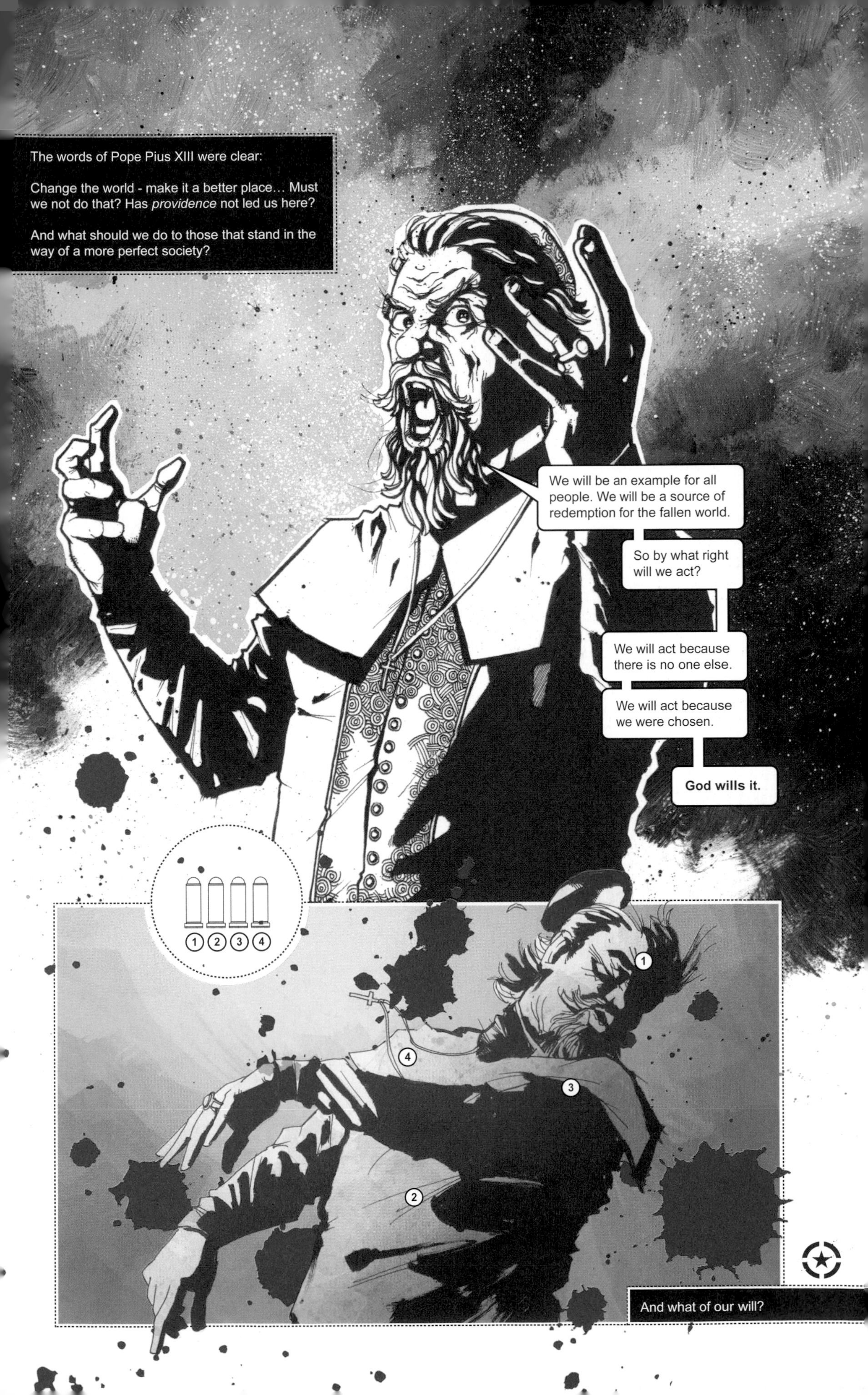
The words of Pope Pius XIII were clear:
Change the world - make it a better place… Must we not do that? Has *providence* not led us here?
And what should we do to those that stand in the way of a more perfect society?
We will be an example for all people. We will be a source of redemption for the fallen world.
So by what right will we act?
We will act because there is no one else.
We will act because we were chosen.
God wills it.
1 2 3 4
1
4
3
2
And what of our will?

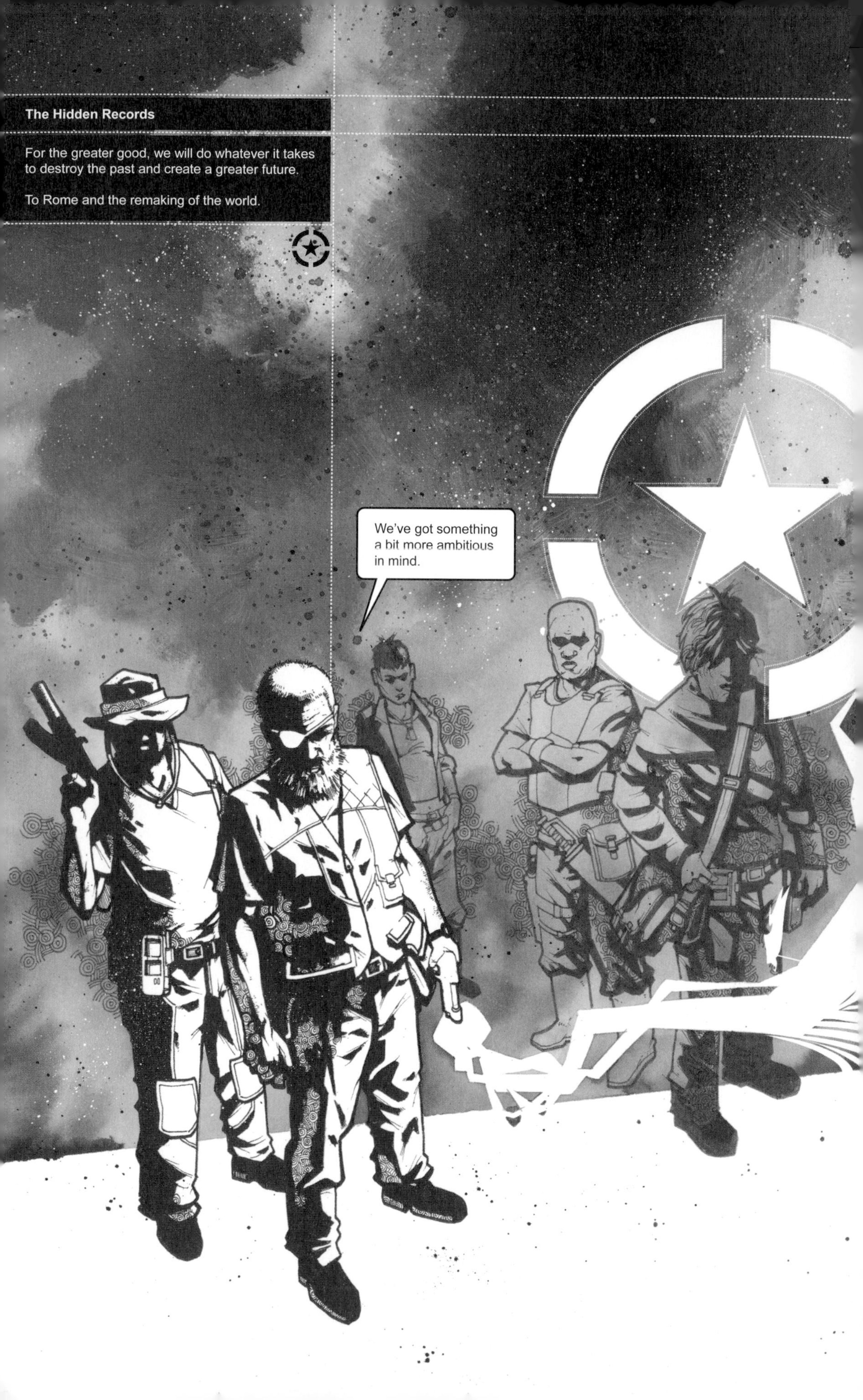
The Hidden Records
For the greater good, we will do whatever it takes to destroy the past and create a greater future.
To Rome and the remaking of the world.
We've got something a bit more ambitious in mind.

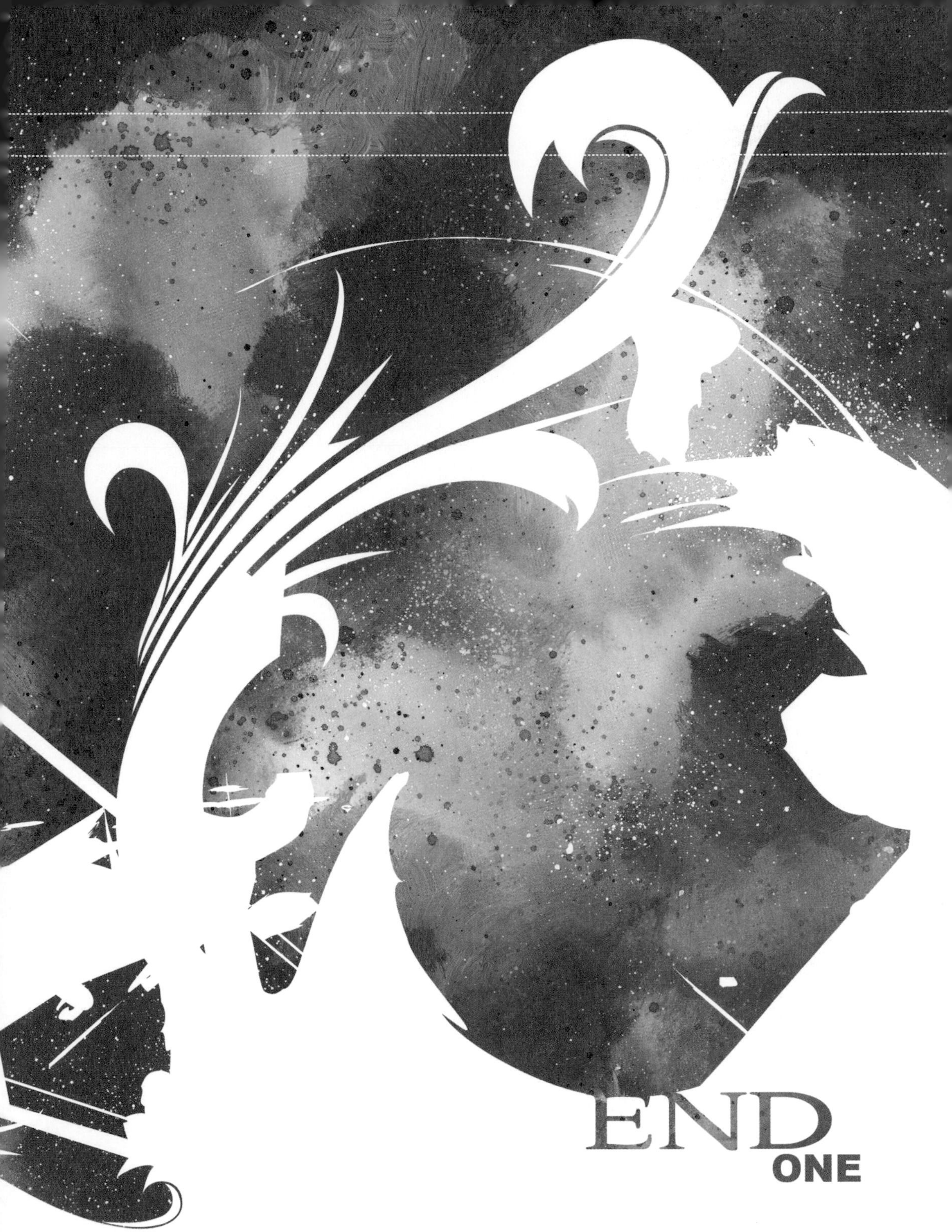

END
ONE

CHAPTER TWO

e megacity Constantinople
ter a snack, before naptime…

education continues...

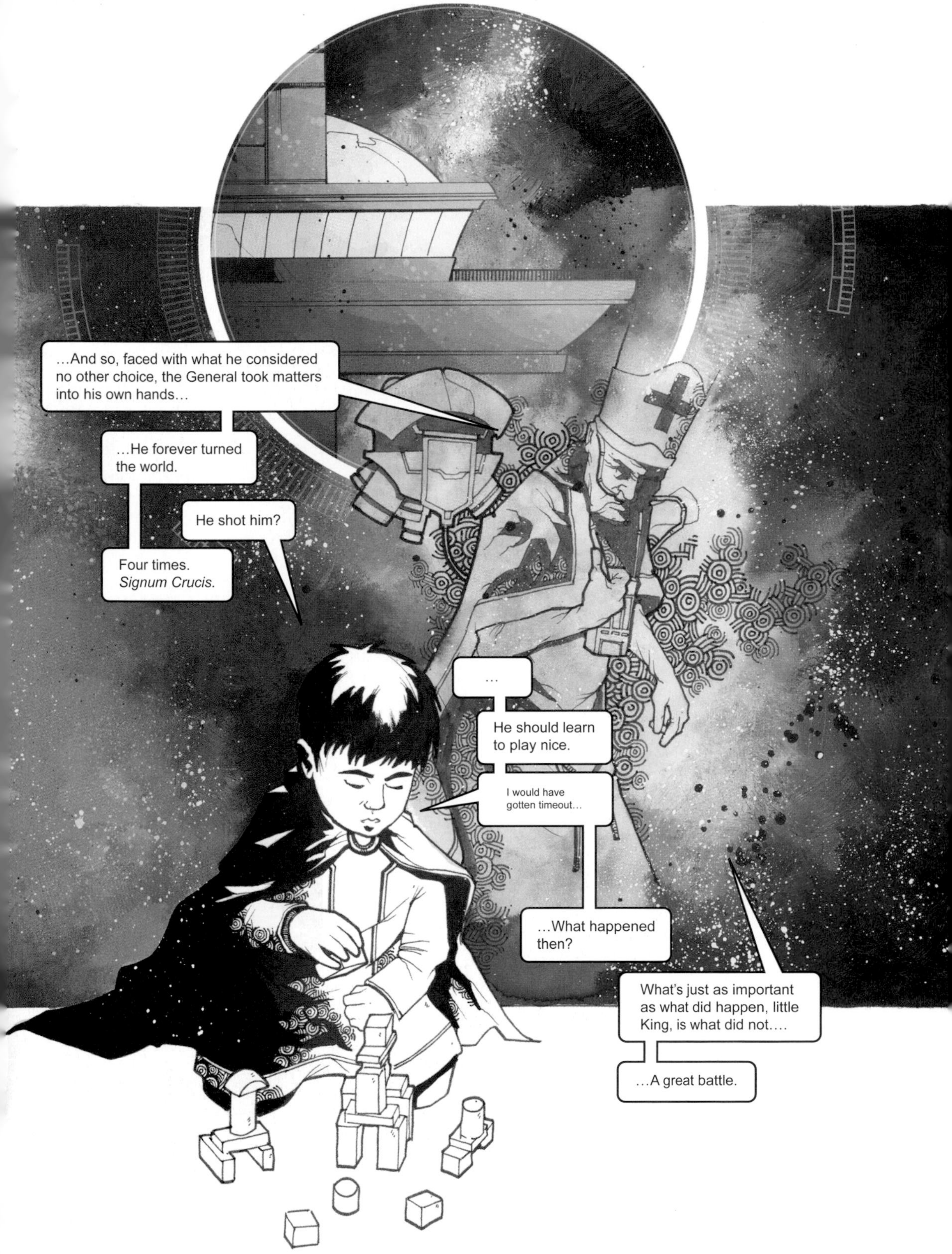

…And so, faced with what he considered no other choice, the General took matters into his own hands…
…He forever turned the world.
He shot him?
Four times. *Signum Crucis.*
…
He should learn to play nice.
I would have gotten timeout…
…What happened then?
What's just as important as what did happen, little King, is what did not….
…A great battle.

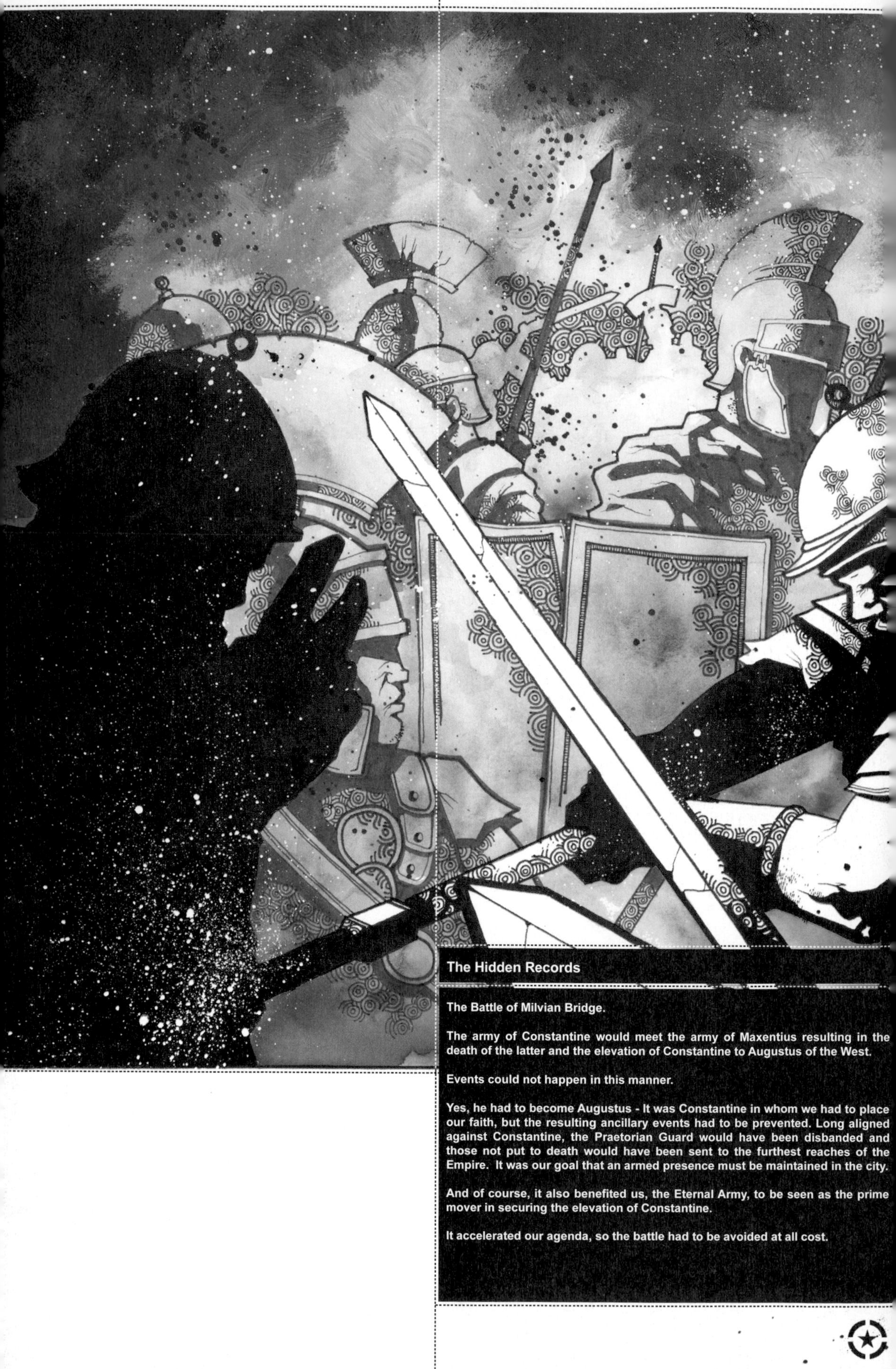

The Hidden Records

The Battle of Milvian Bridge.

The army of Constantine would meet the army of Maxentius resulting in the death of the latter and the elevation of Constantine to Augustus of the West.

Events could not happen in this manner.

Yes, he had to become Augustus - It was Constantine in whom we had to place our faith, but the resulting ancillary events had to be prevented. Long aligned against Constantine, the Praetorian Guard would have been disbanded and those not put to death would have been sent to the furthest reaches of the Empire. It was our goal that an armed presence must be maintained in the city.

And of course, it also benefited us, the Eternal Army, to be seen as the prime mover in securing the elevation of Constantine.

It accelerated our agenda, so the battle had to be avoided at all cost.

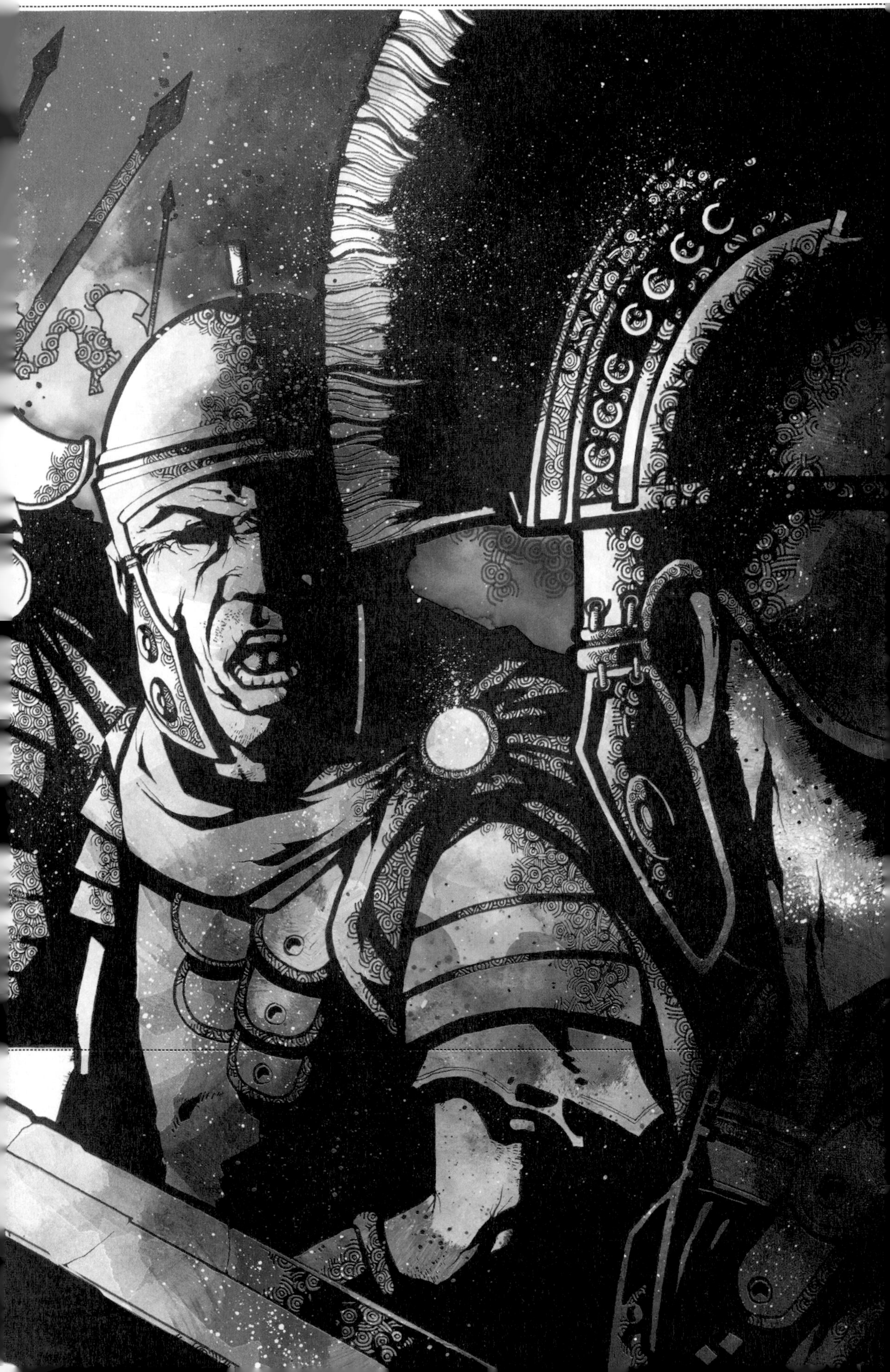

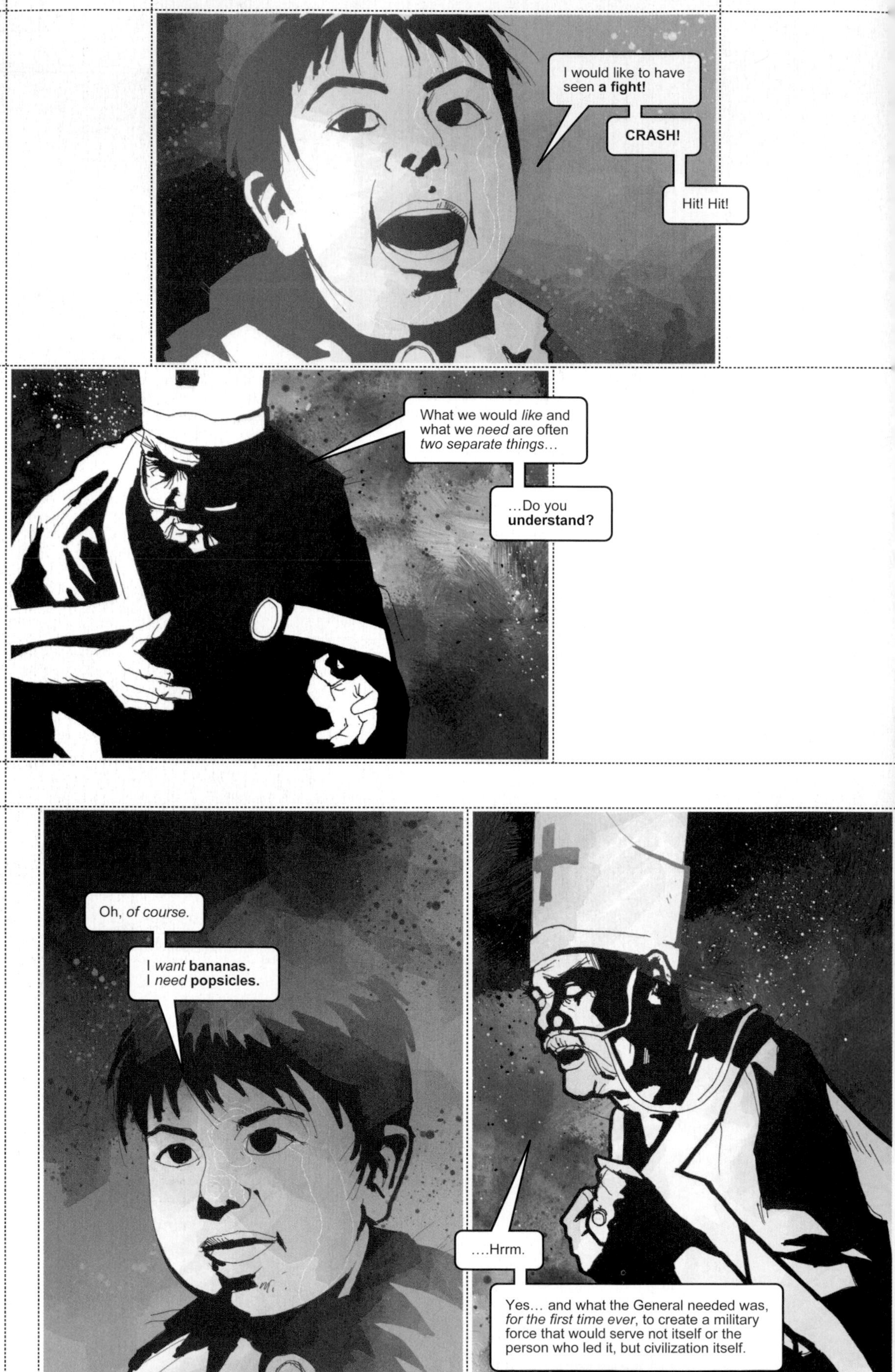
I would like to have seen **a fight!**
CRASH!
Hit! Hit!
What we would *like* and what we *need* are often *two separate things*…
…Do you **understand?**
Oh, *of course.*
I *want* **bananas.** I *need* **popsicles.**
….Hrrm.
Yes… and what the General needed was, *for the first time ever*, to create a military force that would serve not itself or the person who led it, but civilization itself.

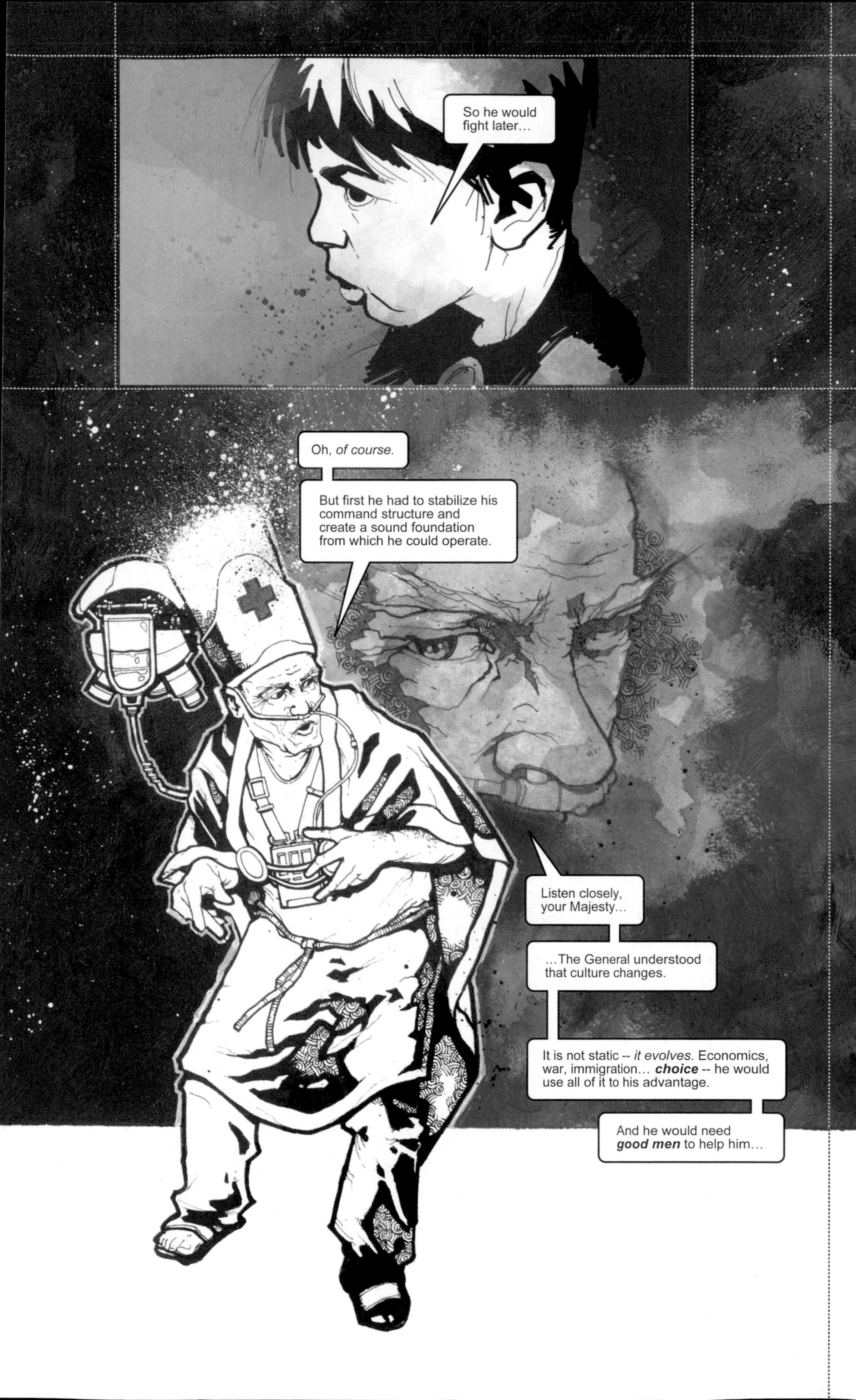
So he would fight later…
Oh, *of course.*
But first he had to stabilize his command structure and create a sound foundation from which he could operate.
Listen closely, your Majesty…
…The General understood that culture changes.
It is not static -- *it evolves.* Economics, war, immigration… ***choice*** -- he would use all of it to his advantage.
And he would need ***good men*** to help him…

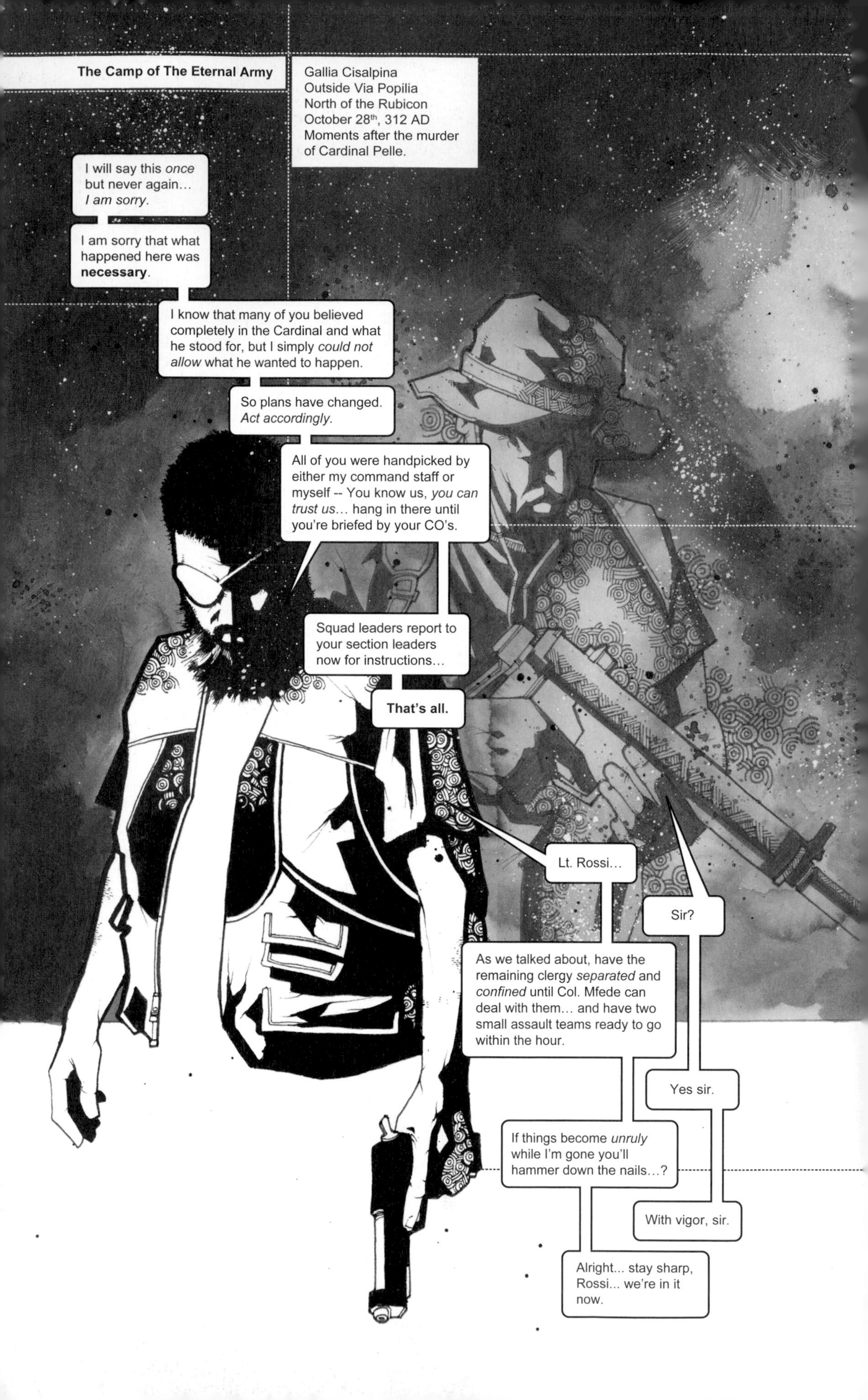
The Camp of The Eternal Army
Gallia Cisalpina
Outside Via Popilia
North of the Rubicon
October 28th, 312 AD
Moments after the murder of Cardinal Pelle.
I will say this *once* but never again… *I am sorry*.
I am sorry that what happened here was **necessary**.
I know that many of you believed completely in the Cardinal and what he stood for, but I simply *could not allow* what he wanted to happen.
So plans have changed. *Act accordingly.*
All of you were handpicked by either my command staff or myself -- You know us, *you can trust us*… hang in there until you're briefed by your CO's.
Squad leaders report to your section leaders now for instructions…
That's all.
Lt. Rossi…
Sir?
As we talked about, have the remaining clergy *separated* and *confined* until Col. Mfede can deal with them… and have two small assault teams ready to go within the hour.
Yes sir.
If things become *unruly* while I'm gone you'll hammer down the nails…?
With vigor, sir.
Alright... stay sharp, Rossi... we're in it now.

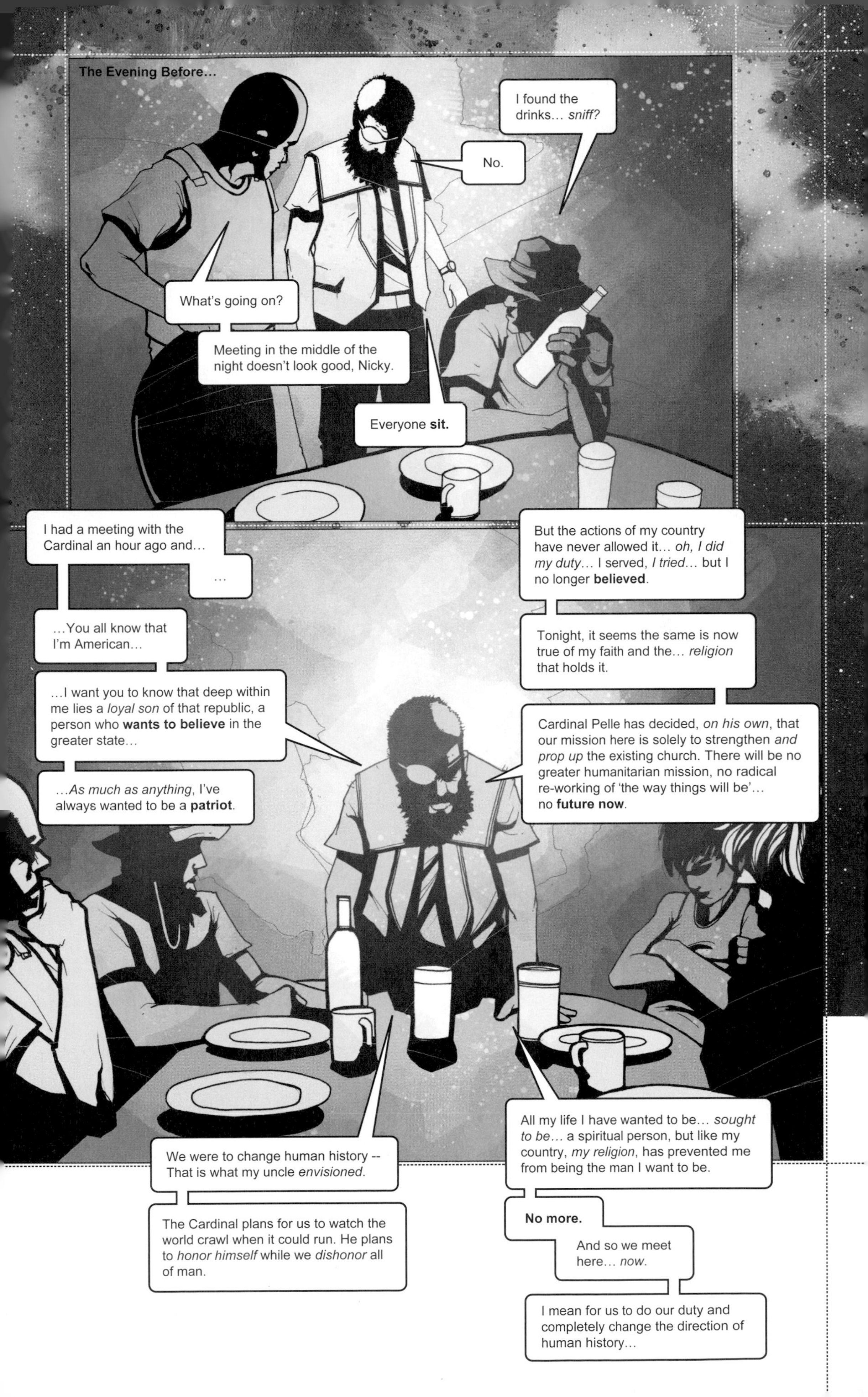
The Evening Before...
What's going on?
Meeting in the middle of the night doesn't look good, Nicky.
No.
I found the drinks... *sniff?*
Everyone **sit.**
I had a meeting with the Cardinal an hour ago and...
...
...You all know that I'm American...
...I want you to know that deep within me lies a *loyal son* of that republic, a person who **wants to believe** in the greater state...
...*As much as anything*, I've always wanted to be a **patriot**.
But the actions of my country have never allowed it... *oh, I did my duty*... I served, *I tried*... but I no longer **believed**.
Tonight, it seems the same is now true of my faith and the... *religion* that holds it.
Cardinal Pelle has decided, *on his own*, that our mission here is solely to strengthen *and prop up* the existing church. There will be no greater humanitarian mission, no radical re-working of 'the way things will be'... no **future now**.
We were to change human history -- That is what my uncle *envisioned*.
The Cardinal plans for us to watch the world crawl when it could run. He plans to *honor himself* while we *dishonor* all of man.
All my life I have wanted to be... *sought to be*... a spiritual person, but like my country, *my religion*, has prevented me from being the man I want to be.
No more.
And so we meet here... *now*.
I mean for us to do our duty and completely change the direction of human history...

The following excerpts were pieced together from the remaining genetic memories of existing participant lines. Even in the fragments that remain, it becomes obvious that what began as 'right cause' quickly became a living experiment in world building.

In attendance:

(NC) – Brigadier General Nicholas Chase
(EM) – Colonel Emmanuel Mfede
(FR) – Colonel Fabio Rossi
(MK) – Colonel Manon Karembeu
(UT) – Lt. Colonel Ulf Tarnat

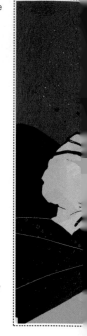

(From left to right: Colonel Emmanuel Mfede, Colonel Fabio Rossi, Brigadier General Nicholas Chase, Colonel Manon Karembeu, Lt. Colonel Ulf Tarnat)

[A Fragment] on Religion and Purpose

EM: General, this… this… is not what was expected.

NC: I know, but each of you is fully aware that I don't make rash decisions. I ask that, in this moment, you believe in me… believe in what I think we should do.

MK: And what's that?

NC: I don't believe in random acts of creation, Manon. I don't believe that something comes from nothing. And that's how it will be with us. We must make a new history.

UT: And our obligations… our mission? What of God?

EM: The equality of all men under the law is an extension of the idea that all believers are equal in the eyes of God. That's not a rationalization, Ulf -- it's an old concept.

NC: But to be clear, equality is a long-term goal.

EM: Long term?

NC: We all here believe that all men are equal. You believe that we are 'born equal' -- I do not. I believe that we are made equal.

EM: Nicholas, you can't rationalize the…

FR: Excuse me, but I fear I have a confession to make. It's been bothering me all day, so I want to get it out there -- I'm an atheist.

MK: Well, aren't you the rebel?

FR: It's true… I'm a wildcard... Why am I the only one drinking?

UT: So, what... you're talking about banning all religions? That's ridiculous.

MK: He's right. Serious decisions -- questions without clear solutions -- have always evoked thoughts of religion.

NC: No, we will embrace them all. The emergence of other religions will only be an effort to draw power away from Rome. They will be started by men possessing political vision and ambition. We must quickly either kill or recruit them and their followers.

UT: You'll only succeed in creating martyrs.

FR: No, General's right. Contemporary martyrs cannot withstand the type of propaganda we will use.

EM: The engineering of beliefs… is this too much?

UT: And what of free will?

FR: Oh, are we still pretending we believe in that?

EM: It doesn't matter. Whether it exists or not, all humans act as if it does. It's the basis of a that thing we call 'moral decisions'.

NC: Our goal is the evolution of human society. That will end when we achieve a type of culture that addresses our deepest and most basic desires. I believe we can do that.

[A Fragment] on Society

UT: I'm going to bring this up once more… why again should we be permitted to do this?

FR: Because we are superior.

UT: That word. It means we are better. It means we act with impunity. It means we are arrogant.

FR: It's not arrogance if it's true.

MK: Listen to yourself... you're a damn fool, Rossi.

EM: If we are so much more evolved, then I can assume we will be wholly substituting our advanced ethics and morality for what passes for acceptable in this time. We will, of course, eliminate slavery, correct?

FR: No.

NC: It's a question of the greater good, Emmanuel. There is infrastructure we must have. Things must be built.

EM: Nicholas, please! This is not a question of a certain time in a society -- of respect for cultural differences or the good we can do -- this is an issue of dignity -- a human cannot own another human. I will not allow it.

FR: It is not your decision to make. Have a drink. Ease the pain.

EM: Listen to me! There is no cyclical nature to human evolution… setbacks, yes. But there will be no return of primate-man. Once you introduce concepts like liberty and equality -- free society, there is no denying the immorality of something like slavery.

FR: Who said anything about a free society?

UT: Come on! He's right. This is not just a question of scientific and technological progress -- that will fail unless we can parallel innovation with moral progress.

EM: There are inherent laws…

FR: Laws are temporary. Vision is eternal.

MK: Don't waste your time arguing with people who know they are right, Emmanuel.

NC: We will eliminate slavery soon, just not yet...

MK: It's assumed there is no inherent order to the long arc of human history... are you saying we will prove that wrong?

NC: We will have many opportunities to do so. We will teach them how to change; and because of our long life spans, if we fail then we will teach our lessons to their children and then their children's children if we were to fail again. With each generation we will be closer to a greater society... by repetition, we will achieve our goals. All of them.

[A Fragment] on Expansion and Control

MK: ...And Constantine?

NC: We will either co-opt him or, at a favorable time, work to have him replaced with someone open to our plans.

FR: [Unintelligible]

EM: Exactly, if necessary, we will permit others the opportunity to rule and implement a radical reworking of government every three generations.

NC: Agreed. One revolutionary. One stabilizing. One status quo. First consolidation, then an ever-accelerating expansion.

FR: [Unintelligible]

UT: I know it's generations away, but what about excessive population growth? Is that sustainable -- we've seen and lived through examples of the dangers of this: Mass starvation in China and Africa...

MK: Yes. Those were burdens of nature... a breaking of the balance.

NC: You're talking about fringe environmental protectionism. Some idea that we are part of and equal to our surroundings. That kind of thinking leads to garbage like a "natural" global population" or "environmental retribution."

MK: Are you saying there's scientifically nothing to that?

NC: No. I'm saying we are man... Are we not here now? Have we not conquered time itself? This planet cannot control or dictate to us. It will not even contain us.

UT: Again... the hubris.

MK: Meh. Be clear. Call it pride and be done with it... let's not sell short what we are attempting here.

EM: But that is not truth. If as a group we maintain our course, we personally are inconsequential. Even with our expanded lives we are short-lived. It is the objective that matters -- not the individual.

NC: Yes, our lives for the goal -- nothing else. And if I ever lose sight of it, I fully expect you to eliminate me, as I will not hesitate to kill you. This is an ultimate sacrifice... there is no pride in it.

UT: Must I say it? Die Weltgeschichte ist das Weltgericht. World history is the final arbiter of the right.

EM: Yes, rest assured, we will be judged.

NC: And as we push man, there will be those that violently oppose us.

MK: We have the benefit of both history and technology. For a while, we should know when they are supposed to come and our satellites will tell us where they are gathering. We will terminate most efforts at conception.

EM: But new enemies will come with every generation. It's inevitable that we will be forced to destroy some of those that choose to stand against us.

NC: Yes. An example will have to be made.

MK: Let's be clear, you're talking about using nuclear weapons... you want to domesticate genocide...

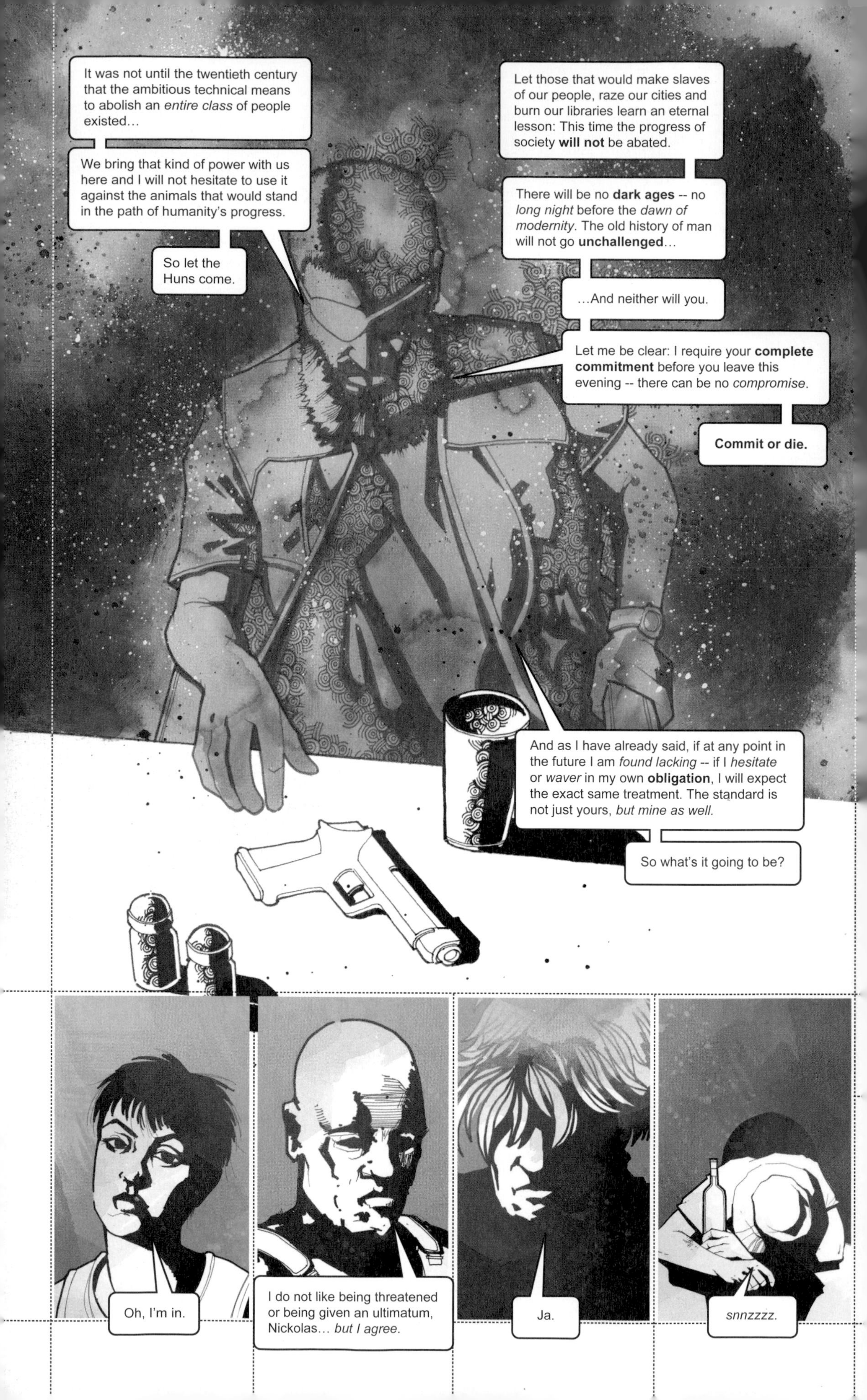
It was not until the twentieth century that the ambitious technical means to abolish an *entire class* of people existed…
We bring that kind of power with us here and I will not hesitate to use it against the animals that would stand in the path of humanity's progress.
So let the Huns come.
Let those that would make slaves of our people, raze our cities and burn our libraries learn an eternal lesson: This time the progress of society **will not** be abated.
There will be no **dark ages** -- no *long night* before the *dawn of modernity*. The old history of man will not go **unchallenged**…
…And neither will you.
Let me be clear: I require your **complete commitment** before you leave this evening -- there can be no *compromise*.
Commit or die.
And as I have already said, if at any point in the future I am *found lacking* -- if I *hesitate* or *waver* in my own **obligation**, I will expect the exact same treatment. The standard is not just yours, *but mine as well.*
So what's it going to be?
Oh, I'm in.
I do not like being threatened or being given an ultimatum, Nickolas… *but I agree.*
Ja.
snnzzzz.

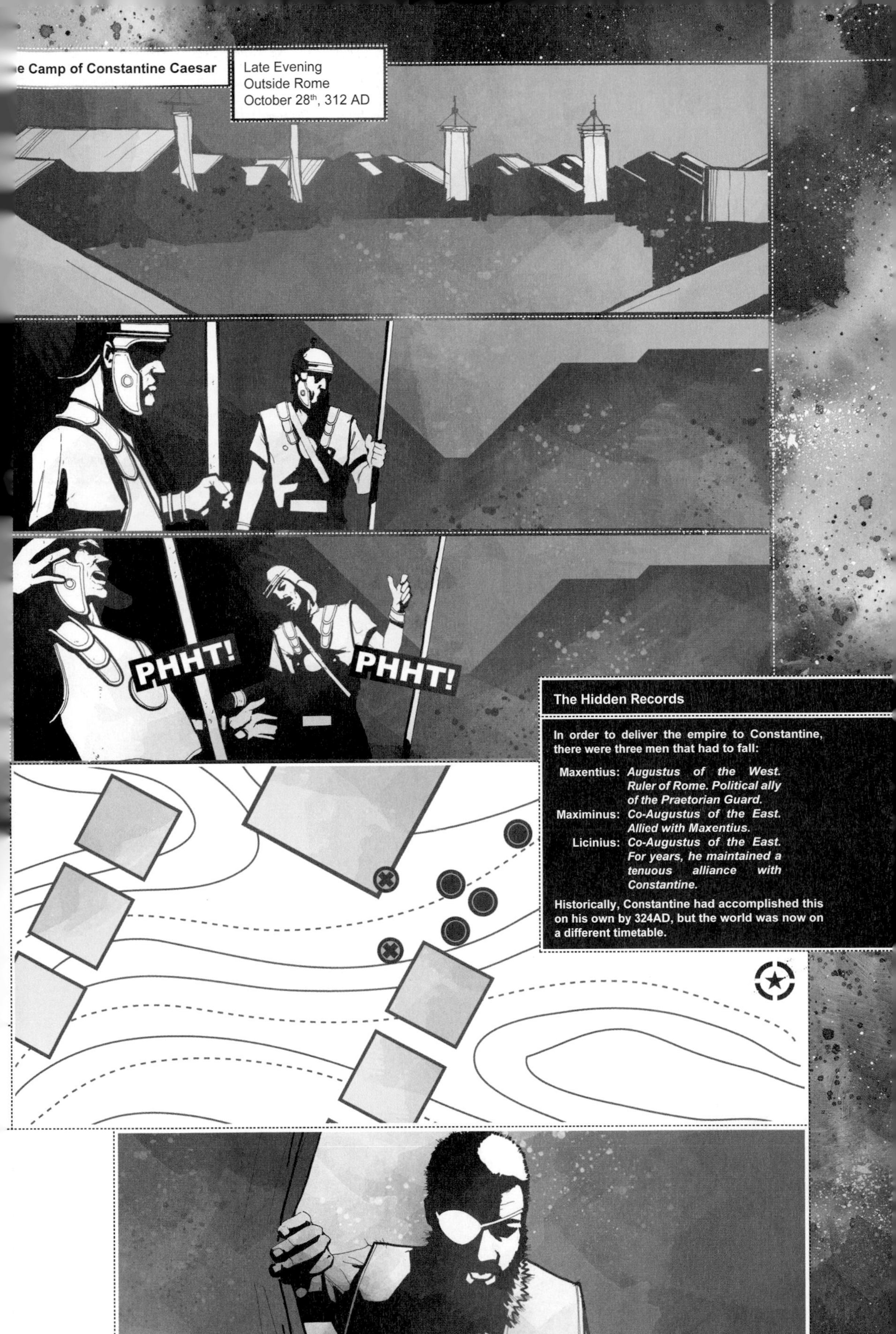
e Camp of Constantine Caesar
Late Evening
Outside Rome
October 28th, 312 AD
PHHT!
PHHT!
The Hidden Records
In order to deliver the empire to Constantine, there were three men that had to fall:
Maxentius: *Augustus of the West. Ruler of Rome. Political ally of the Praetorian Guard.*
Maximinus: *Co-Augustus of the East. Allied with Maxentius.*
Licinius: *Co-Augustus of the East. For years, he maintained a tenuous alliance with Constantine.*
Historically, Constantine had accomplished this on his own by 324AD, but the world was now on a different timetable.

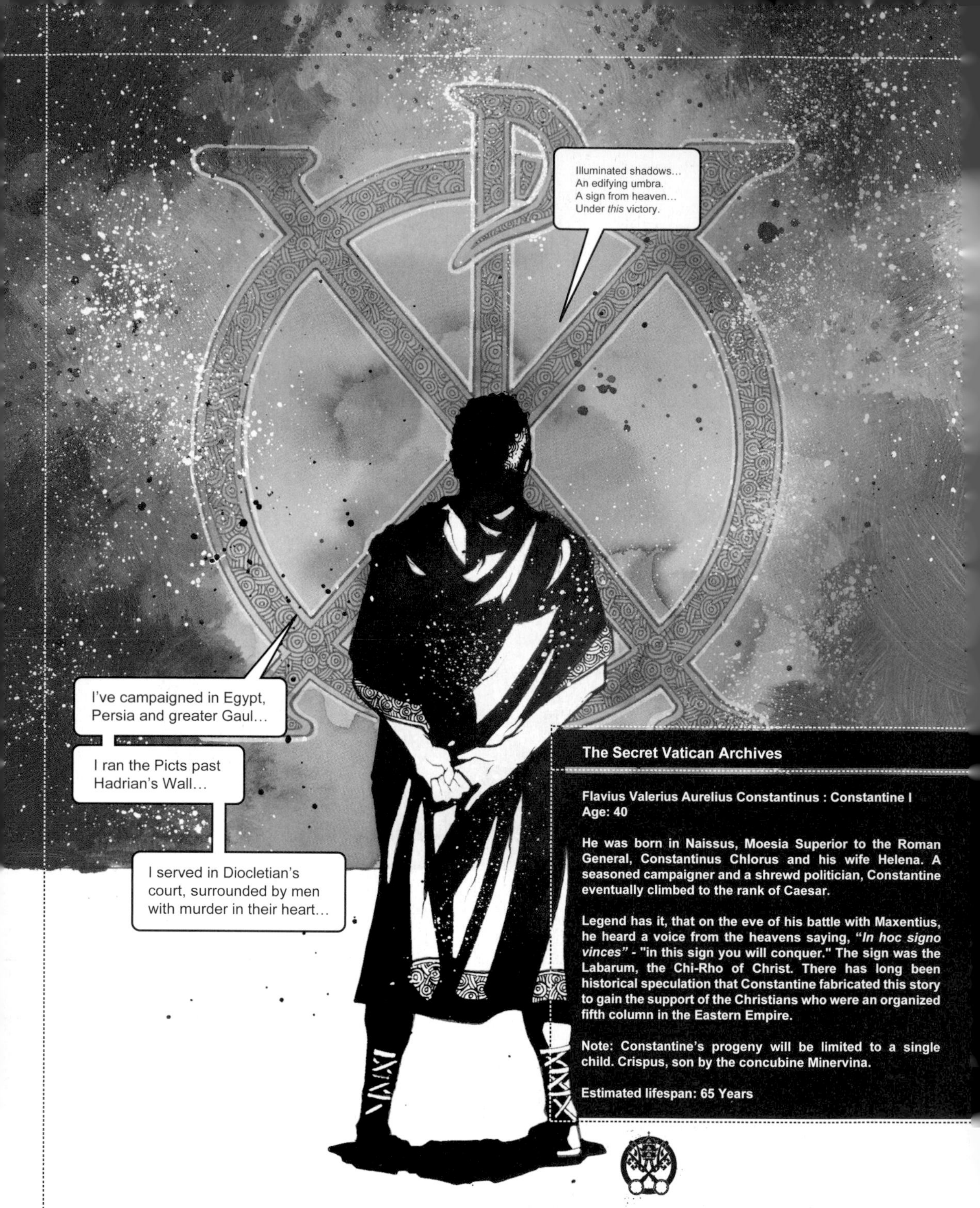

Illuminated shadows...
An edifying umbra.
A sign from heaven...
Under *this* victory.
I've campaigned in Egypt, Persia and greater Gaul...
I ran the Picts past Hadrian's Wall...
I served in Diocletian's court, surrounded by men with murder in their heart...
The Secret Vatican Archives
Flavius Valerius Aurelius Constantinus : Constantine I
Age: 40
He was born in Naissus, Moesia Superior to the Roman General, Constantinus Chlorus and his wife Helena. A seasoned campaigner and a shrewd politician, Constantine eventually climbed to the rank of Caesar.
Legend has it, that on the eve of his battle with Maxentius, he heard a voice from the heavens saying, *"In hoc signo vinces"* - "in this sign you will conquer." The sign was the Labarum, the Chi-Rho of Christ. There has long been historical speculation that Constantine fabricated this story to gain the support of the Christians who were an organized fifth column in the Eastern Empire.
Note: Constantine's progeny will be limited to a single child. Crispus, son by the concubine Minervina.
Estimated lifespan: 65 Years

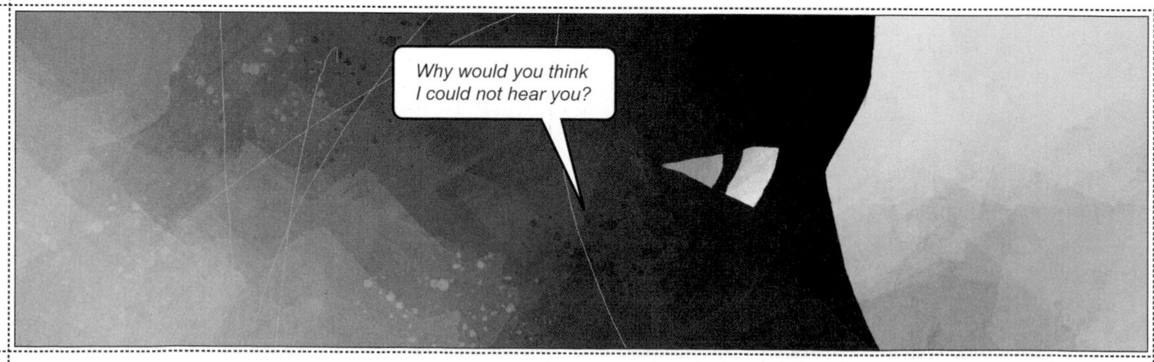

Why would you think I could not hear you?

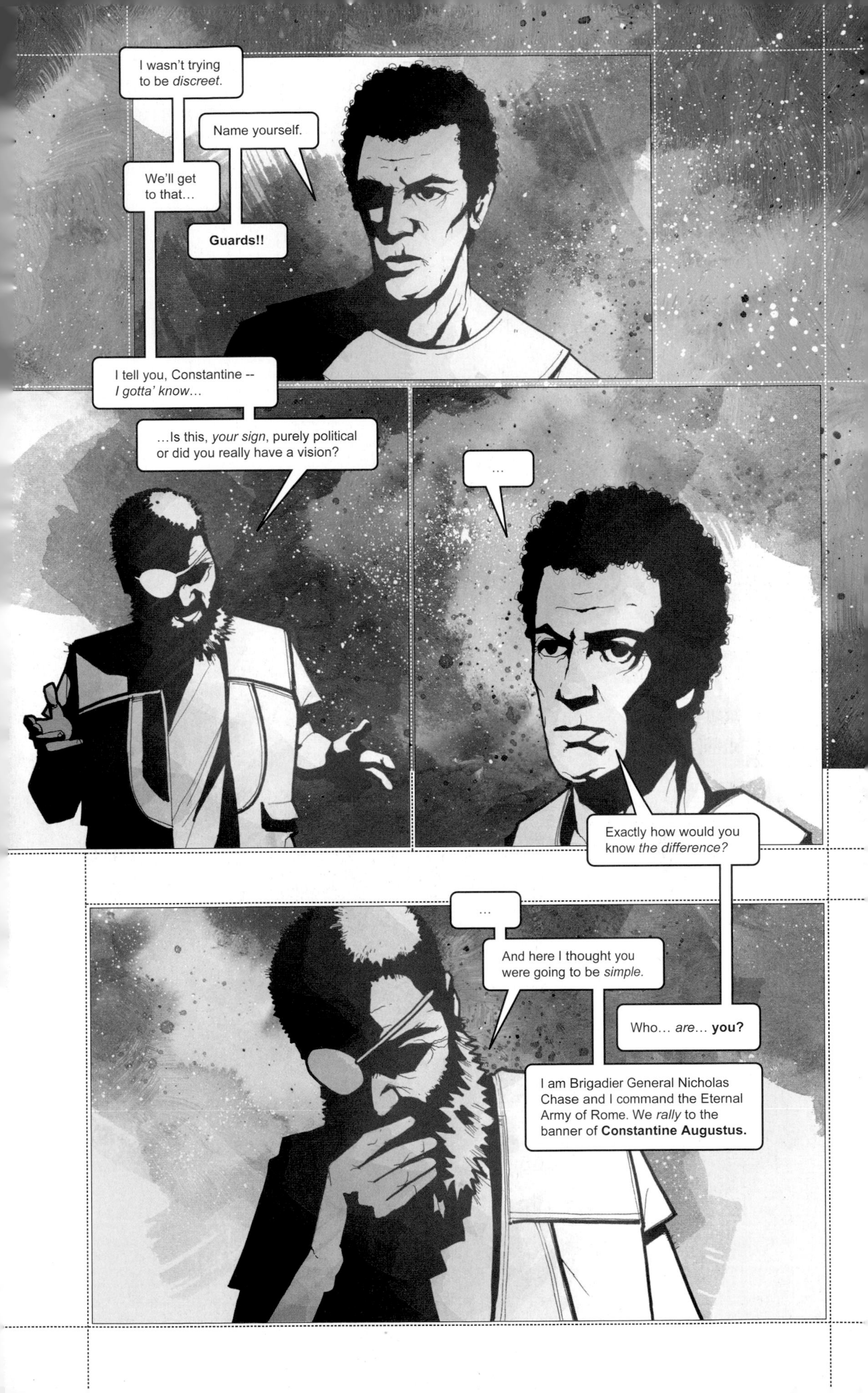

I wasn't trying to be *discreet*.
Name yourself.
We'll get to that…
Guards!!
I tell you, Constantine -- *I gotta' know*…
…Is this, *your sign*, purely political or did you really have a vision?
…
Exactly how would you know *the difference?*
…
And here I thought you were going to be *simple*.
Who… *are*… **you?**
I am Brigadier General Nicholas Chase and I command the Eternal Army of Rome. We *rally* to the banner of **Constantine Augustus.**

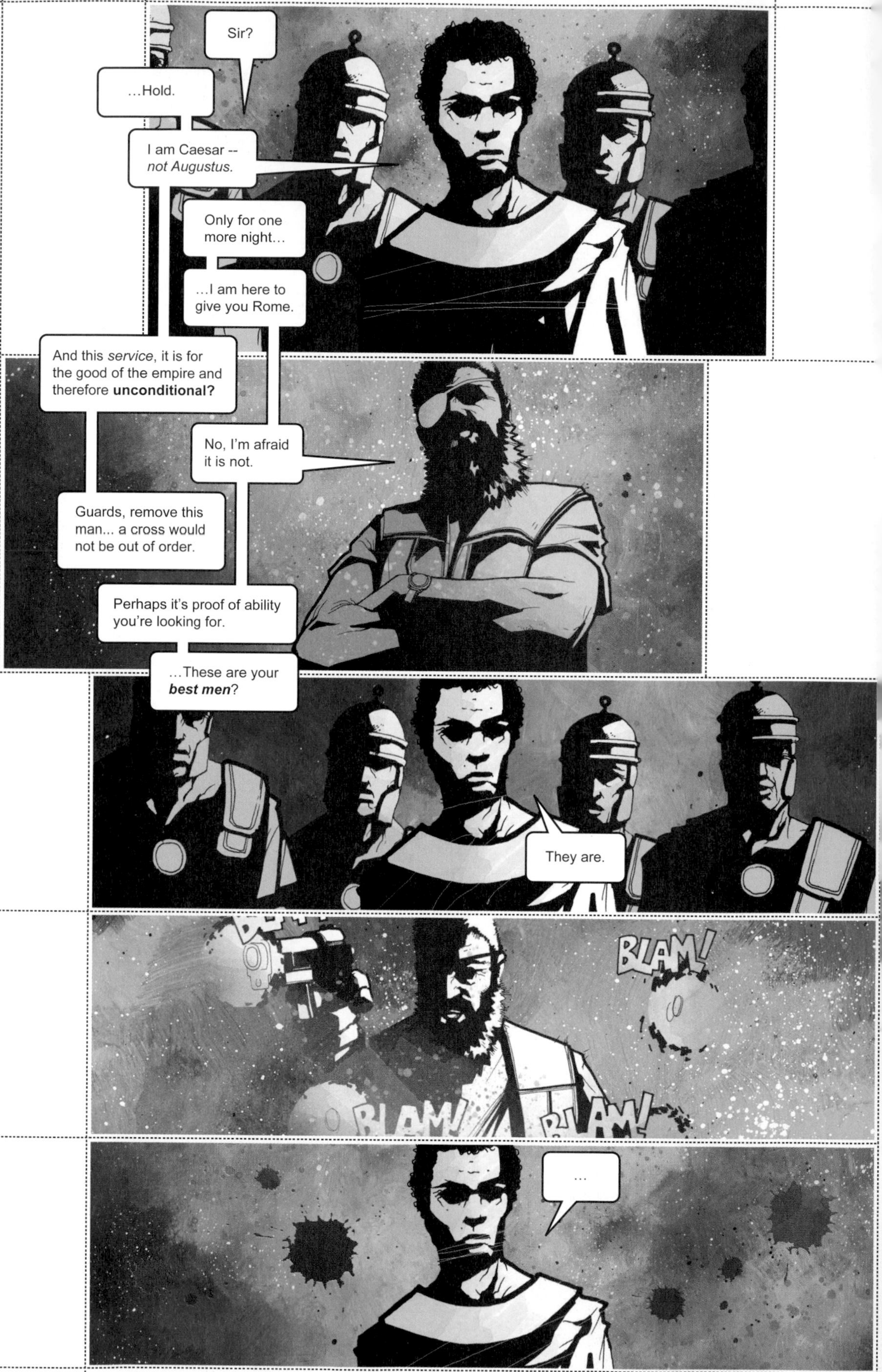
Sir?
...Hold.
I am Caesar -- *not Augustus.*
Only for one more night...
...I am here to give you Rome.
And this *service*, it is for the good of the empire and therefore **unconditional?**
No, I'm afraid it is not.
Guards, remove this man... a cross would not be out of order.
Perhaps it's proof of ability you're looking for.
...These are your ***best men***?
They are.
BLAM!
BLAM!
BLAM!
...

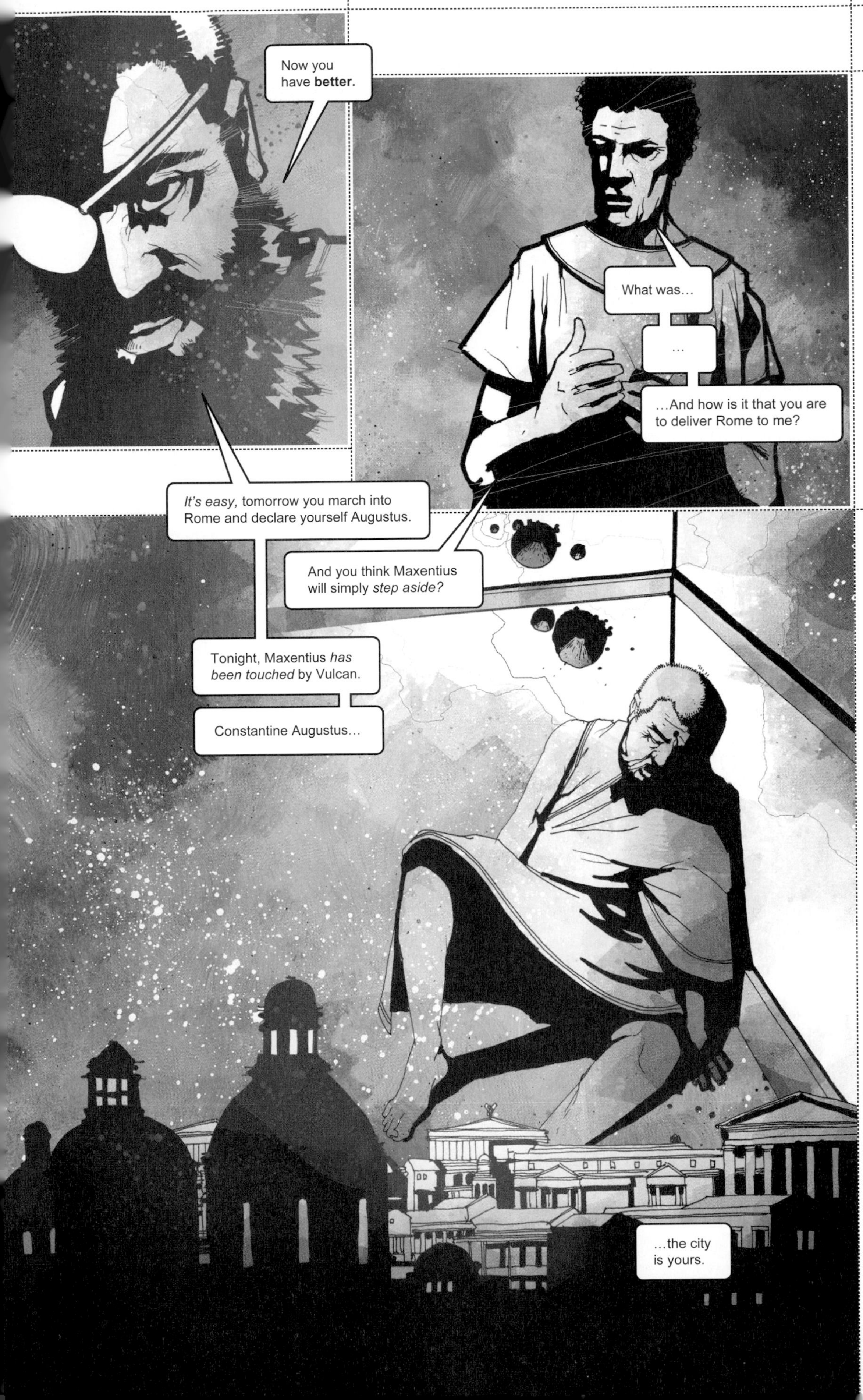
Now you have **better.**
What was…
…
…And how is it that you are to deliver Rome to me?
It's easy, tomorrow you march into Rome and declare yourself Augustus.
And you think Maxentius will simply *step aside?*
Tonight, Maxentius *has been touched* by Vulcan.
Constantine Augustus…
…the city is yours.

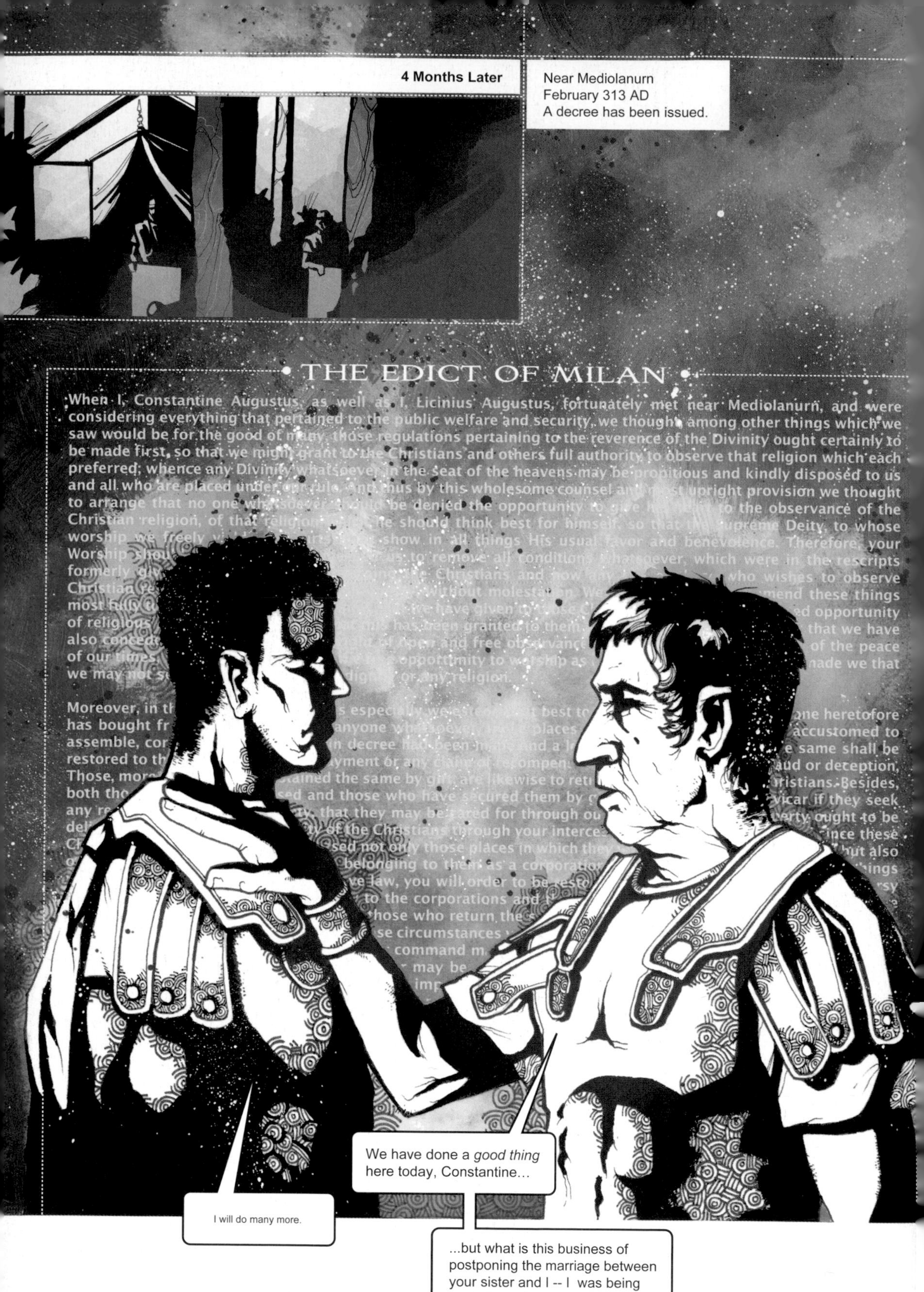
4 Months Later
Near Mediolanurn
February 313 AD
A decree has been issued.
THE EDICT OF MILAN
When I, Constantine Augustus, as well as I, Licinius Augustus, fortunately met near Mediolanurn, and were considering everything that pertained to the public welfare and security, we thought among other things which we saw would be for the good of many, those regulations pertaining to the reverence of the Divinity ought certainly to be made first, so that we might grant to the Christians and others full authority to observe that religion which each preferred; whence any Divinity whatsoever in the seat of the heavens may be propitious and kindly disposed to us
We have done a *good thing* here today, Constantine...
I will do many more.
...but what is this business of postponing the marriage between your sister and I -- I was being *very clear* when...

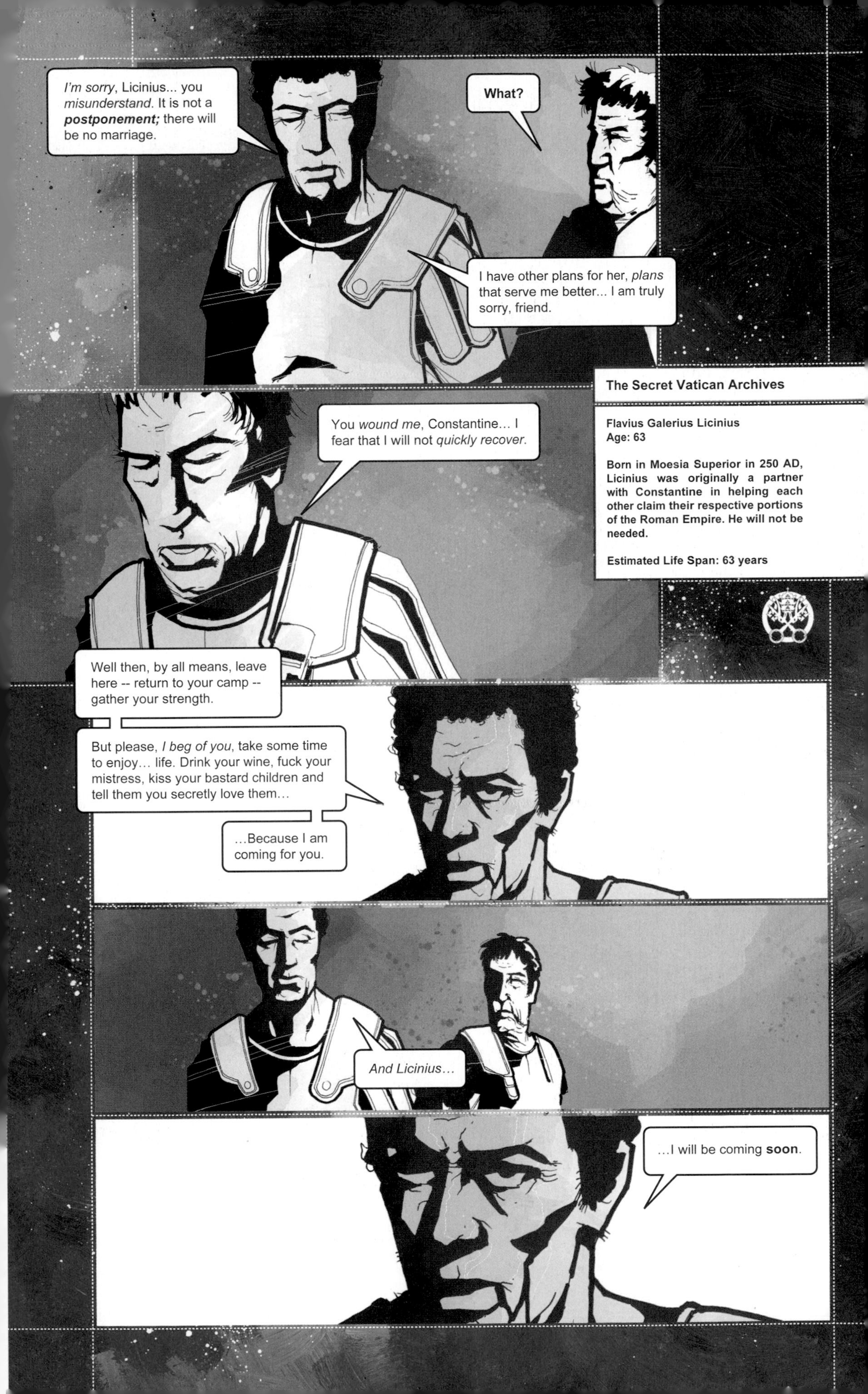
I'm sorry, Licinius... you *misunderstand*. It is not a ***postponement;*** there will be no marriage.
What?
I have other plans for her, *plans* that serve me better... I am truly sorry, friend.
You *wound me*, Constantine... I fear that I will not *quickly recover*.
The Secret Vatican Archives
Flavius Galerius Licinius
Age: 63
Born in Moesia Superior in 250 AD, Licinius was originally a partner with Constantine in helping each other claim their respective portions of the Roman Empire. He will not be needed.
Estimated Life Span: 63 years
Well then, by all means, leave here -- return to your camp -- gather your strength.
But please, *I beg of you*, take some time to enjoy… life. Drink your wine, fuck your mistress, kiss your bastard children and tell them you secretly love them…
…Because I am coming for you.
And Licinius…
…I will be coming **soon**.

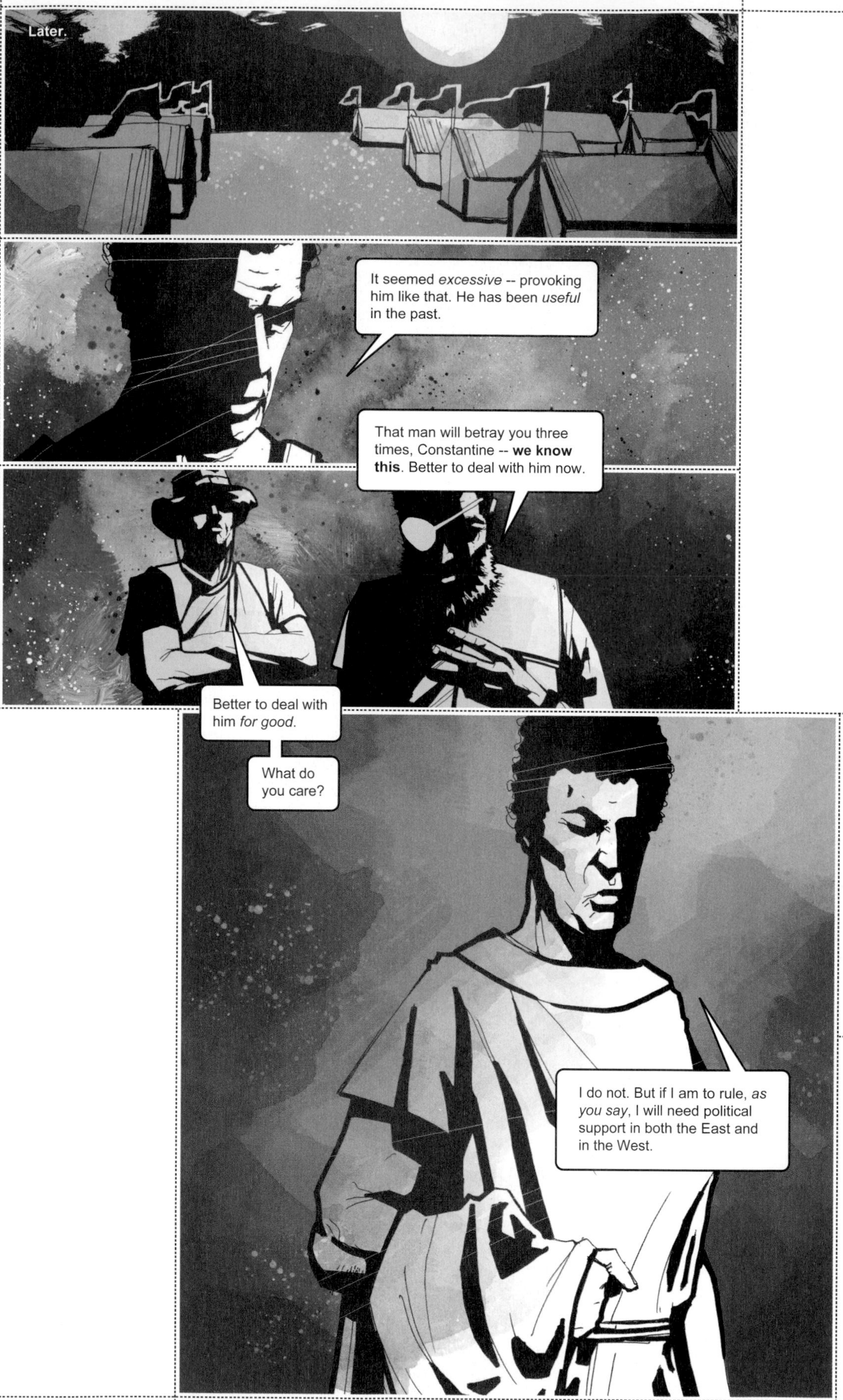
Later.
It seemed *excessive* -- provoking him like that. He has been *useful* in the past.
That man will betray you three times, Constantine -- **we know this**. Better to deal with him now.
Better to deal with him *for good*.
What do you care?
I do not. But if I am to rule, *as you say*, I will need political support in both the East and in the West.

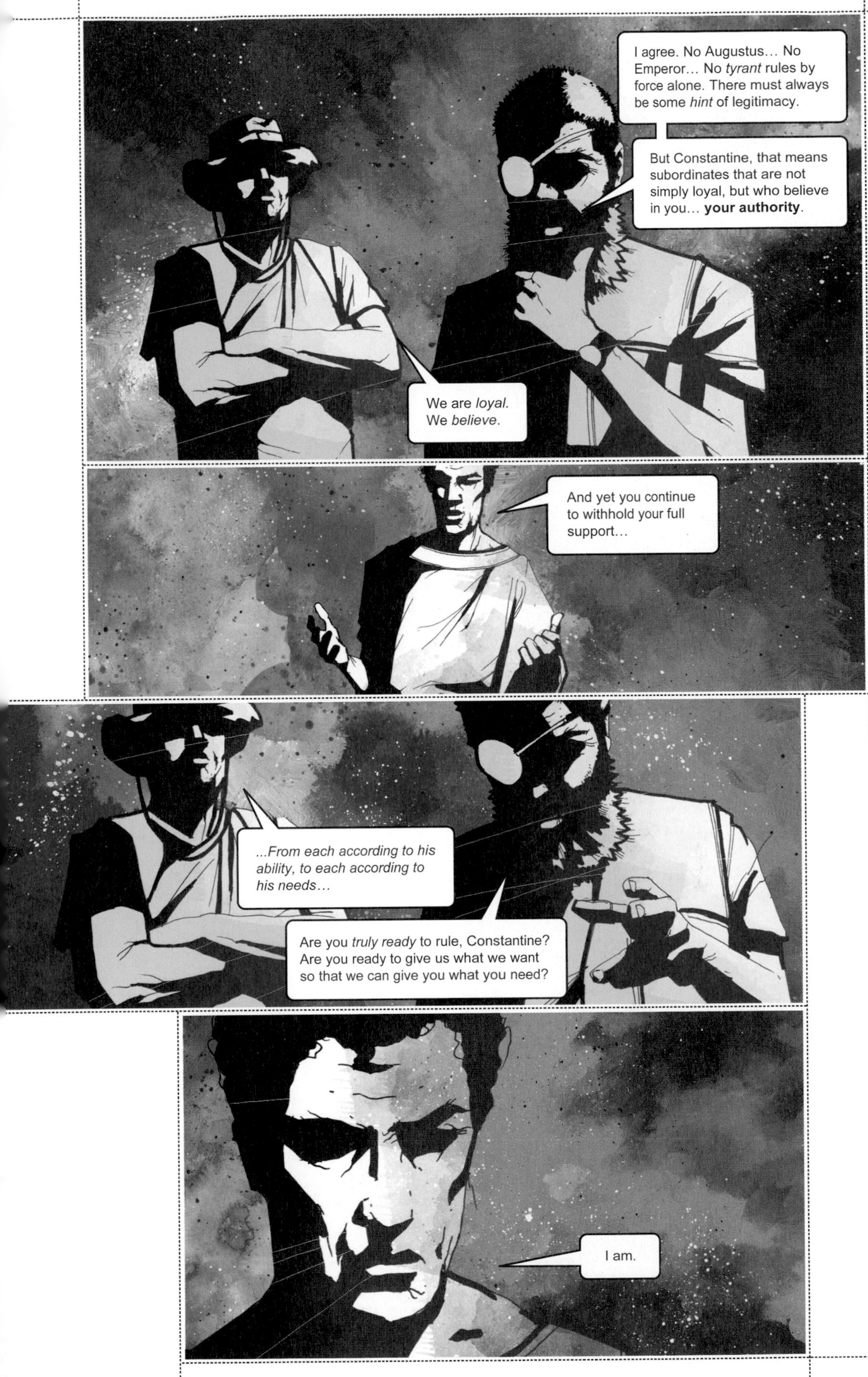
I agree. No Augustus… No Emperor… No *tyrant* rules by force alone. There must always be some *hint* of legitimacy.
But Constantine, that means subordinates that are not simply loyal, but who believe in you… **your authority**.
We are *loyal.* We *believe*.
And yet you continue to withhold your full support…
...From each according to his ability, to each according to his needs…
Are you *truly ready* to rule, Constantine? Are you ready to give us what we want so that we can give you what you need?
I am.

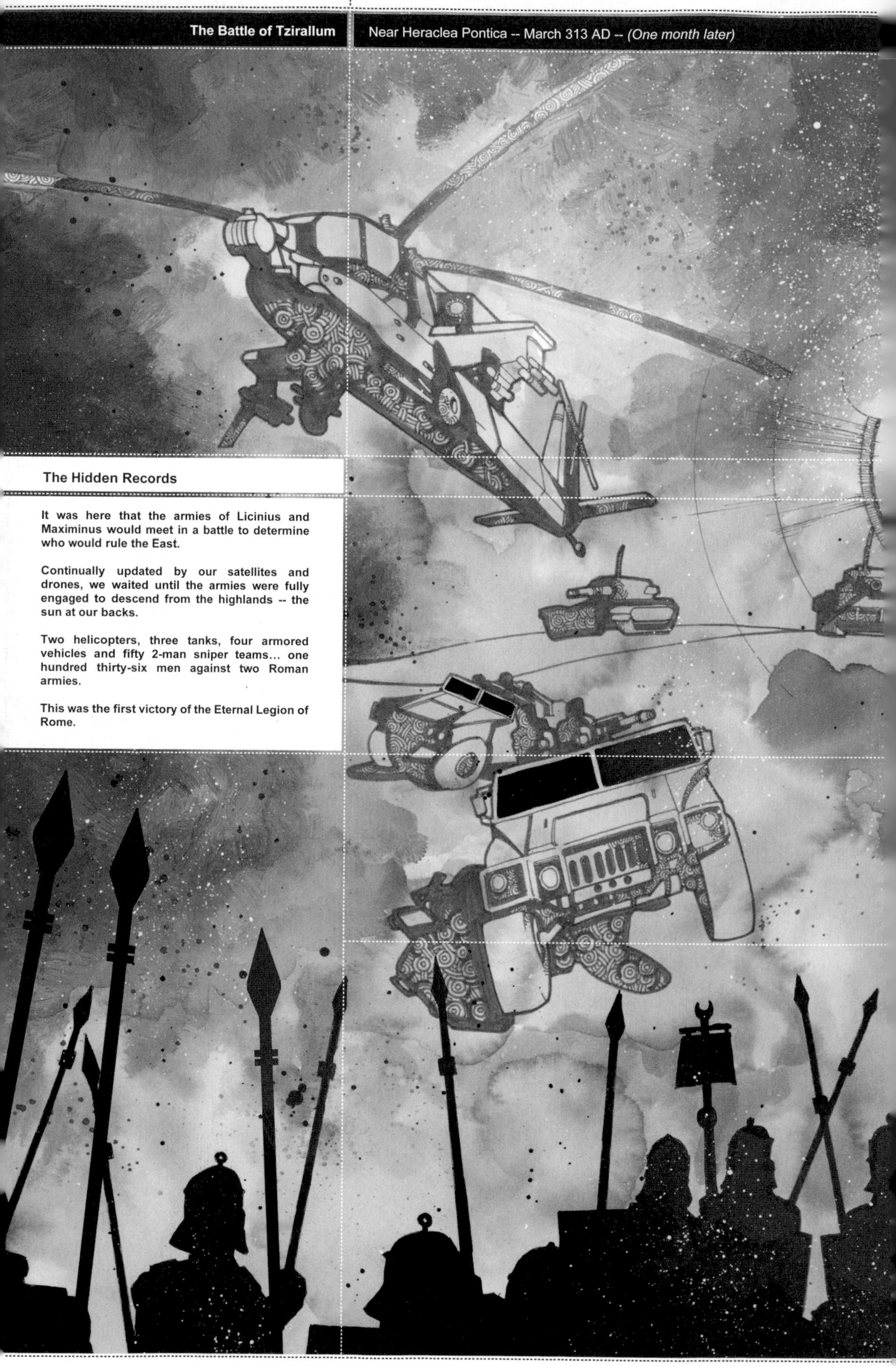
The Battle of Tzirallum
Near Heraclea Pontica -- March 313 AD -- (One month later)
The Hidden Records
It was here that the armies of Licinius and Maximinus would meet in a battle to determine who would rule the East.
Continually updated by our satellites and drones, we waited until the armies were fully engaged to descend from the highlands -- the sun at our backs.
Two helicopters, three tanks, four armored vehicles and fifty 2-man sniper teams... one hundred thirty-six men against two Roman armies.
This was the first victory of the Eternal Legion of Rome.

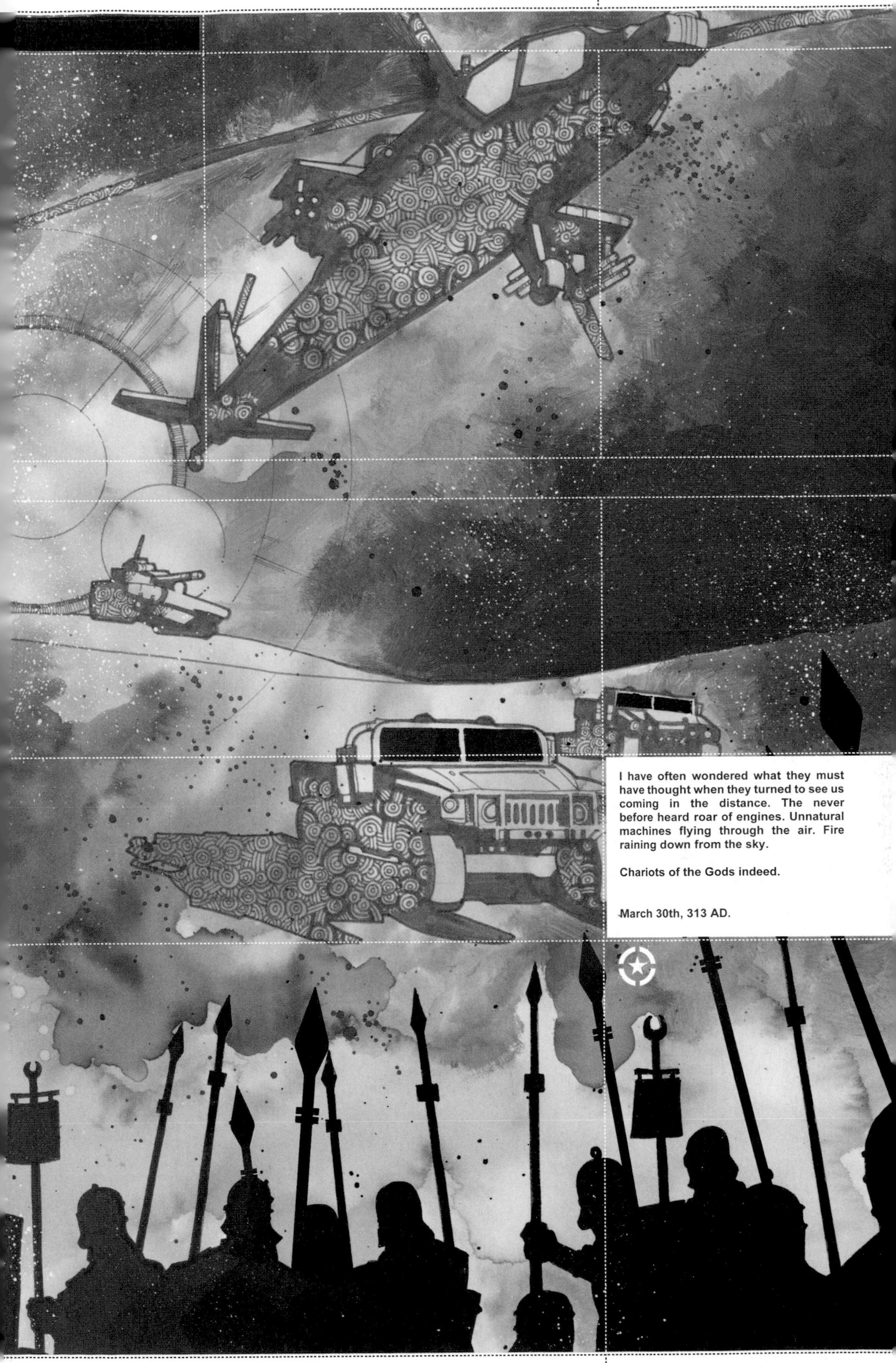
I have often wondered what they must have thought when they turned to see us coming in the distance. The never before heard roar of engines. Unnatural machines flying through the air. Fire raining down from the sky.
Chariots of the Gods indeed.
March 30th, 313 AD.

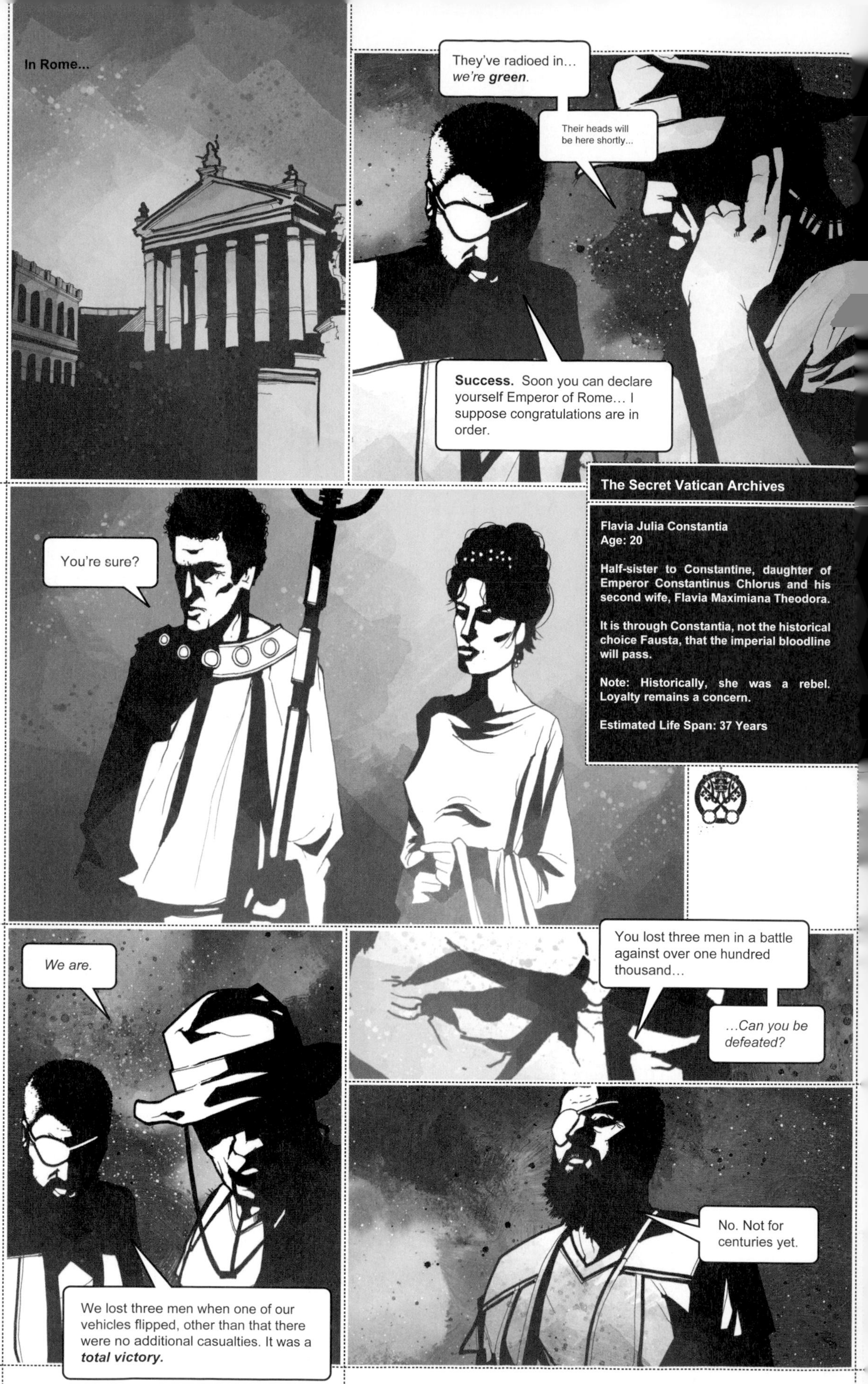
In Rome...
They've radioed in... *we're* ***green***.
Their heads will be here shortly...
Success. Soon you can declare yourself Emperor of Rome... I suppose congratulations are in order.
The Secret Vatican Archives
Flavia Julia Constantia
Age: 20
Half-sister to Constantine, daughter of Emperor Constantinus Chlorus and his second wife, Flavia Maximiana Theodora.
It is through Constantia, not the historical choice Fausta, that the imperial bloodline will pass.
Note: Historically, she was a rebel. Loyalty remains a concern.
Estimated Life Span: 37 Years
You're sure?
We are.
We lost three men when one of our vehicles flipped, other than that there were no additional casualties. It was a ***total victory.***
You lost three men in a battle against over one hundred thousand...
...Can you be defeated?
No. Not for centuries yet.

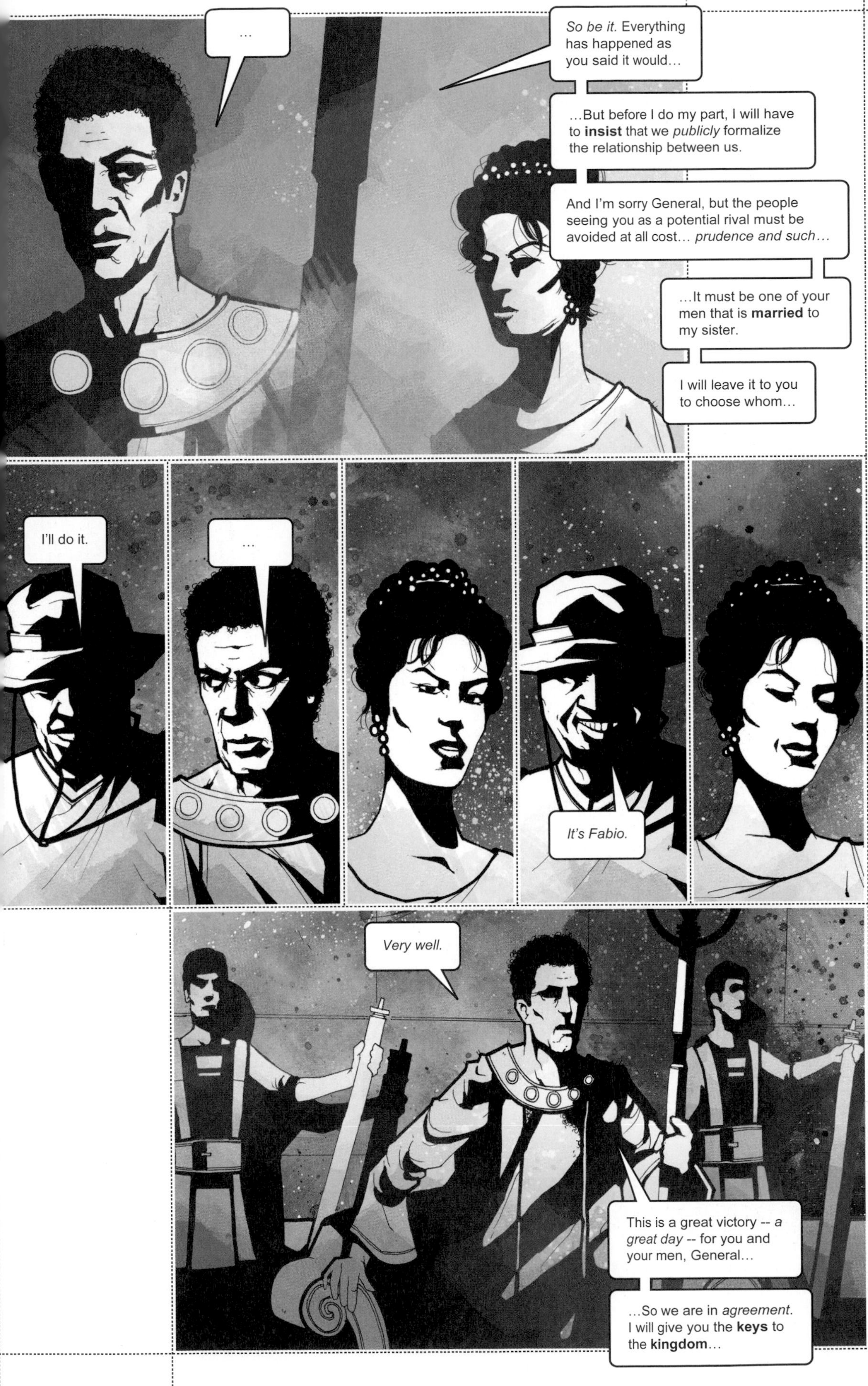

...
So be it. Everything has happened as you said it would...
...But before I do my part, I will have to **insist** that we *publicly* formalize the relationship between us.
And I'm sorry General, but the people seeing you as a potential rival must be avoided at all cost... *prudence and such*...
...It must be one of your men that is **married** to my sister.
I will leave it to you to choose whom...
I'll do it.
...
It's Fabio.
Very well.
This is a great victory -- *a great day* -- for you and your men, General...
...So we are in *agreement*. I will give you the **keys** to the **kingdom**...

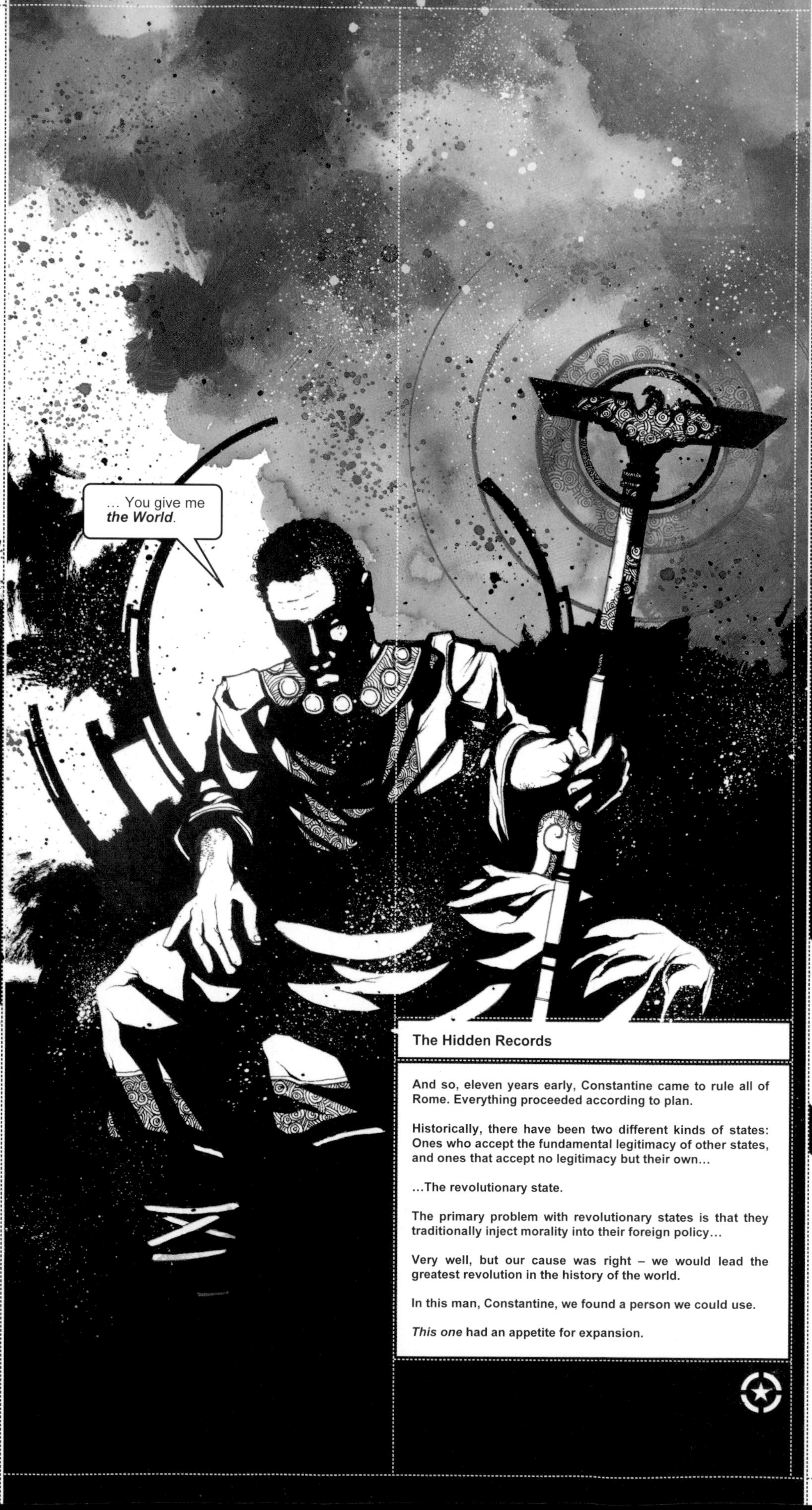
... You give me *the World*.
The Hidden Records
And so, eleven years early, Constantine came to rule all of Rome. Everything proceeded according to plan.
Historically, there have been two different kinds of states: Ones who accept the fundamental legitimacy of other states, and ones that accept no legitimacy but their own...
...The revolutionary state.
The primary problem with revolutionary states is that they traditionally inject morality into their foreign policy...
Very well, but our cause was right – we would lead the greatest revolution in the history of the world.
In this man, Constantine, we found a person we could use.
This one had an appetite for expansion.

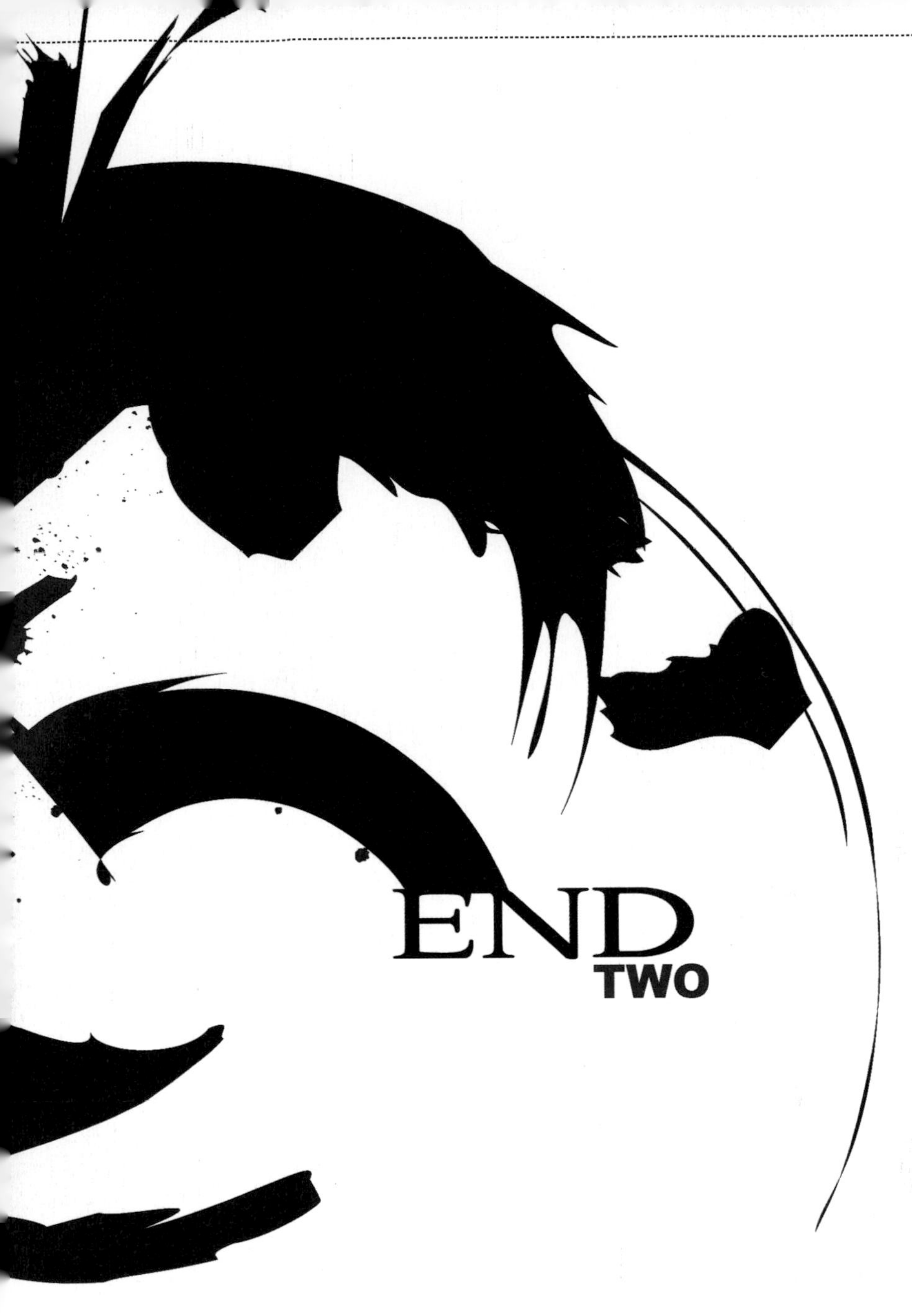

END
TWO

CHAPTER THREE

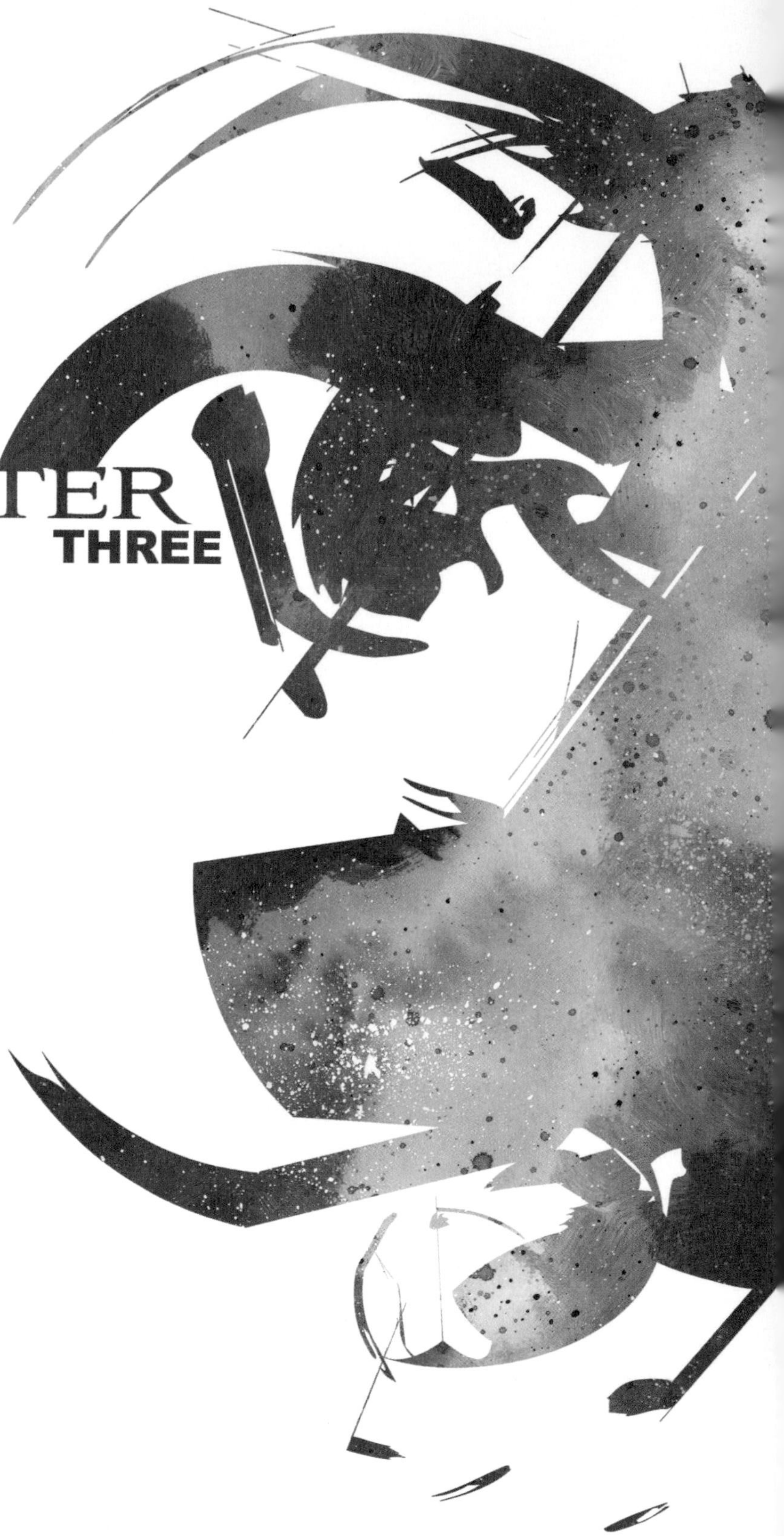

caea
ne 9th, 325 AD

e First Ecumenical Conference of Bishops
e Council of Nicaea

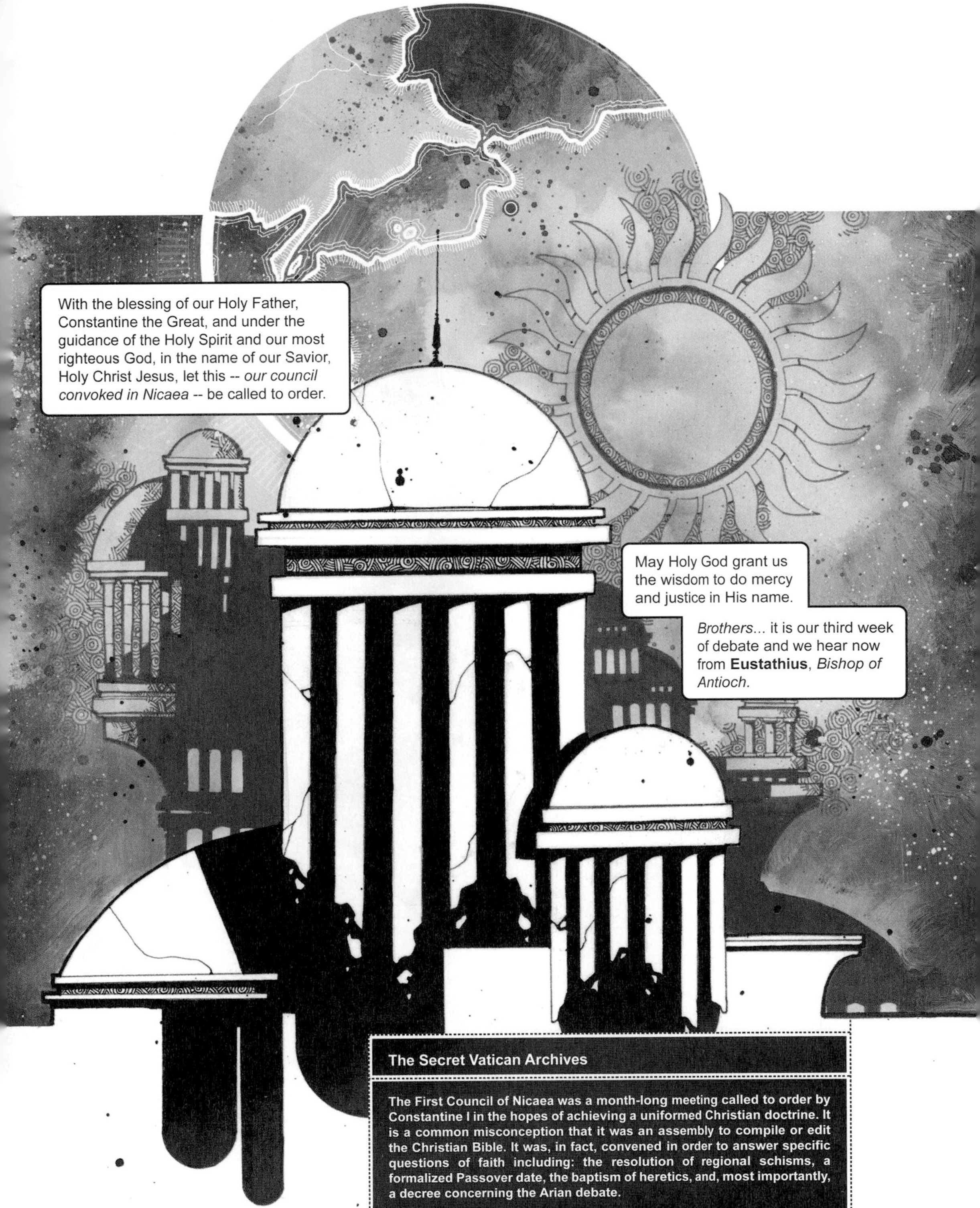
With the blessing of our Holy Father, Constantine the Great, and under the guidance of the Holy Spirit and our most righteous God, in the name of our Savior, Holy Christ Jesus, let this -- *our council convoked in Nicaea* -- be called to order.
May Holy God grant us the wisdom to do mercy and justice in His name.
Brothers... it is our third week of debate and we hear now from **Eustathius**, *Bishop of Antioch*.

The Secret Vatican Archives

The First Council of Nicaea was a month-long meeting called to order by Constantine I in the hopes of achieving a uniformed Christian doctrine. It is a common misconception that it was an assembly to compile or edit the Christian Bible. It was, in fact, convened in order to answer specific questions of faith including: the resolution of regional schisms, a formalized Passover date, the baptism of heretics, and, most importantly, a decree concerning the Arian debate.

Arian belief originated from the competing beliefs that either Christ Jesus was the same as God, or that He was merely composed of the same material -- a product of His father's divinity.

The resulting support of the first position was the point of origin for the guidelines of a unified Christendom -- The clear delineation of what was Orthodox belief and what was heretical. A distinction that had to be manipulated.

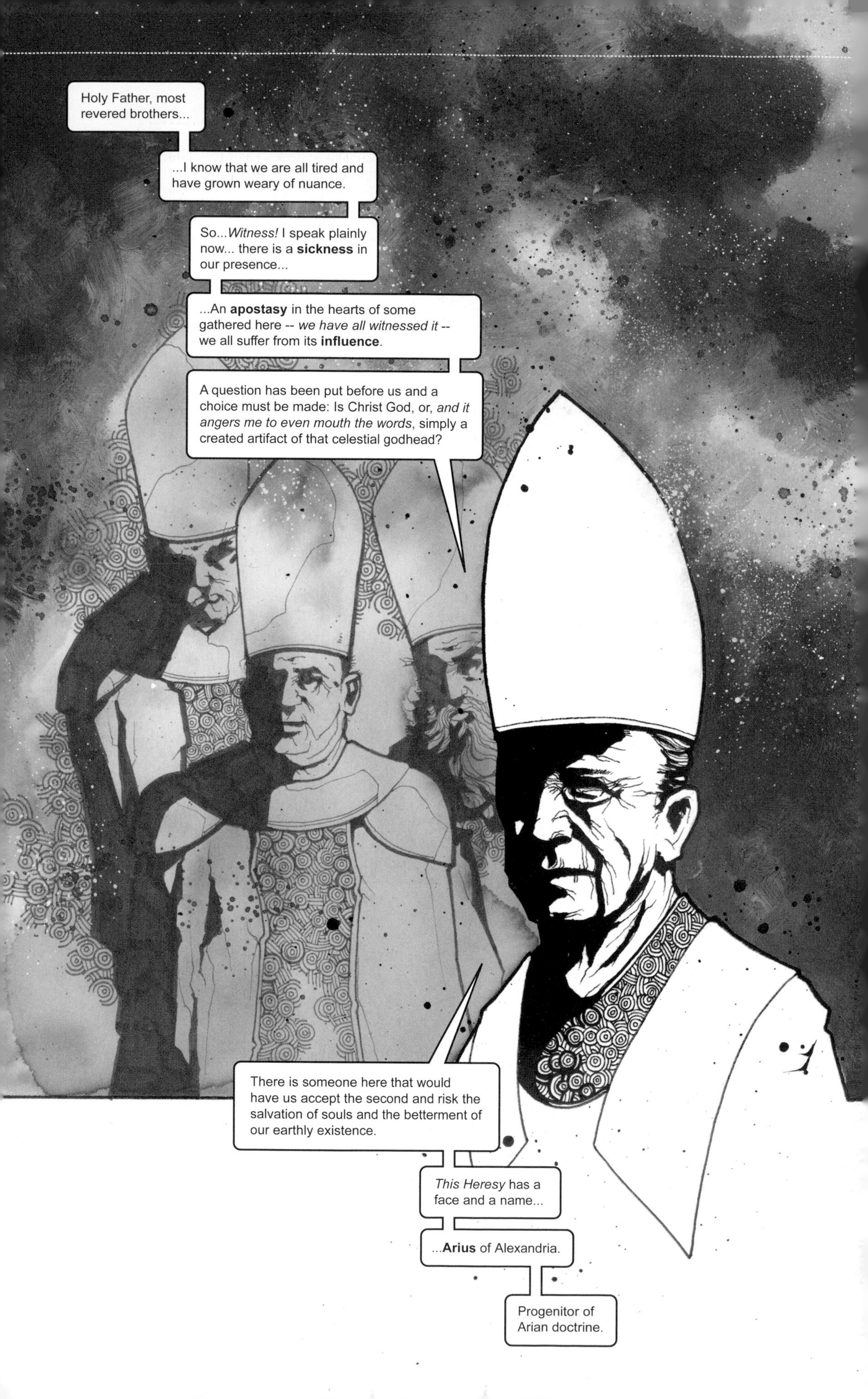

Holy Father, most revered brothers...
...I know that we are all tired and have grown weary of nuance.
So...*Witness!* I speak plainly now... there is a **sickness** in our presence...
...An **apostasy** in the hearts of some gathered here -- *we have all witnessed it* -- we all suffer from its **influence**.
A question has been put before us and a choice must be made: Is Christ God, or, *and it angers me to even mouth the words*, simply a created artifact of that celestial godhead?
There is someone here that would have us accept the second and risk the salvation of souls and the betterment of our earthly existence.
This Heresy has a face and a name...
...**Arius** of Alexandria.
Progenitor of Arian doctrine.

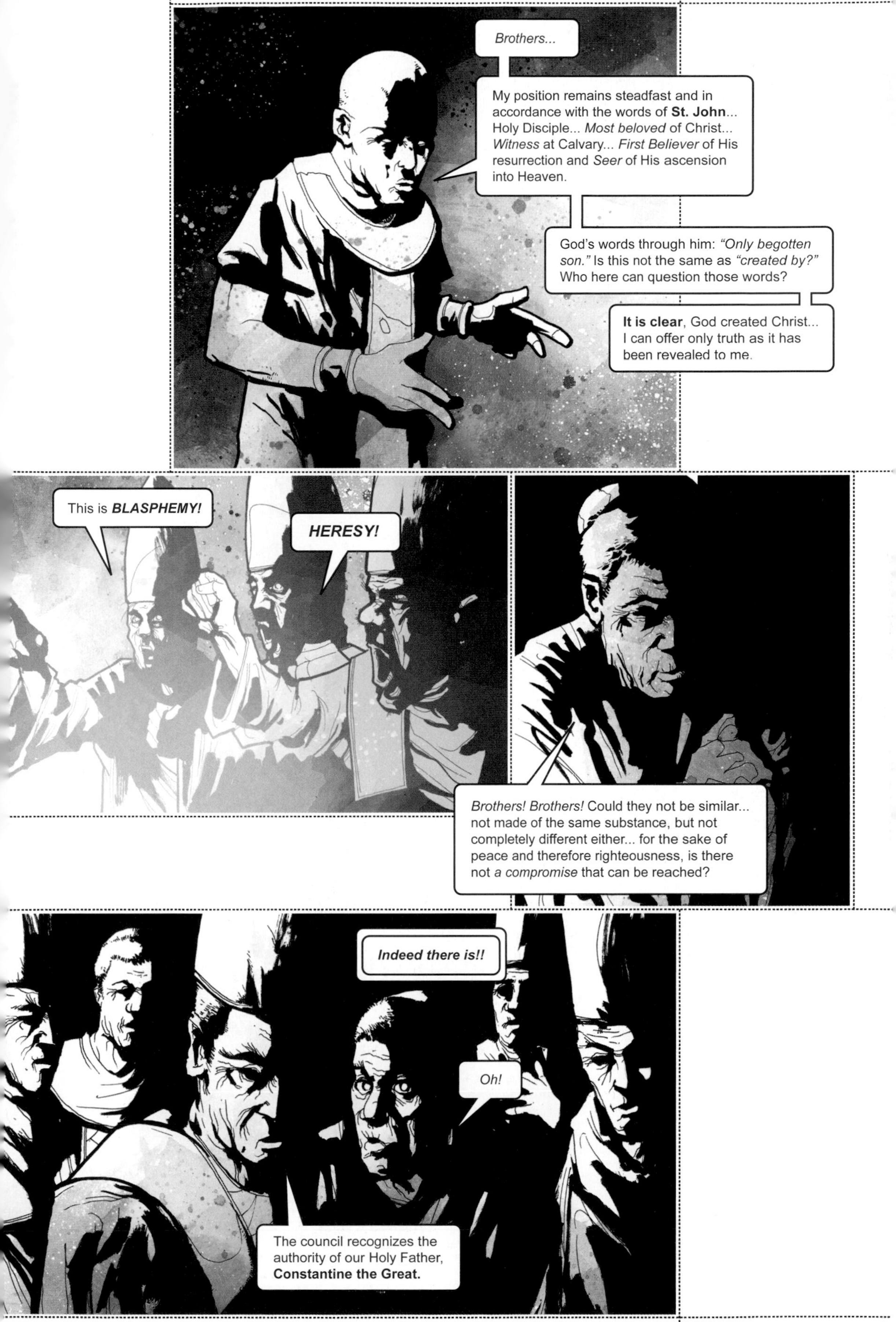
Brothers...
My position remains steadfast and in accordance with the words of **St. John**... Holy Disciple... *Most beloved* of Christ... *Witness* at Calvary... *First Believer* of His resurrection and *Seer* of His ascension into Heaven.
God's words through him: *"Only begotten son."* Is this not the same as *"created by?"* Who here can question those words?
It is clear, God created Christ... I can offer only truth as it has been revealed to me.
This is ***BLASPHEMY!***
HERESY!
Brothers! Brothers! Could they not be similar... not made of the same substance, but not completely different either... for the sake of peace and therefore righteousness, is there not *a compromise* that can be reached?
Indeed there is!!
Oh!
The council recognizes the authority of our Holy Father, **Constantine the Great.**

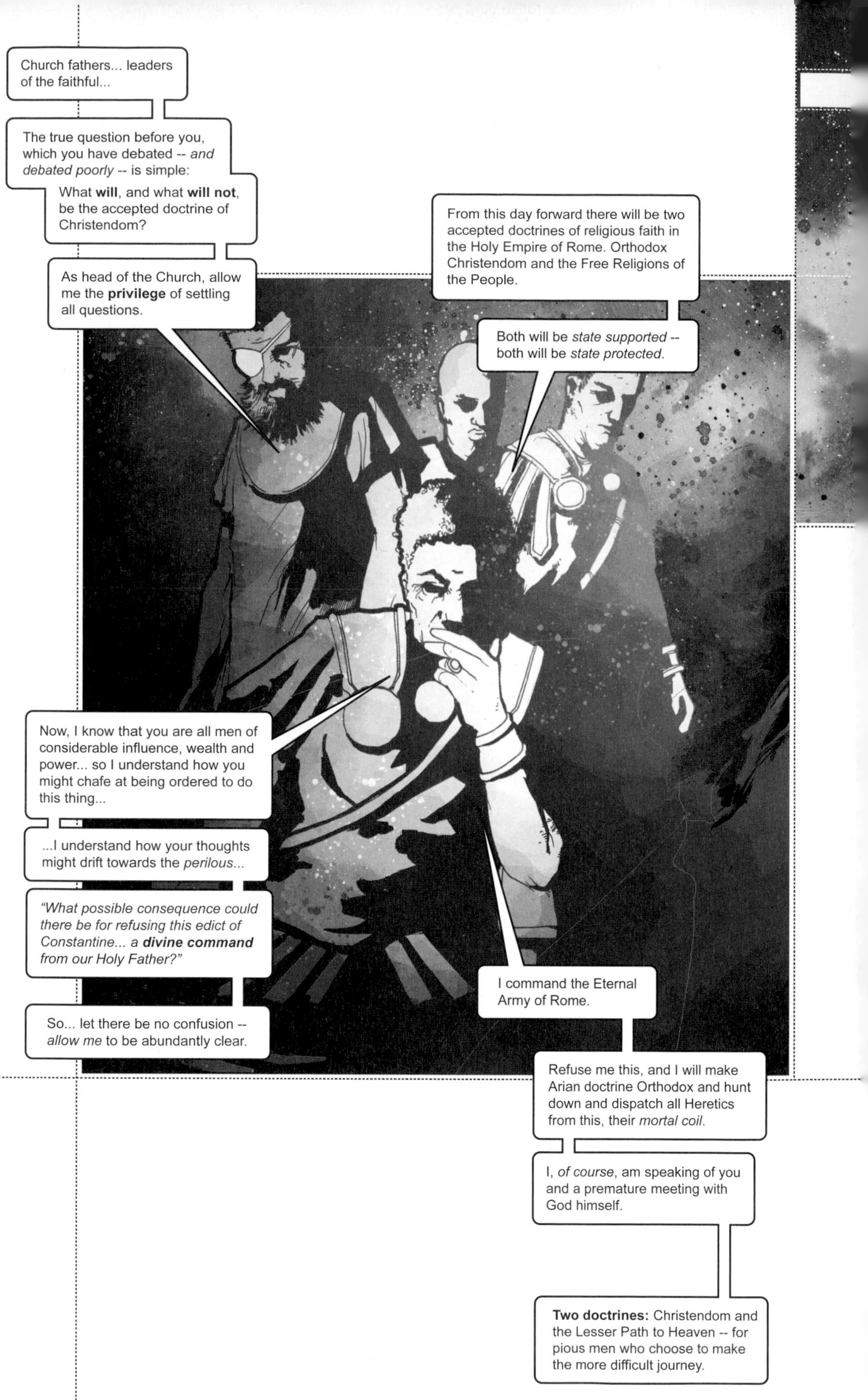
Church fathers... leaders of the faithful...
The true question before you, which you have debated -- *and debated poorly* -- is simple:
What **will**, and what **will not**, be the accepted doctrine of Christendom?
As head of the Church, allow me the **privilege** of settling all questions.
From this day forward there will be two accepted doctrines of religious faith in the Holy Empire of Rome. Orthodox Christendom and the Free Religions of the People.
Both will be *state supported* -- both will be *state protected*.
Now, I know that you are all men of considerable influence, wealth and power... so I understand how you might chafe at being ordered to do this thing...
...I understand how your thoughts might drift towards the *perilous*...
"What possible consequence could there be for refusing this edict of Constantine... a ***divine command*** *from our Holy Father?"*
So... let there be no confusion -- *allow me* to be abundantly clear.
I command the Eternal Army of Rome.
Refuse me this, and I will make Arian doctrine Orthodox and hunt down and dispatch all Heretics from this, their *mortal coil*.
I, *of course*, am speaking of you and a premature meeting with God himself.
Two doctrines: Christendom and the Lesser Path to Heaven -- for pious men who choose to make the more difficult journey.

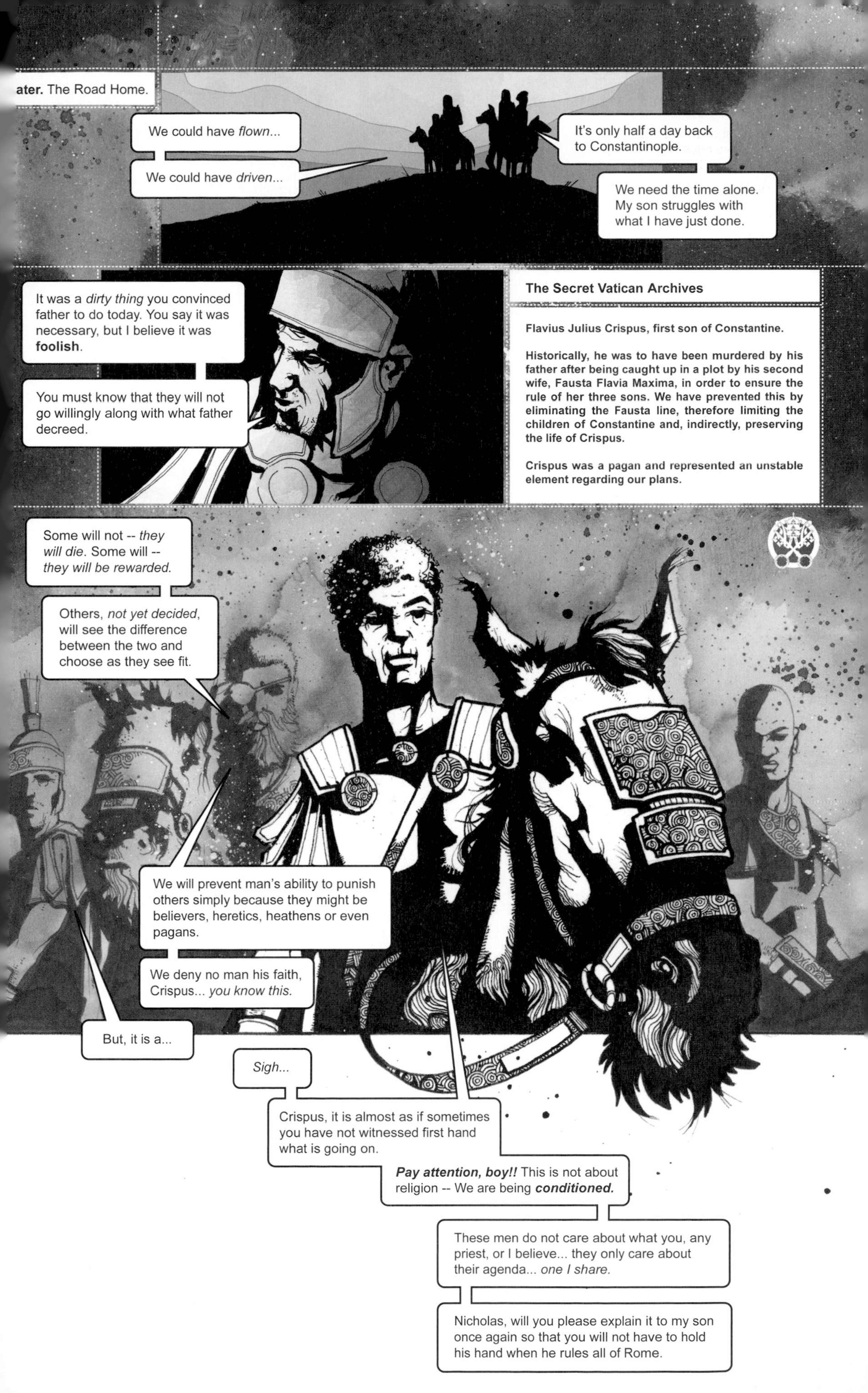
ater. The Road Home.
We could have *flown*...
We could have *driven*...
It's only half a day back to Constantinople.
We need the time alone. My son struggles with what I have just done.
It was a *dirty thing* you convinced father to do today. You say it was necessary, but I believe it was **foolish**.
You must know that they will not go willingly along with what father decreed.
The Secret Vatican Archives
Flavius Julius Crispus, first son of Constantine.
Historically, he was to have been murdered by his father after being caught up in a plot by his second wife, Fausta Flavia Maxima, in order to ensure the rule of her three sons. We have prevented this by eliminating the Fausta line, therefore limiting the children of Constantine and, indirectly, preserving the life of Crispus.
Crispus was a pagan and represented an unstable element regarding our plans.
Some will not -- *they will die*. Some will -- *they will be rewarded.*
Others, *not yet decided*, will see the difference between the two and choose as they see fit.
We will prevent man's ability to punish others simply because they might be believers, heretics, heathens or even pagans.
We deny no man his faith, Crispus... *you know this.*
But, it is a...
Sigh...
Crispus, it is almost as if sometimes you have not witnessed first hand what is going on.
Pay attention, boy!! This is not about religion -- We are being ***conditioned.***
These men do not care about what you, any priest, or I believe... they only care about their agenda... *one I share.*
Nicholas, will you please explain it to my son once again so that you will not have to hold his hand when he rules all of Rome.

The following conversation was reconstructed from the journals of Constantine and the unauthorized biography of Emmanuel Mfede, To Raise a People.

In attendance:

(CA) - Constantine Augustus
(CR) - Crispus Ceasar
(NC) - General Nicholas Chase
(EM) - Colonel Emmanuel Mfede

These are the relevant excerpts from that conversation in regards to:

The Death of Religion

NC: Crispus, tell me again what your opposition is to what we do.

CR: I don't think you and your men realize what you might possibly unleash -- I don't know how you think you could control...

EM: [Interrupts] We are not hoping to control anything -- we want to eliminate religion as a method of control.

CA: Crispus, religion hides evil behind a veil of righteousness. It attacks legitimate questions by simply calling them immoral. It demands examples to be made of men who fail to meet hypocritical standards.

NC: It's worse than that. Religion feeds off of that within us which cries out to understand our place in the universe, but crushes that spirituality under false rules and demands of acceptable behavior.

CR: ...People should be able to believe what they want.

CA: Son, the people can believe whatever they want, but there will be no authority higher than the laws of the state from this day forward.

EM: Authority -- power -- always attracts people who wish to control others. We geld religion becuase it has always been the easiest path to gaining that. When you appoint yourself a religious authority... do you not speak for God?

CR: I still do not see how you could be successful.

NC: Until now, no one has ever solved the problem of creating culture as a matter of public policy. What we will do is create an internal state morality with revolution as a generational catalyst.

The Goal and Government

CR: And father, you believe this is possible.

CA: I do, and in the many conversations Nicholas and I have had about this, he has never once wavered on his position or failed to answer questions truthfully.

CR: Very well, explain it to me.

NC: To be clear: Our end-goal is the ultimate Republic. But that cannot be achieved without major upheaval. We have to facilitate a rapid progression of political thought.

CR: Progression?

EM: In the future, the true inheritor of the republic was something called democracy. Two other political movements attempted to challenge its rise: they were called fascism and communism. We intend to systematically use of the strengths of those to enact radical socio-political change and then use their inherent weaknesses to directly implement progressively better systems. Every three to five generations we will change the government of Rome until we achieve this. Revolution -- Stabilization -- Consolidation.

CR: How can you possibly hope to manipulate people on such a massive scale?

NC: Historically, the world is rife with cultural conflicts based on ideological differences that have derived primarily from the disparity of resources.

CA: Some have, while others do not.

EM: Our first goal is to enhance this condition by creating a separation between Rome and the world. To do this, we will need to create the greatest disparity in the history of the man.

NC: Our technology makes it possible for us, in this time, to accumulate limitless wealth. This allows us to provide, address and satisfy the ever-increasing appetite of evolving man in a way no others can.

CR: I don't understand how that helps...

NC: We will make all of this free to those who want it, all they have to do is join us. We will assimilate their culture -- not eradicate it -- as Rome is all things to all enlightened people.

CR: And this is the first form our new government will take?

CA: The Fascist state.

EM: And it's important to know that Fascism is not a universal doctrine. Its only source of legitimacy is race or nation -- specifically the right of certain peoples to rule over others. So, it is with fascism we will begin -- you are either Roman or you are not.

CR: How do you expect men to want to change from this into another form of government? You speak as if the difference will be like comparing paradise with the squalor of slaves.

NC: We appeal to that which makes us human. The discoverer. Man is not comfortable staying in one place, or living just one life... It is human to not simply want to exist, but to become something more than what you are. We feed humanity a perfect diet of change. We will feed them revolution.

EM: The young always rebel against authority and the old always want to feel young. There will be no trouble finding radicals.

CA: What they do not tell you is that they intend to lead the radicals themselves.

CR: What?

EM: It's true. We do not believe in the governments we are creating, we are simply using them to accelerate man's progress. We are agents of change.

NC: So, we will replace the Fascist state with a Communist state -- a form of pseudo-socialism.

CR: And that is?

NC: Ehhh, it's a form of government where all institutions are collectively owned and run by the state. It's silly utopianism that runs contrary to the natural state of man, but centralized economies have always been excellent at rapidly creating an internal industrial revolution.

CR: I don't understand what…

CA: The machines they use. To be able to create things of that nature, you have to have industry.

CR: It seems impossible that this could happen so quickly.

EM: Centralized economies, educational institutions and armies working towards a single goal: The engine of industry.

NC: The problem will not be achieving an industrial state. We have the knowledge to achieve this, the problem will be with predicting what follows.

CR: How so?

EM: Communist governments quickly become obsolete in post-industrial economies. There must be greater freedom for technological innovation to flourish.

NC: So we will then leave behind our communist state for democracy -- one where for the first time all men will be truly free. A return, and the rebirth, of the Republic of Rome.

CR: And how will you instigate this revolution?

CA: It is the very nature of man to be free, Crispus.

CR: You think so?

EM: We know so. There are many economic reasons why man evolves to a certain point. In the future, he works in an office and not a field, he is a member of a union or professional organization rather than a tribe or clan. He comes to obey bureaucrats instead of priests, and become literate in a common language. But even this kind of thinking, Crispus, is limited… man is not simply an economic animal. There are greater questions to be asked.

NC: Why are we greater than the animals that exist out there in the world? Because a Roman is the only animal able to overcome his instinct for self-preservation and take up higher, complex purposes and goals.

CA: Right now, out there in the world exists the age-old patrician-pleb paradigm. Here, here in our New Rome, there will be respect for all men.

NC: We believe Rome can be the first 'universal state.'

The Republic

CR: So you can do this -- achieve what seems impossible?

NC: We do not believe that achieving it is the problem -- maintaining it will be.

EM: We will have to manufacture a fluid social and ethnic structure to eliminate the standard problems of most older societies like rigid social classes and subnationalism -- plus, others will arise.

NC: Yes, man will evolve quickly, so as soon as possible we need a support structure in place for clearly identifying the most talented and ambitious citizens. We must keep them personally satisfied and out of the government and our higher military ranks until our democracy is established.

CA: Then the problem will take care of itself.

CR: And that's it, then. The course of human history -- plotted

NC: Crispus, we're not saying that…

CR: [Interrupts] Are there no flaws in your universal state?

EM: Of course there are.

NC: The tyranny of the majority…

CR: Ah, the mob.

EM: Yes, there is also the problem of mediocrity.

NC: But we believe that both of these are controllable… we have other plans.

CA: The Empire will still need a guiding hand, Crispus. There are things that only a man such as yourself can do.

CR: And how would we start?

EM: Well, it's too late for that, I introduced the scientific method to a group of scholars last week a full 1300 years early.

CA: And?

EM: Went well.

NC: Crispus, there are those that say it takes maturity to see the world as it is and not how we want it to be… We say those men are blind and lack ambition.

They may have a semblance of being human, but they are not Roman.

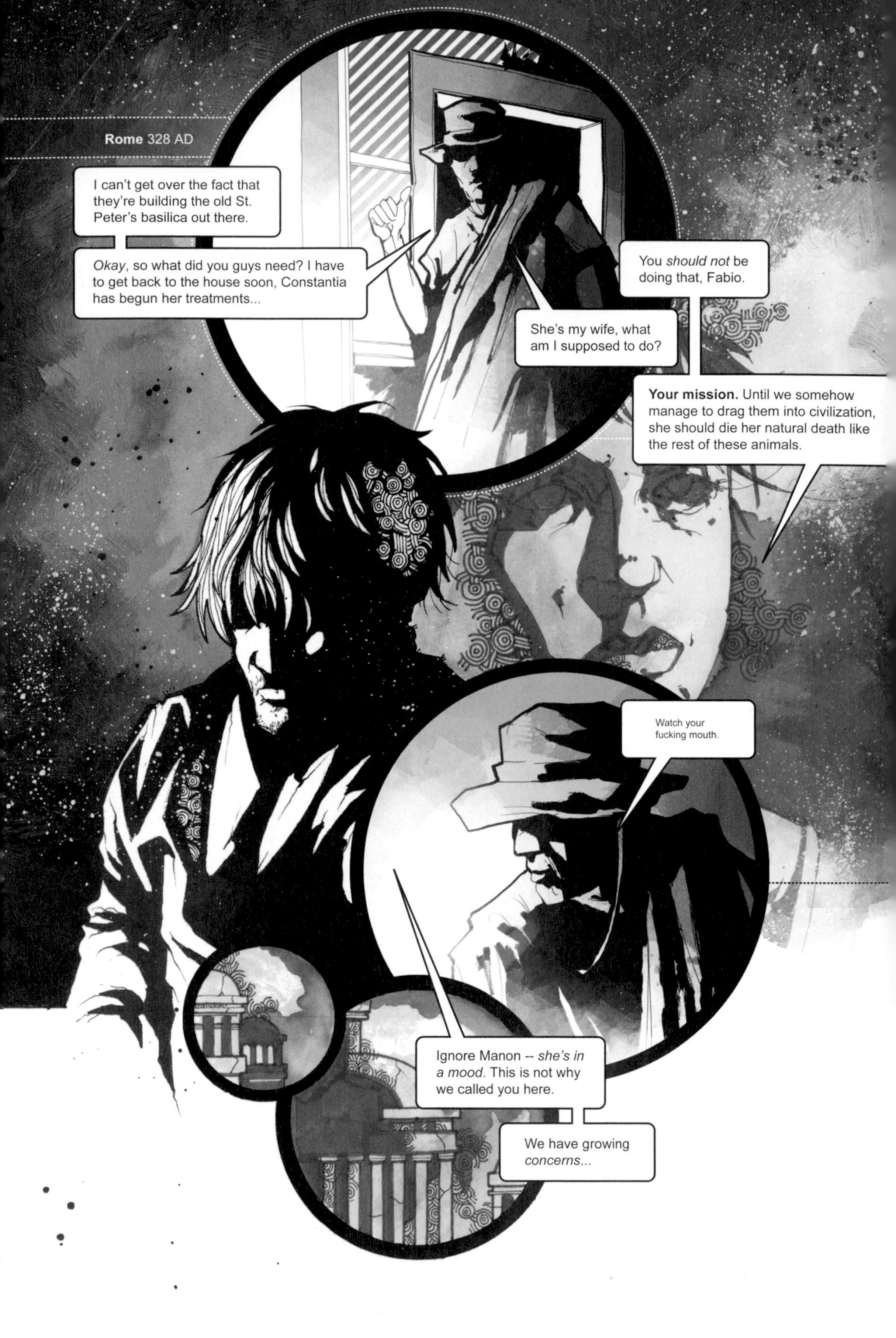
Rome 328 AD
I can't get over the fact that they're building the old St. Peter's basilica out there.
Okay, so what did you guys need? I have to get back to the house soon, Constantia has begun her treatments...
You *should not* be doing that, Fabio.
She's my wife, what am I supposed to do?
Your mission. Until we somehow manage to drag them into civilization, she should die her natural death like the rest of these animals.
Watch your fucking mouth.
Ignore Manon -- *she's in a mood*. This is not why we called you here.
We have growing *concerns*...

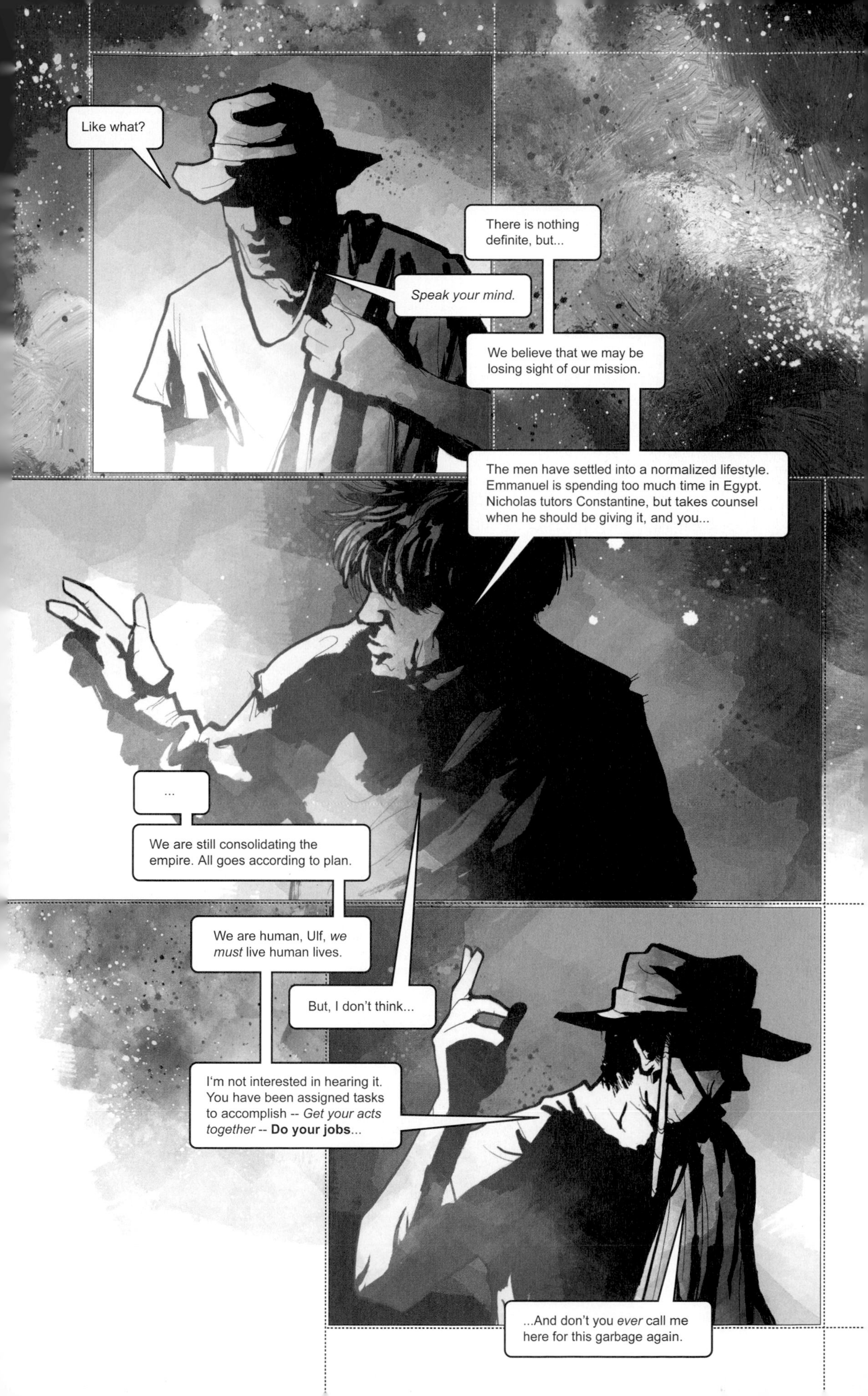
Like what?
There is nothing definite, but...
Speak your mind.
We believe that we may be losing sight of our mission.
The men have settled into a normalized lifestyle. Emmanuel is spending too much time in Egypt. Nicholas tutors Constantine, but takes counsel when he should be giving it, and you...
...
We are still consolidating the empire. All goes according to plan.
We are human, Ulf, *we must* live human lives.
But, I don't think...
I'm not interested in hearing it. You have been assigned tasks to accomplish -- *Get your acts together* -- **Do your jobs**...
...And don't you *ever* call me here for this garbage again.

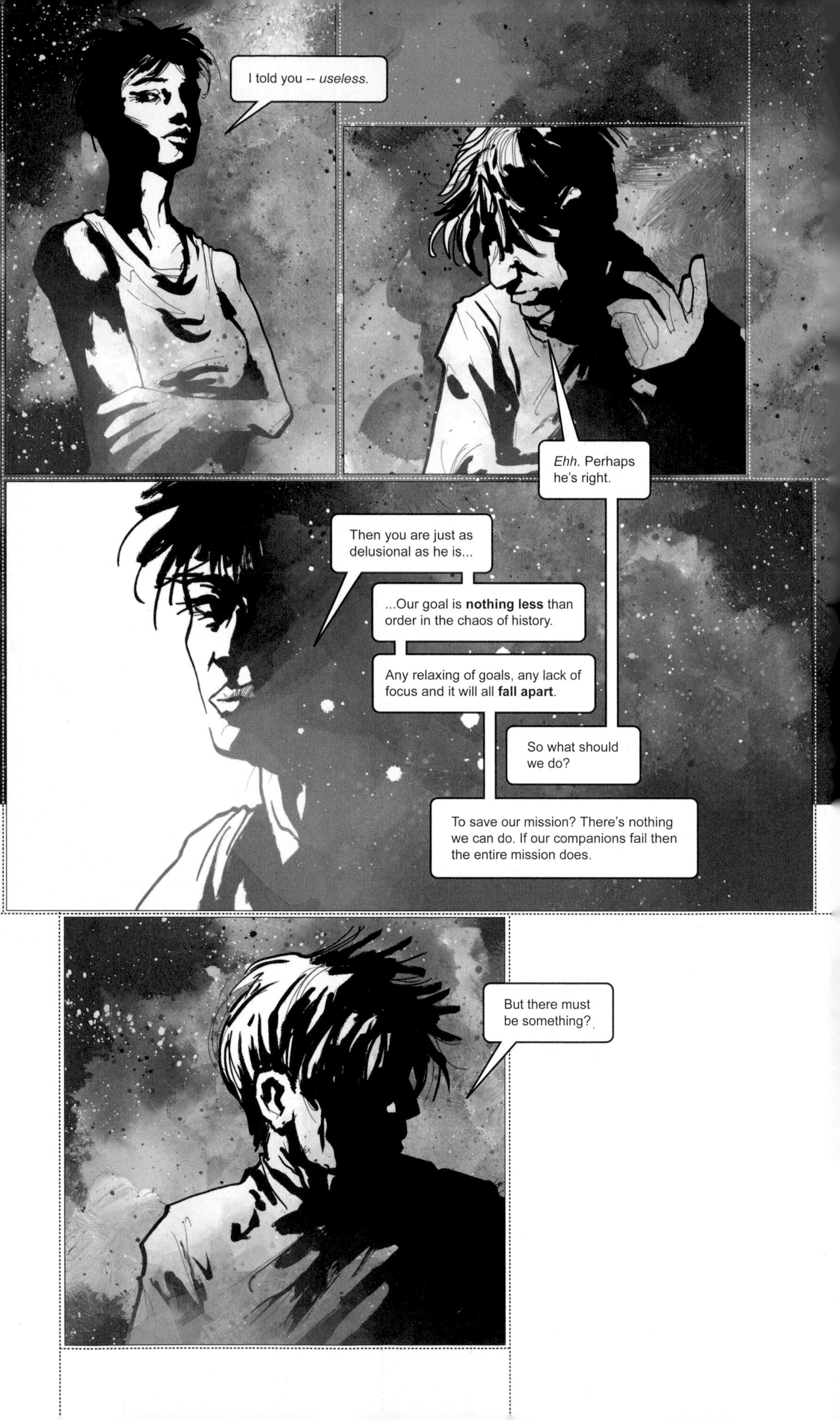
I told you -- *useless*.
Ehh. Perhaps he's right.
Then you are just as delusional as he is...
...Our goal is **nothing less** than order in the chaos of history.
Any relaxing of goals, any lack of focus and it will all **fall apart**.
So what should we do?
To save our mission? There's nothing we can do. If our companions fail then the entire mission does.
But there must be something?

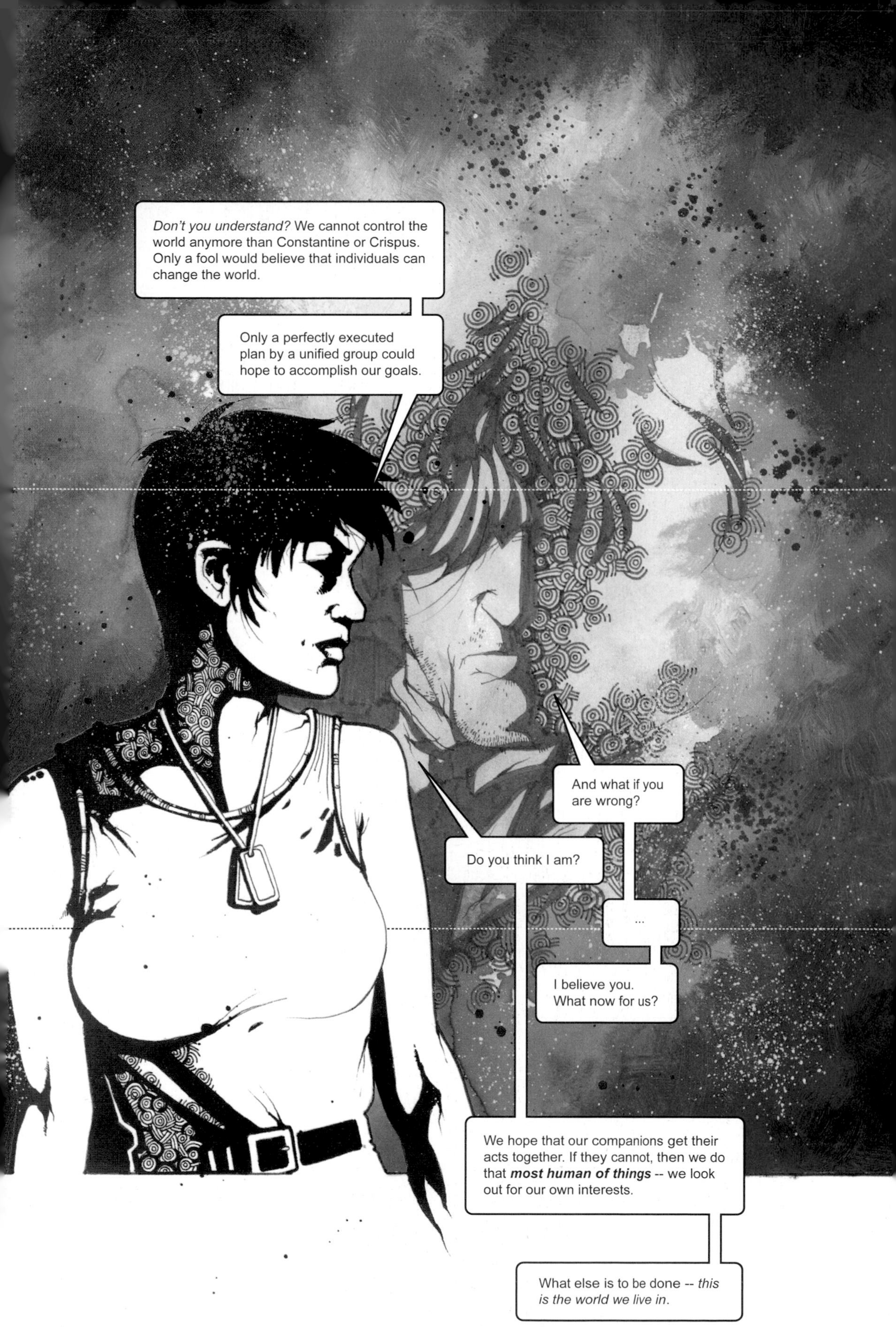
Don't you understand? We cannot control the world anymore than Constantine or Crispus. Only a fool would believe that individuals can change the world.
Only a perfectly executed plan by a unified group could hope to accomplish our goals.
And what if you are wrong?
Do you think I am?
...
I believe you. What now for us?
We hope that our companions get their acts together. If they cannot, then we do that ***most human of things*** -- we look out for our own interests.
What else is to be done -- *this is the world we live in*.

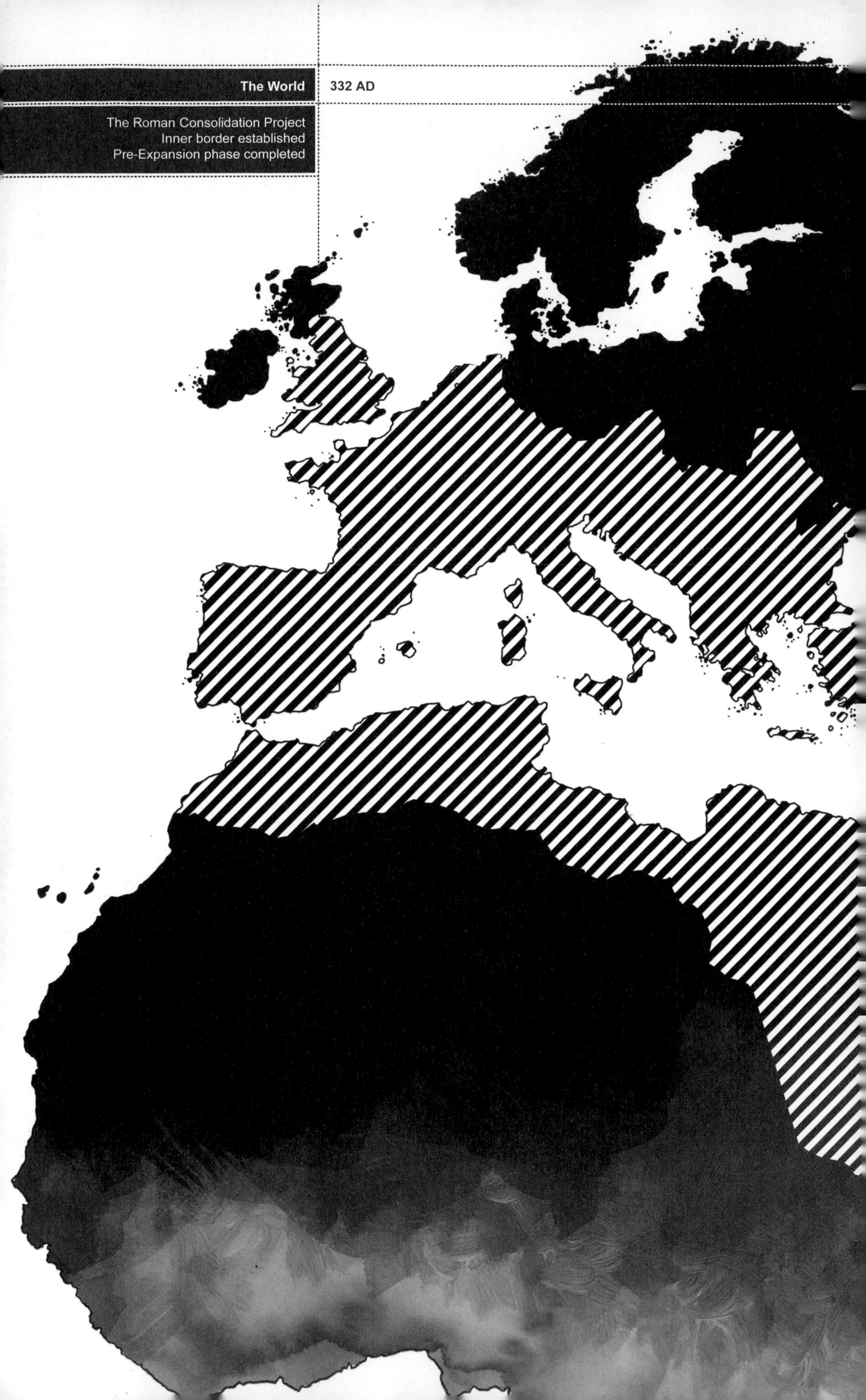
The World
332 AD
The Roman Consolidation Project
Inner border established
Pre-Expansion phase completed

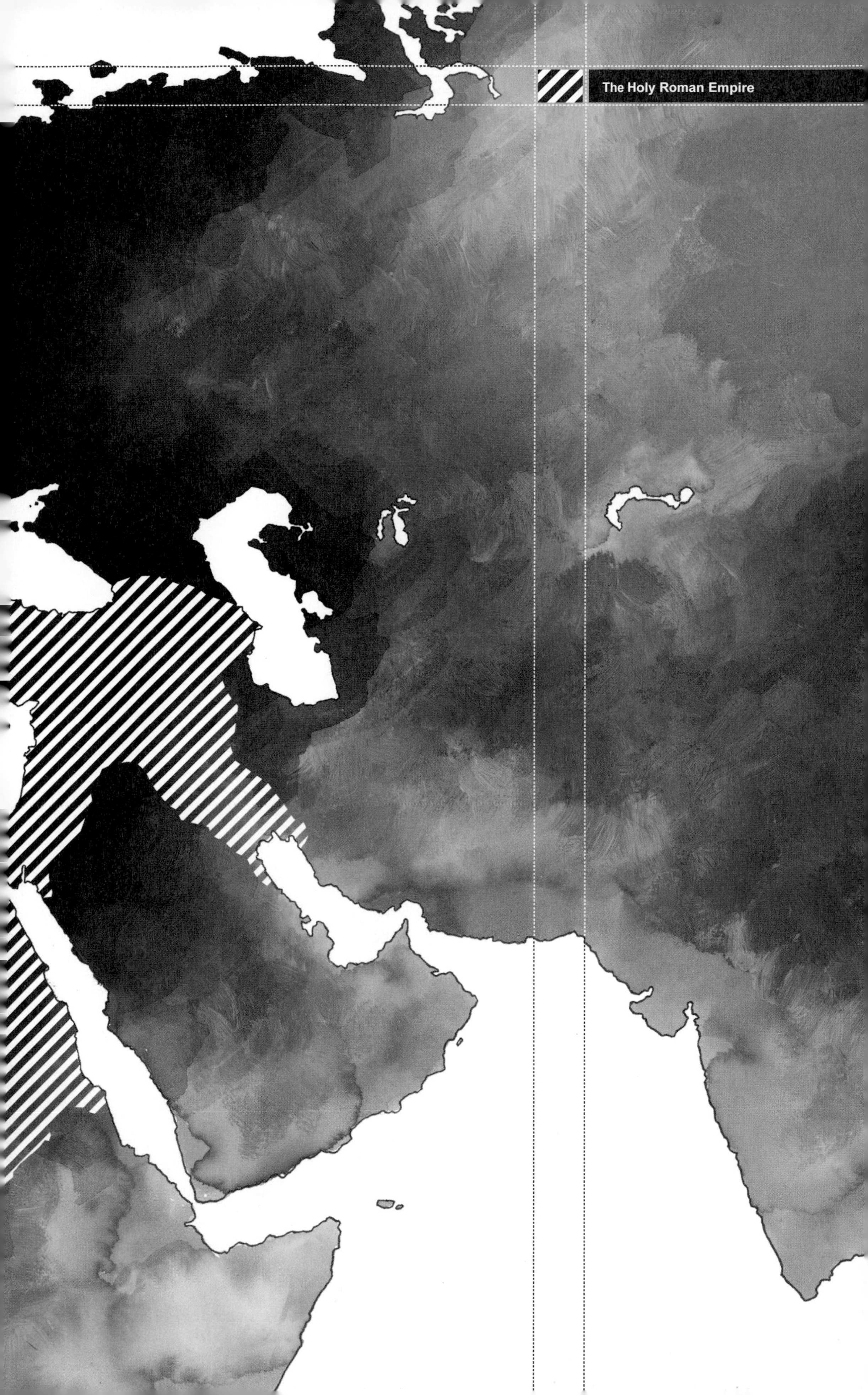
The Holy Roman Empire

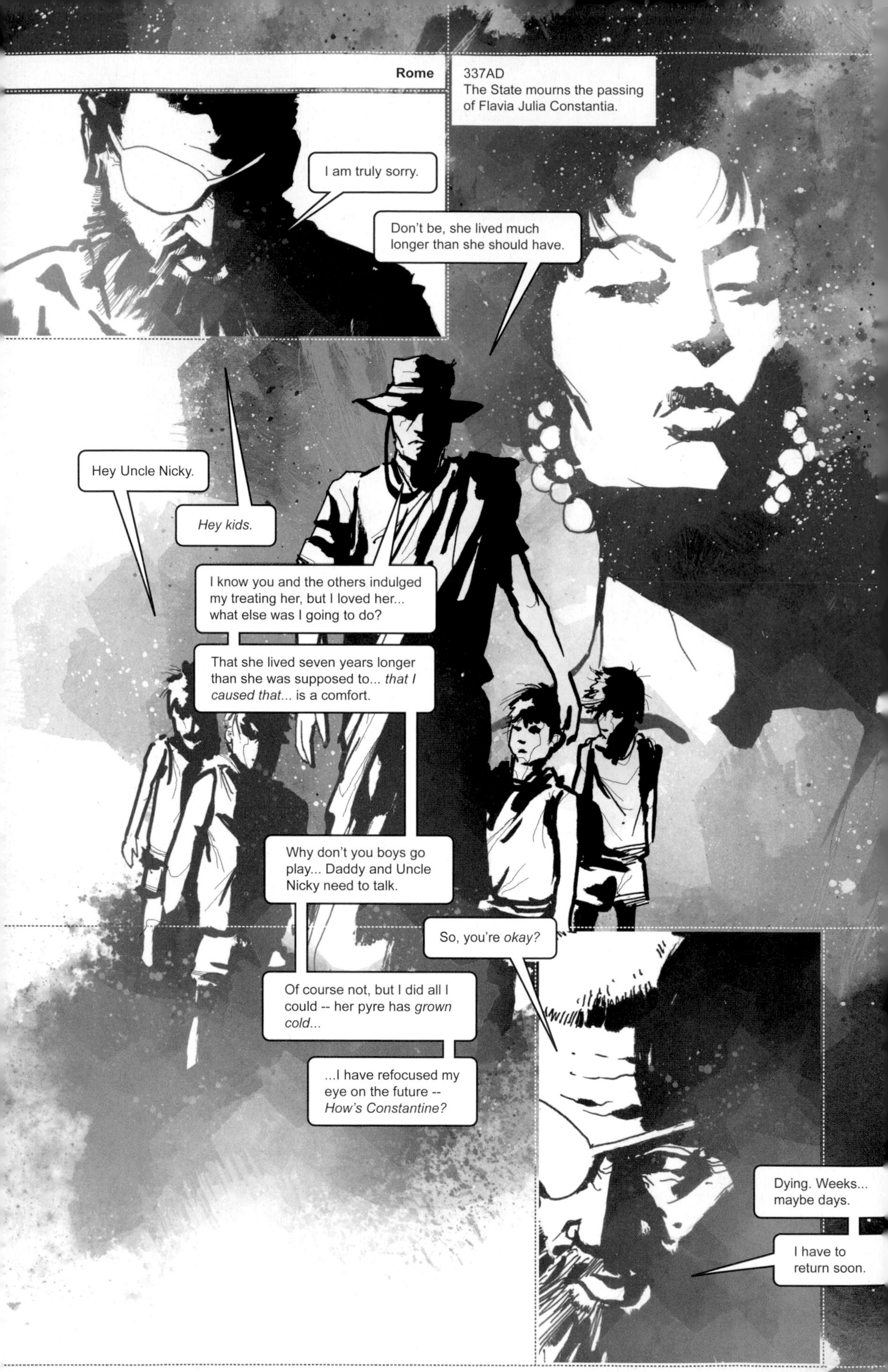
Rome
337AD
The State mourns the passing of Flavia Julia Constantia.
I am truly sorry.
Don't be, she lived much longer than she should have.
Hey Uncle Nicky.
Hey kids.
I know you and the others indulged my treating her, but I loved her... what else was I going to do?
That she lived seven years longer than she was supposed to... *that I caused that...* is a comfort.
Why don't you boys go play... Daddy and Uncle Nicky need to talk.
So, you're *okay?*
Of course not, but I did all I could -- her pyre has *grown cold...*
...I have refocused my eye on the future -- *How's Constantine?*
Dying. Weeks... maybe days.
I have to return soon.

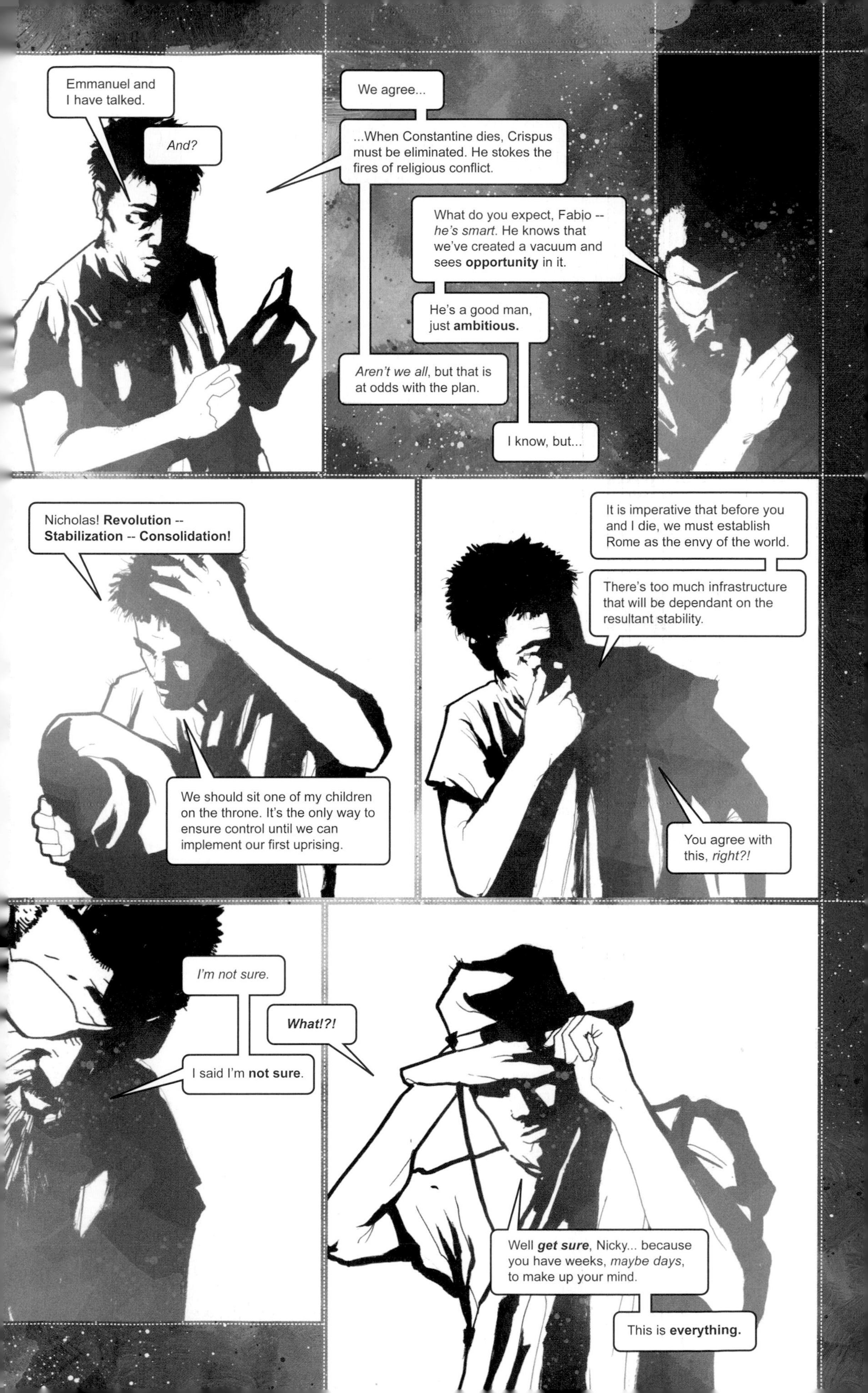
Emmanuel and I have talked.
And?
We agree...
...When Constantine dies, Crispus must be eliminated. He stokes the fires of religious conflict.
What do you expect, Fabio -- *he's smart.* He knows that we've created a vacuum and sees **opportunity** in it.
He's a good man, just **ambitious.**
Aren't we all, but that is at odds with the plan.
I know, but...
Nicholas! **Revolution -- Stabilization -- Consolidation!**
We should sit one of my children on the throne. It's the only way to ensure control until we can implement our first uprising.
It is imperative that before you and I die, we must establish Rome as the envy of the world.
There's too much infrastructure that will be dependant on the resultant stability.
You agree with this, *right?!*
I'm not sure.
What!?!
I said I'm **not sure**.
Well ***get sure***, Nicky... because you have weeks, *maybe days*, to make up your mind.
This is **everything.**

ONE
WEEK L

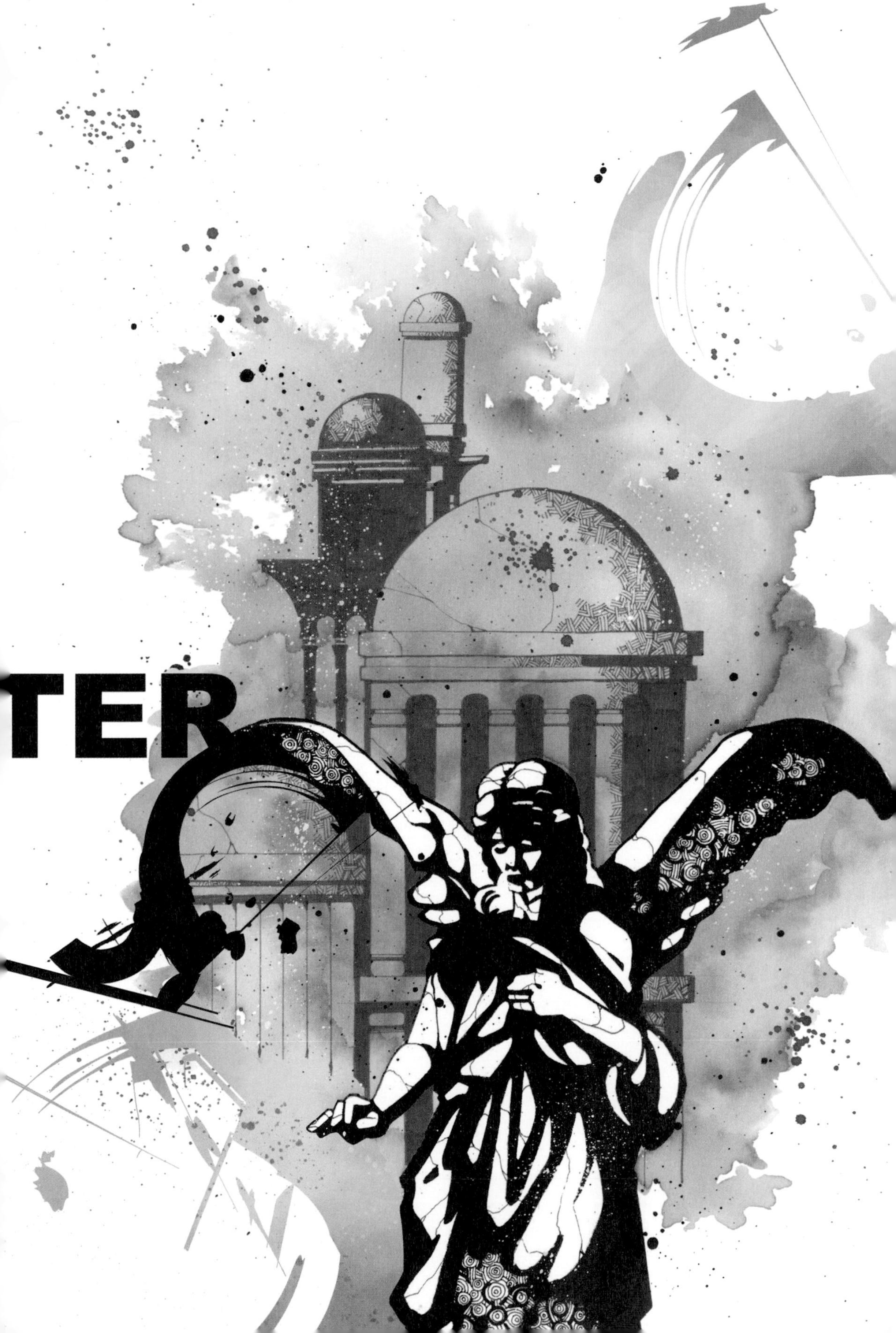
TER

Constantinople
337 AD
The end of an era.

Ah, Nicholas...

And so, it is like this that the greatest emperor in the history of the world passes... I thought for certain it would be with sword and shield in hand -- that you would dare death to try and take you.

Kaff!... Flatterer.

All of Rome weeps, *friend.*

Rome...

Nicholas... time grows short... there are things I **must know** -- Things that we have **not discussed**.

Yes?

You are a leader of men, and we both know that means you do not have the luxury of confiding in those beneath you.

It corrupts morale, it weakens you in their eyes... it compromises the ability to achieve your goals.

As we are both leaders, let us speak -- and speak truthfully one last time.

Of course, old friend... ask anything.

Your plan... the plan... do you know you will succeed? Do you believe that you cannot fail?

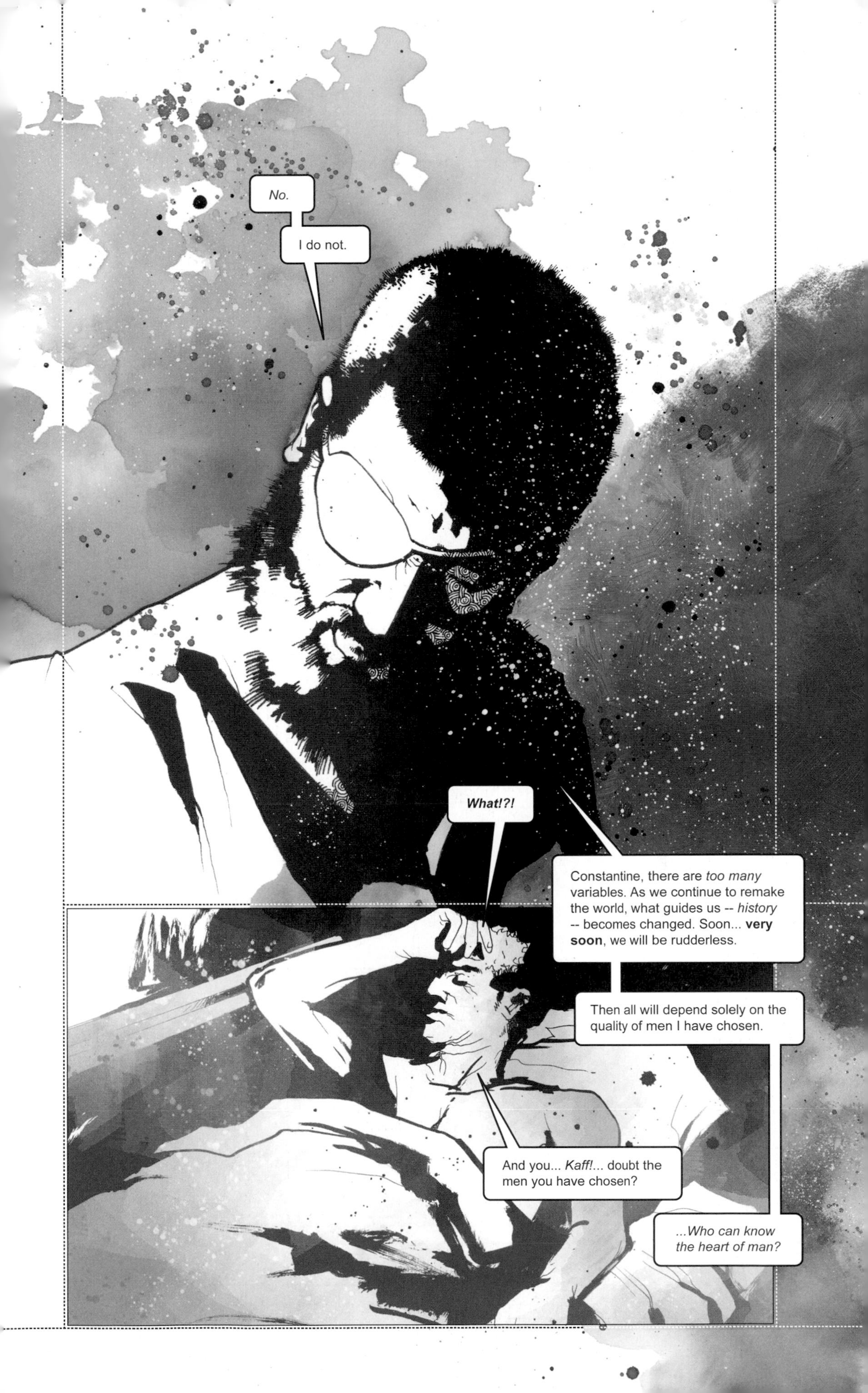
No.
I do not.
What!?!
Constantine, there are too many variables. As we continue to remake the world, what guides us -- history -- becomes changed. Soon... very soon, we will be rudderless.
Then all will depend solely on the quality of men I have chosen.
And you... Kaff!... doubt the men you have chosen?
...Who can know the heart of man?

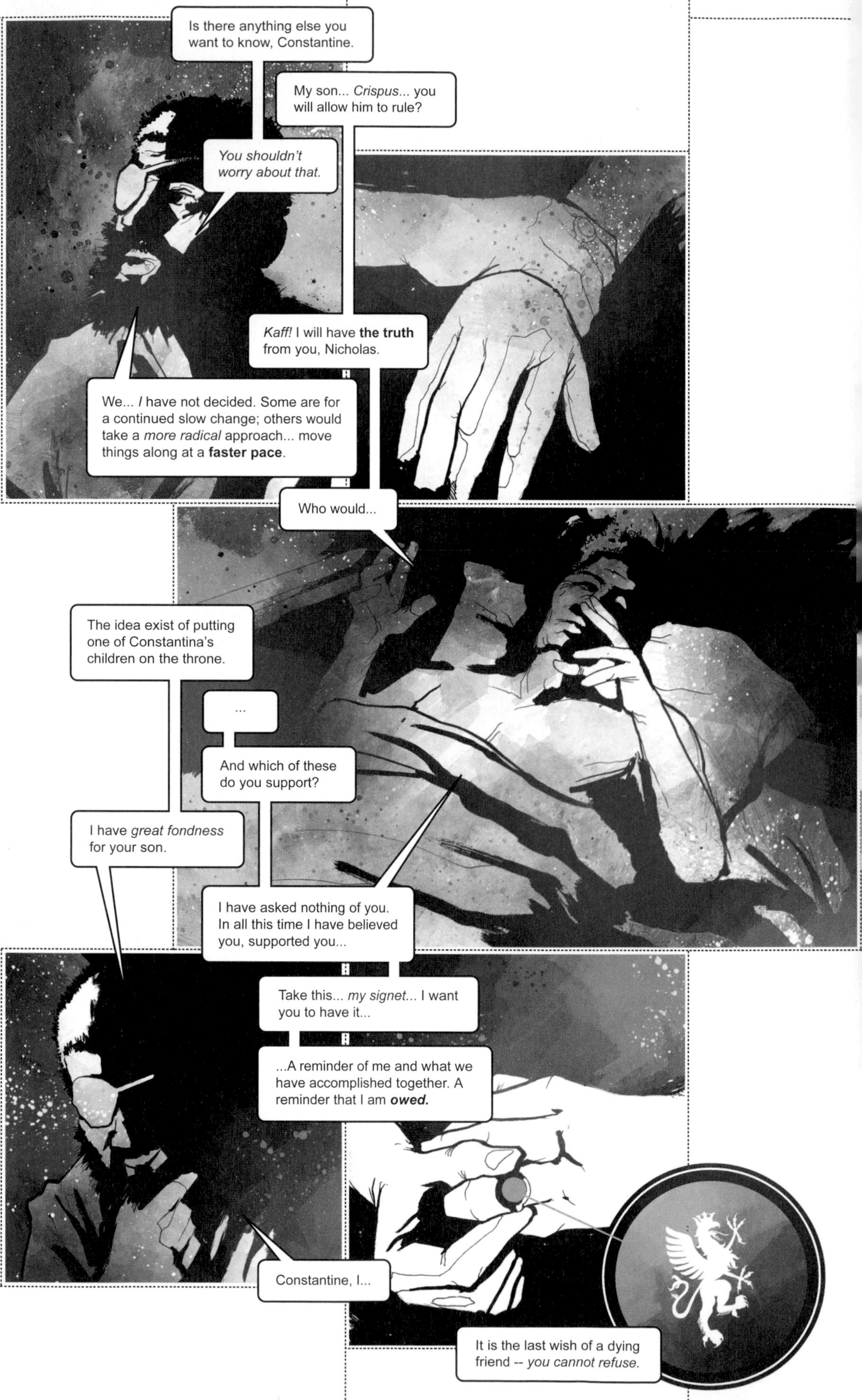
Is there anything else you want to know, Constantine.
My son... *Crispus*... you will allow him to rule?
You shouldn't worry about that.
Kaff! I will have **the truth** from you, Nicholas.
We... *I* have not decided. Some are for a continued slow change; others would take a *more radical* approach... move things along at a **faster pace**.
Who would...
The idea exist of putting one of Constantina's children on the throne.
...
And which of these do you support?
I have *great fondness* for your son.
I have asked nothing of you. In all this time I have believed you, supported you...
Take this... *my signet*... I want you to have it...
...A reminder of me and what we have accomplished together. A reminder that I am ***owed.***
Constantine, I...
It is the last wish of a dying friend -- *you cannot refuse.*

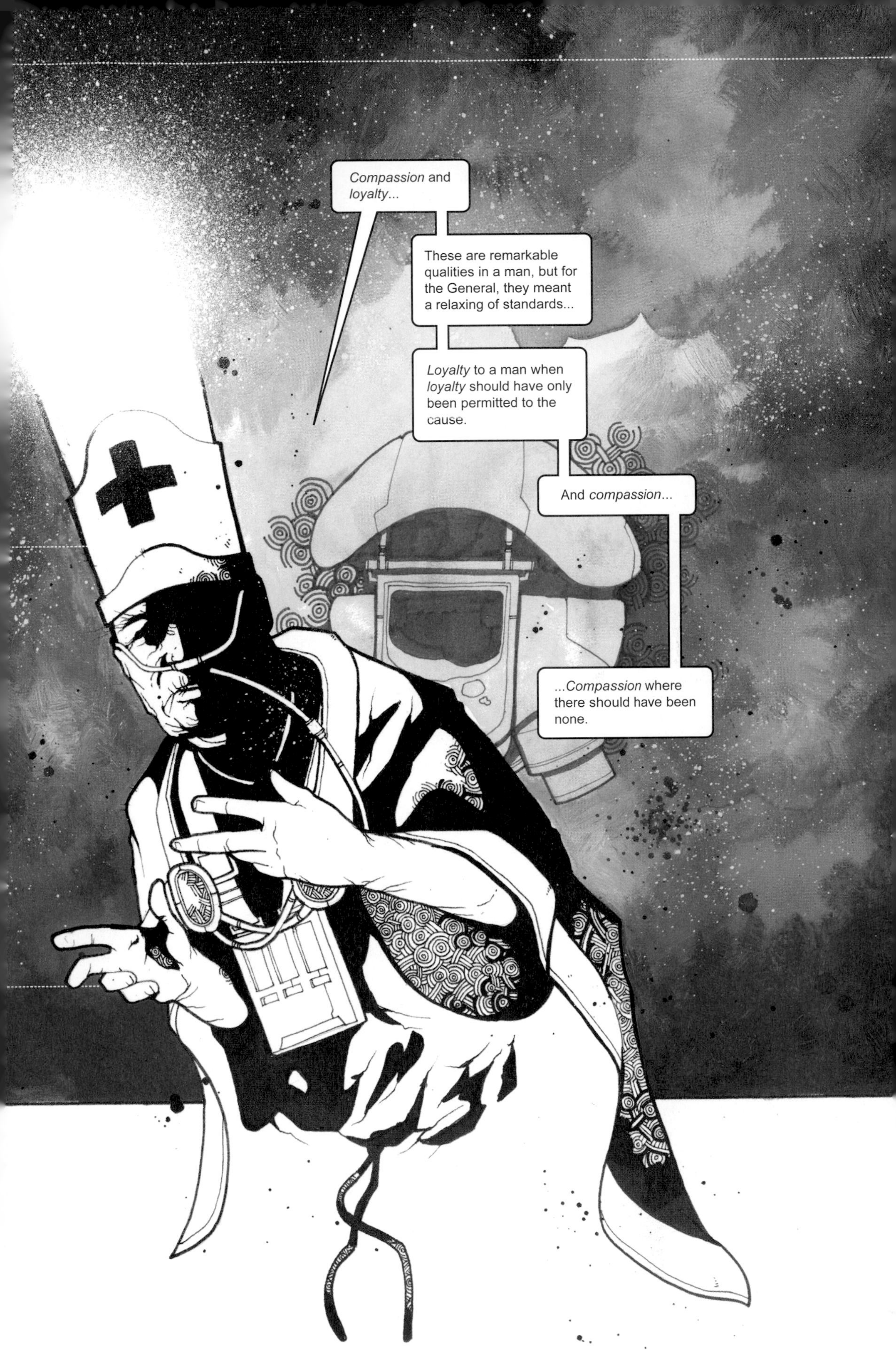
Compassion and *loyalty*...
These are remarkable qualities in a man, but for the General, they meant a relaxing of standards...
Loyalty to a man when *loyalty* should have only been permitted to the cause.
And *compassion*...
...*Compassion* where there should have been none.

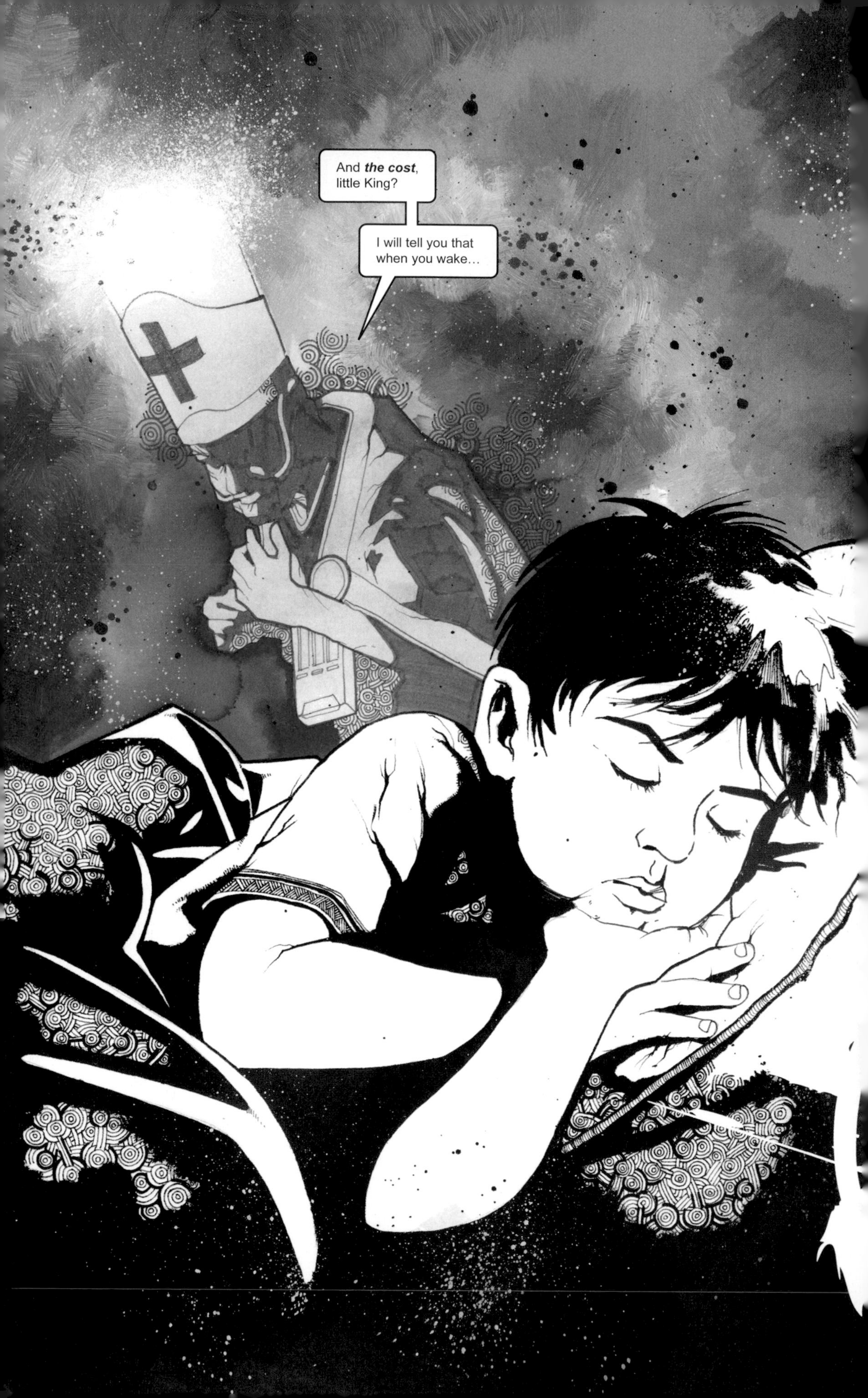
And **the cost**, little King?
I will tell you that when you wake…

OVE

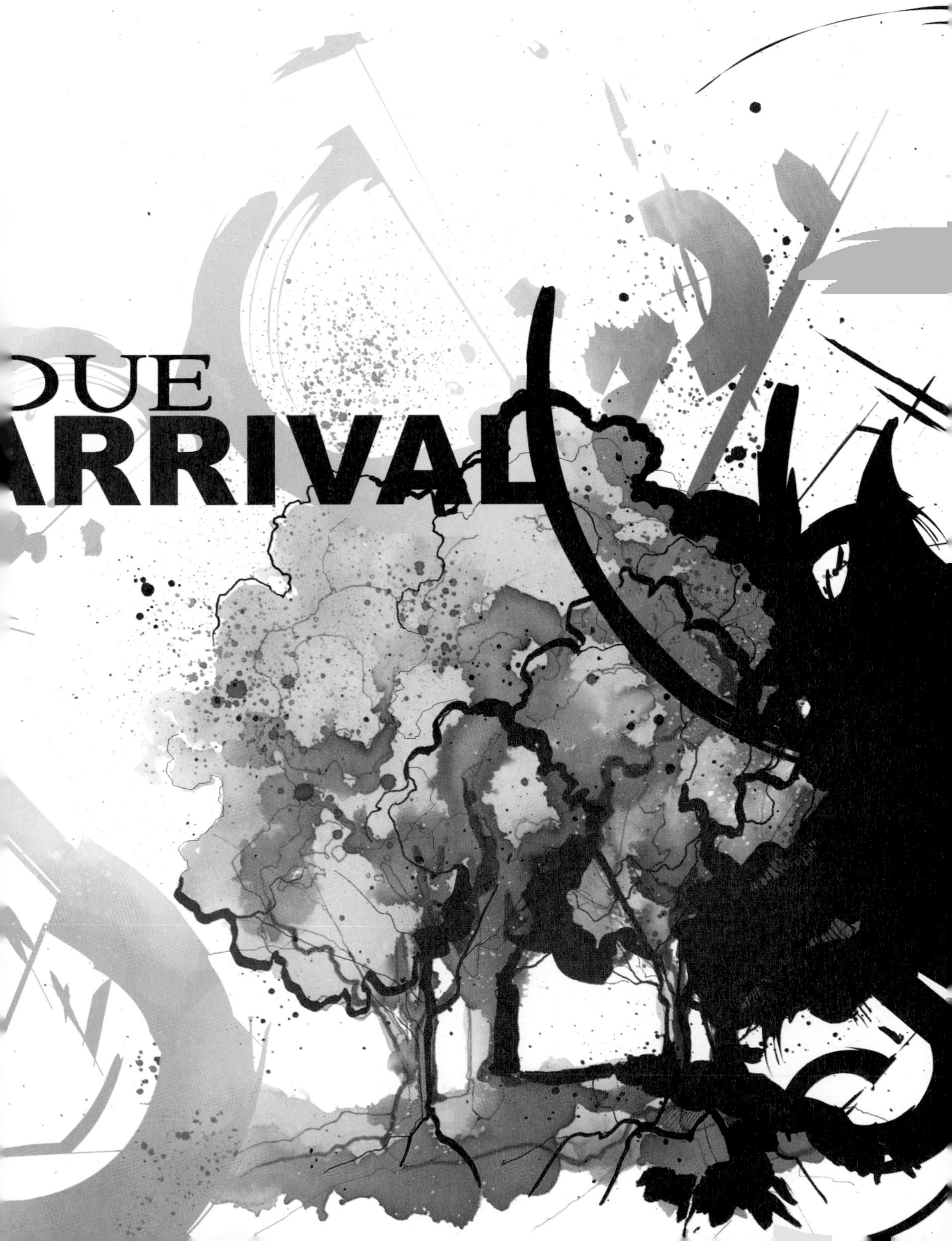
DUE
ARRIVAL

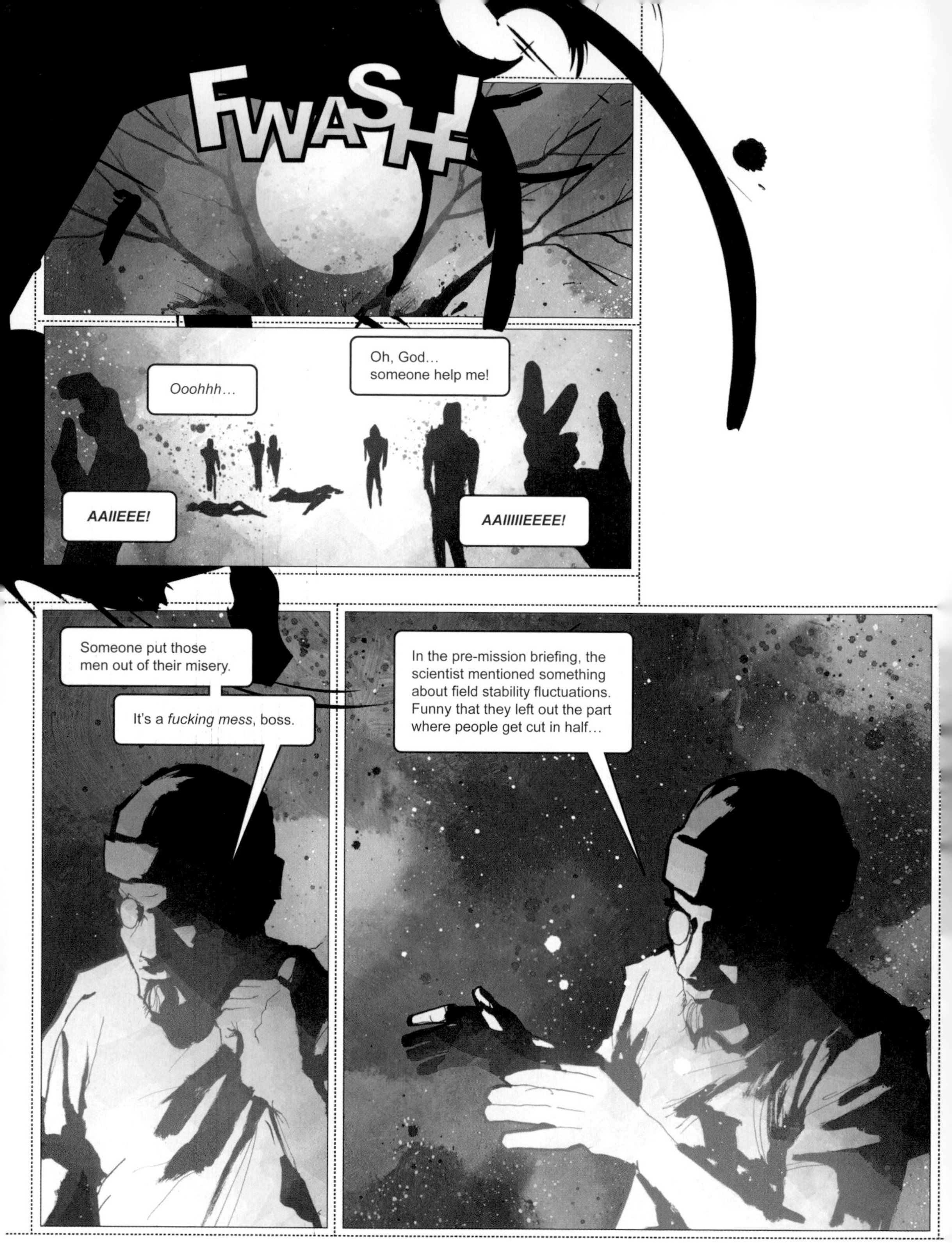
FWASH!
Ooohhh…
Oh, God…
someone help me!
AAIIEEE!
AAIIIIIEEEE!
Someone put those
men out of their misery.
It's a *fucking mess*, boss.
In the pre-mission briefing, the
scientist mentioned something
about field stability fluctuations.
Funny that they left out the part
where people get cut in half…

…Regardless, there's no doubt that's why they stuck us on the outside.

And we'll have landed up-time… meaning they've been here a while.

Which means the mission could have already succeeded or failed. Which means there's a decision to be made as far as what to do…

Well boss, what's it *gonna' be?*

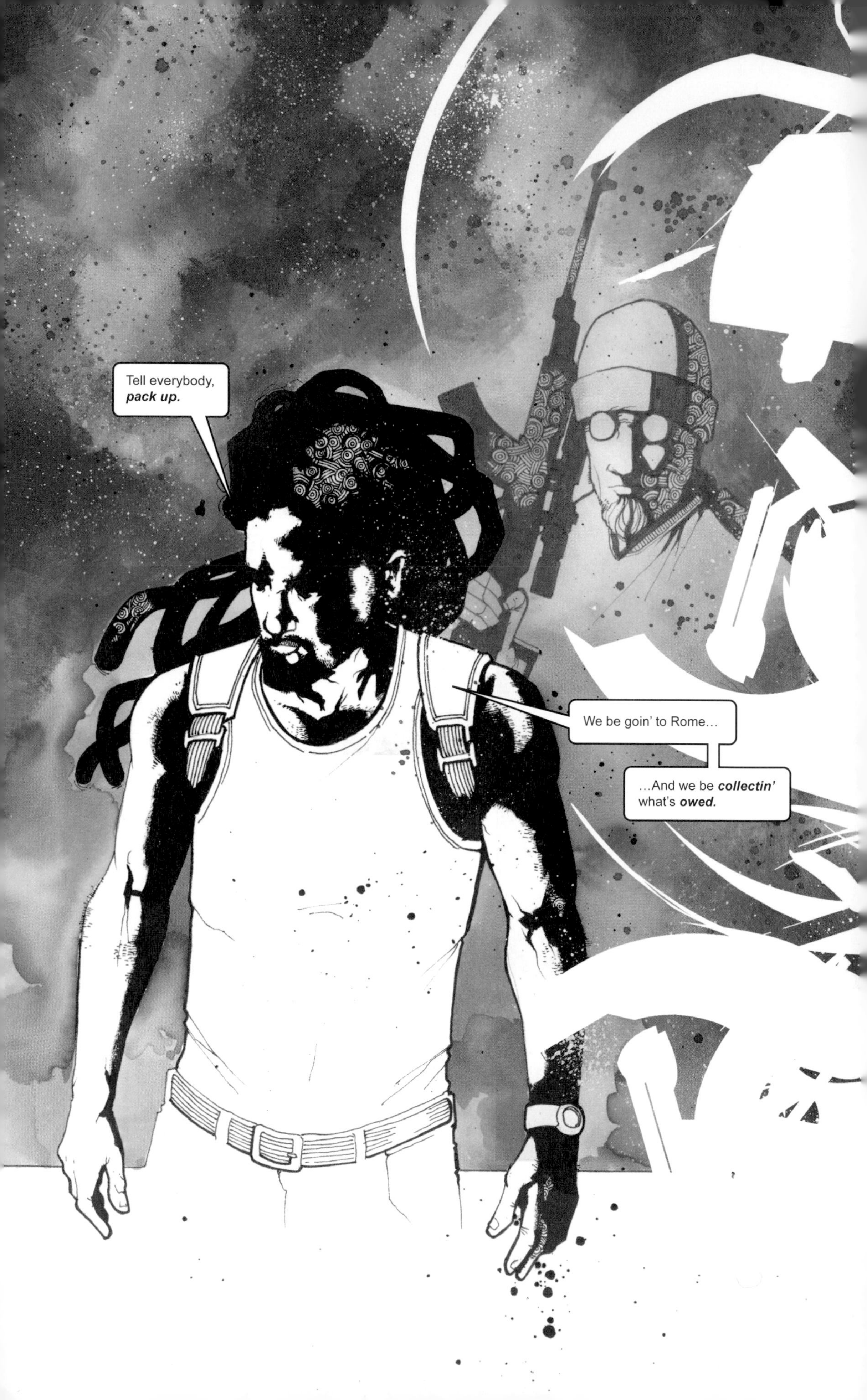
Tell everybody, ***pack up.***
We be goin' to Rome…
…And we be ***collectin'*** what's ***owed.***

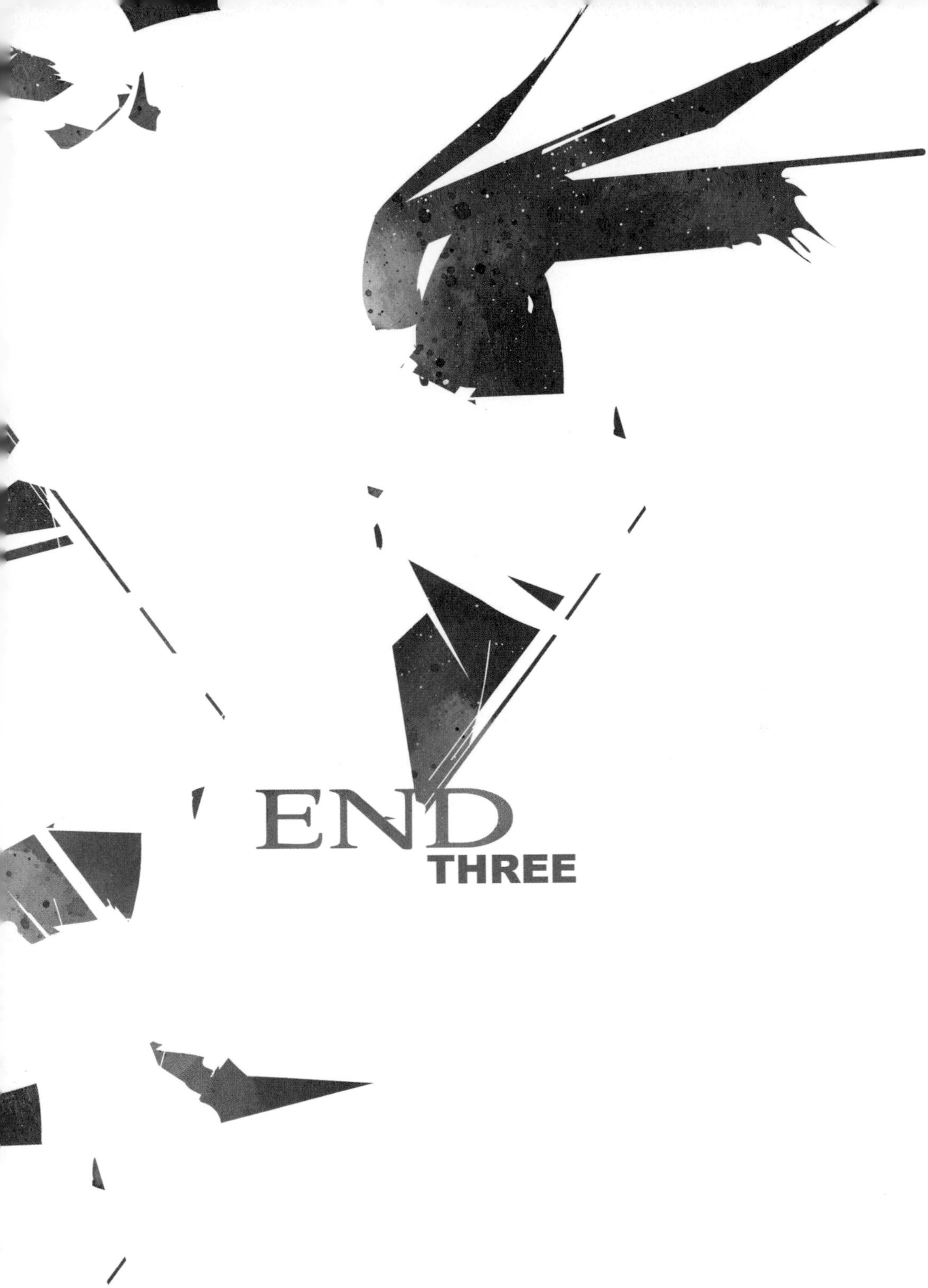
END
THREE

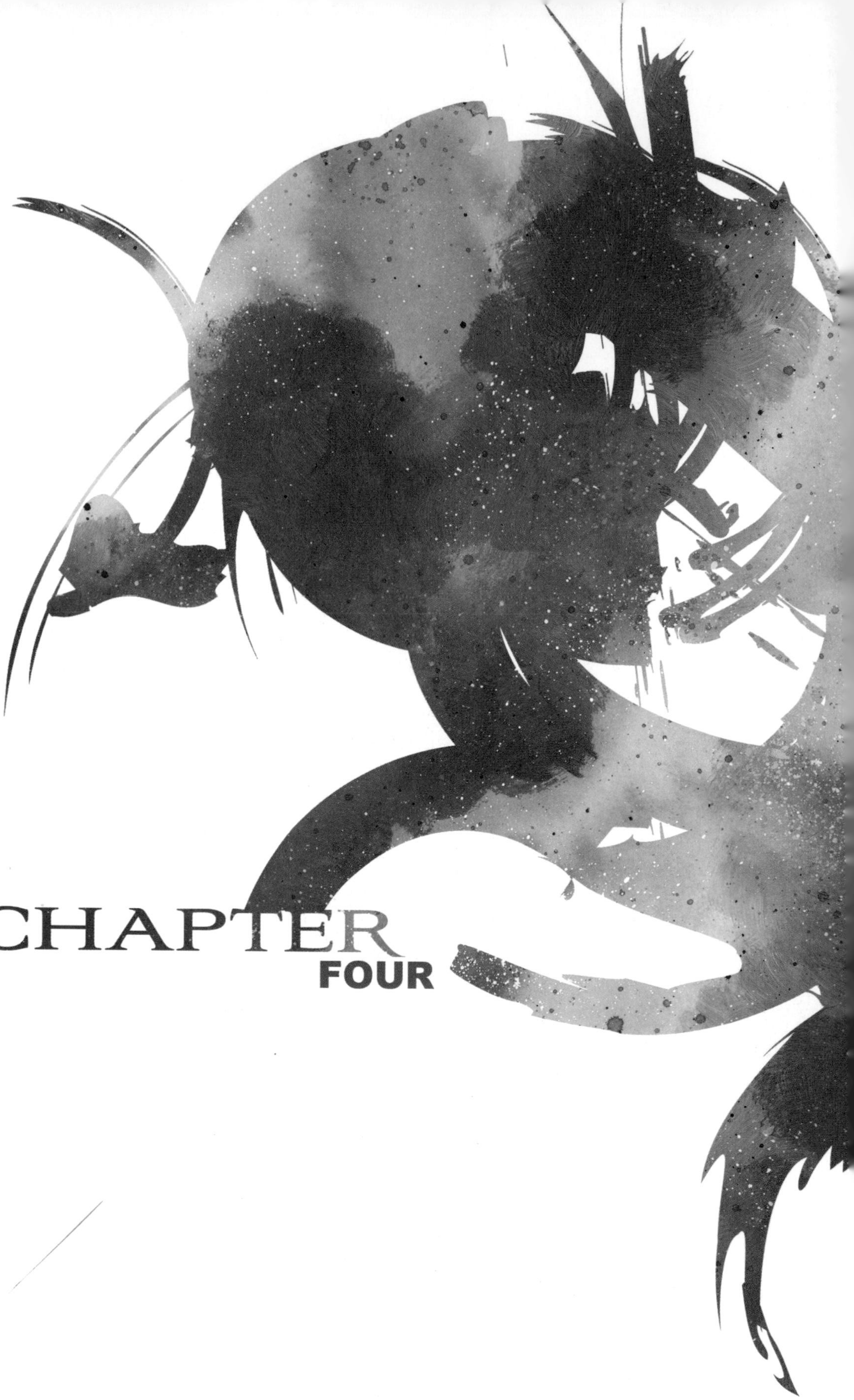

CHAPTER FOUR

ome.
he coronation of Augustus Crispus.
37 AD

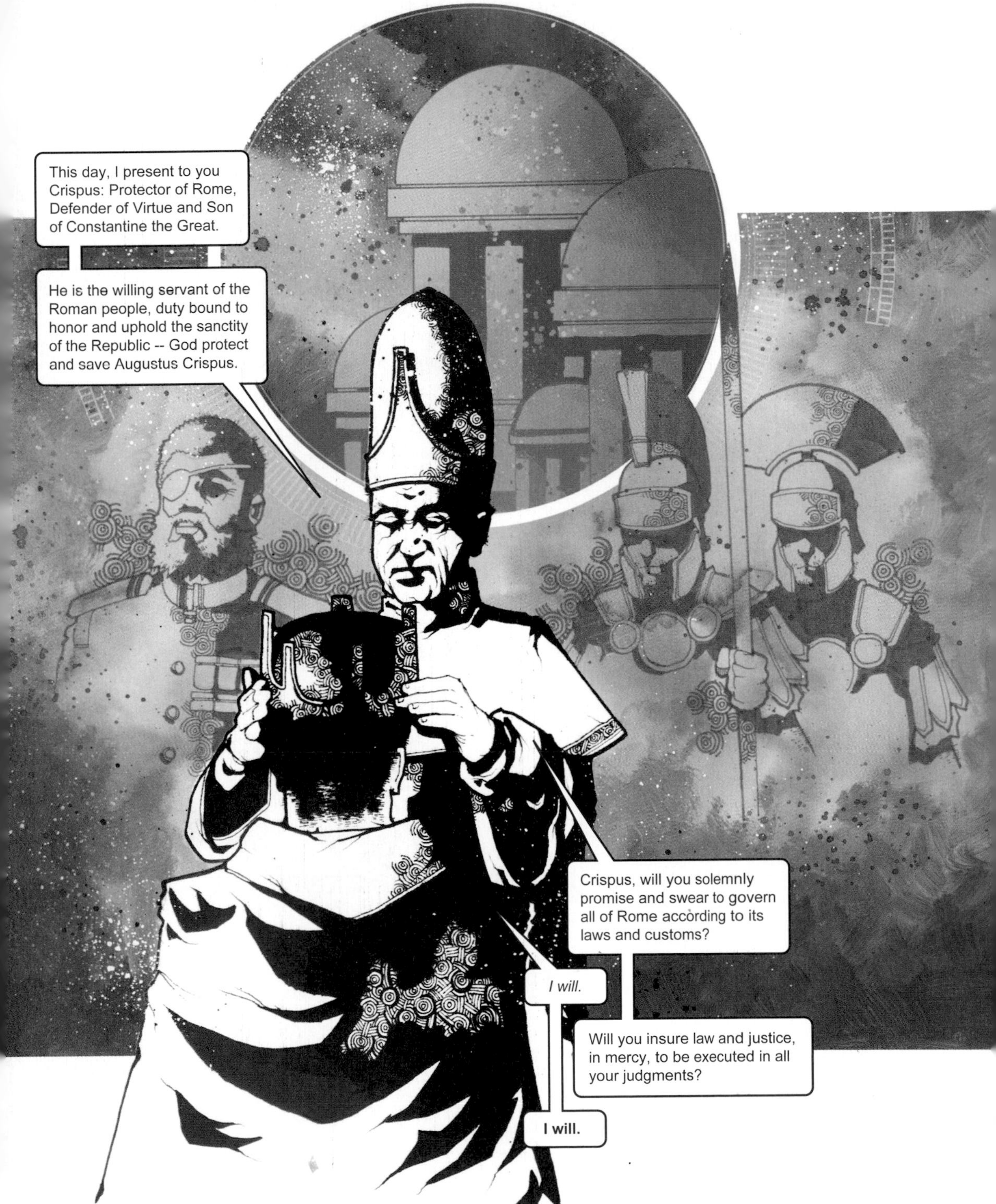

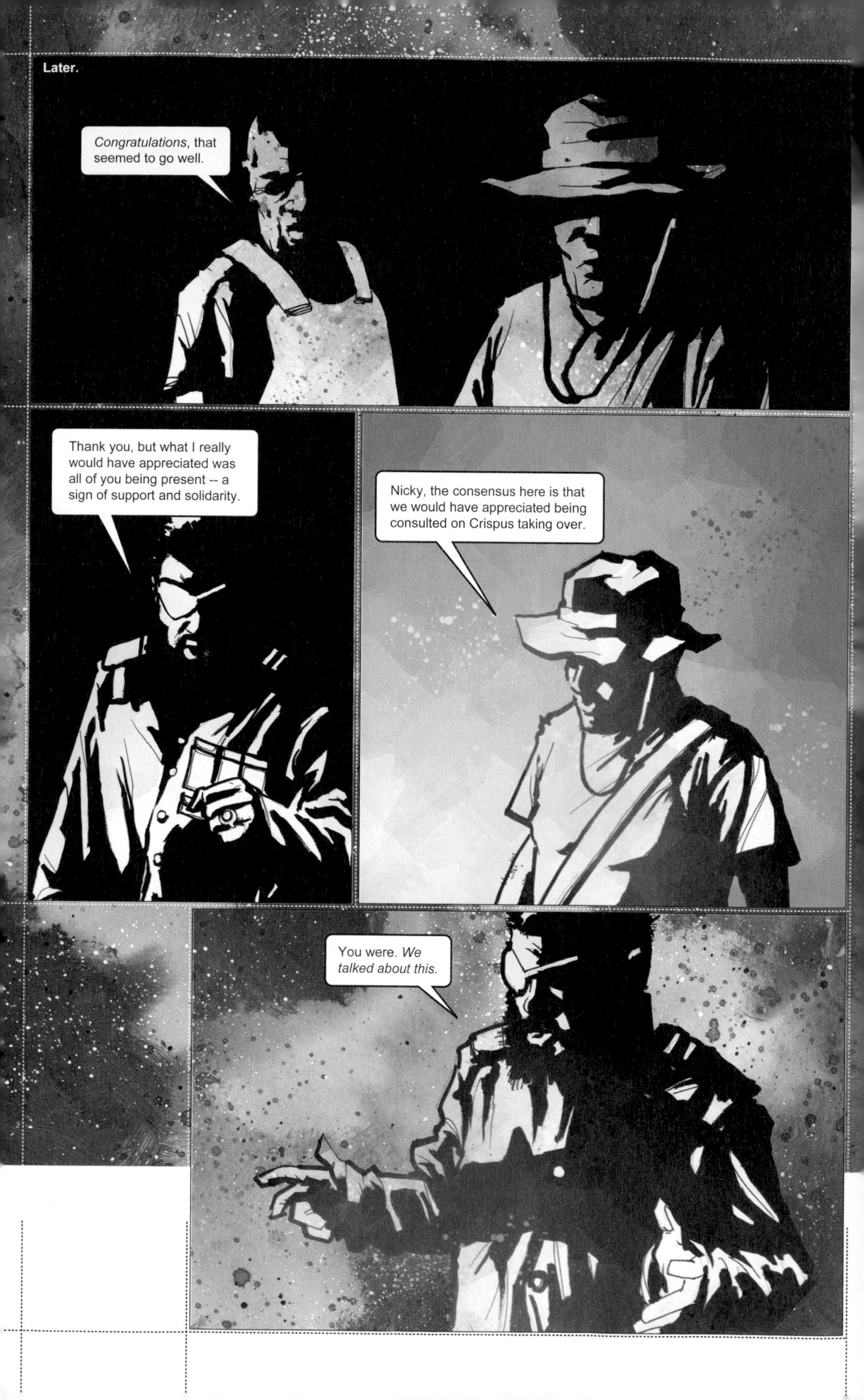
Later.
Congratulations, that seemed to go well.
Thank you, but what I really would have appreciated was all of you being present -- a sign of support and solidarity.
Nicky, the consensus here is that we would have appreciated being consulted on Crispus taking over.
You were. *We talked about this.*

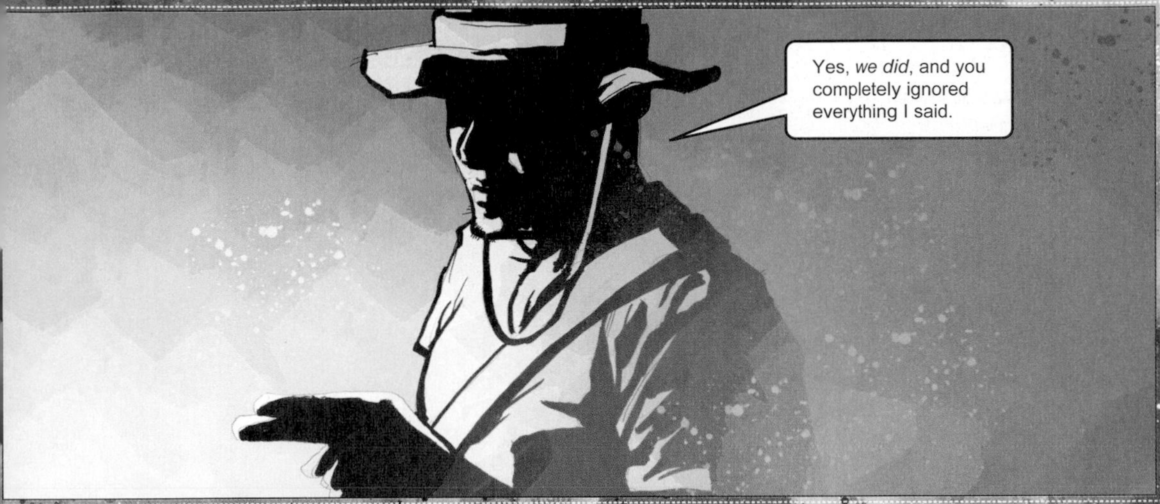
Yes, *we did*, and you completely ignored everything I said.

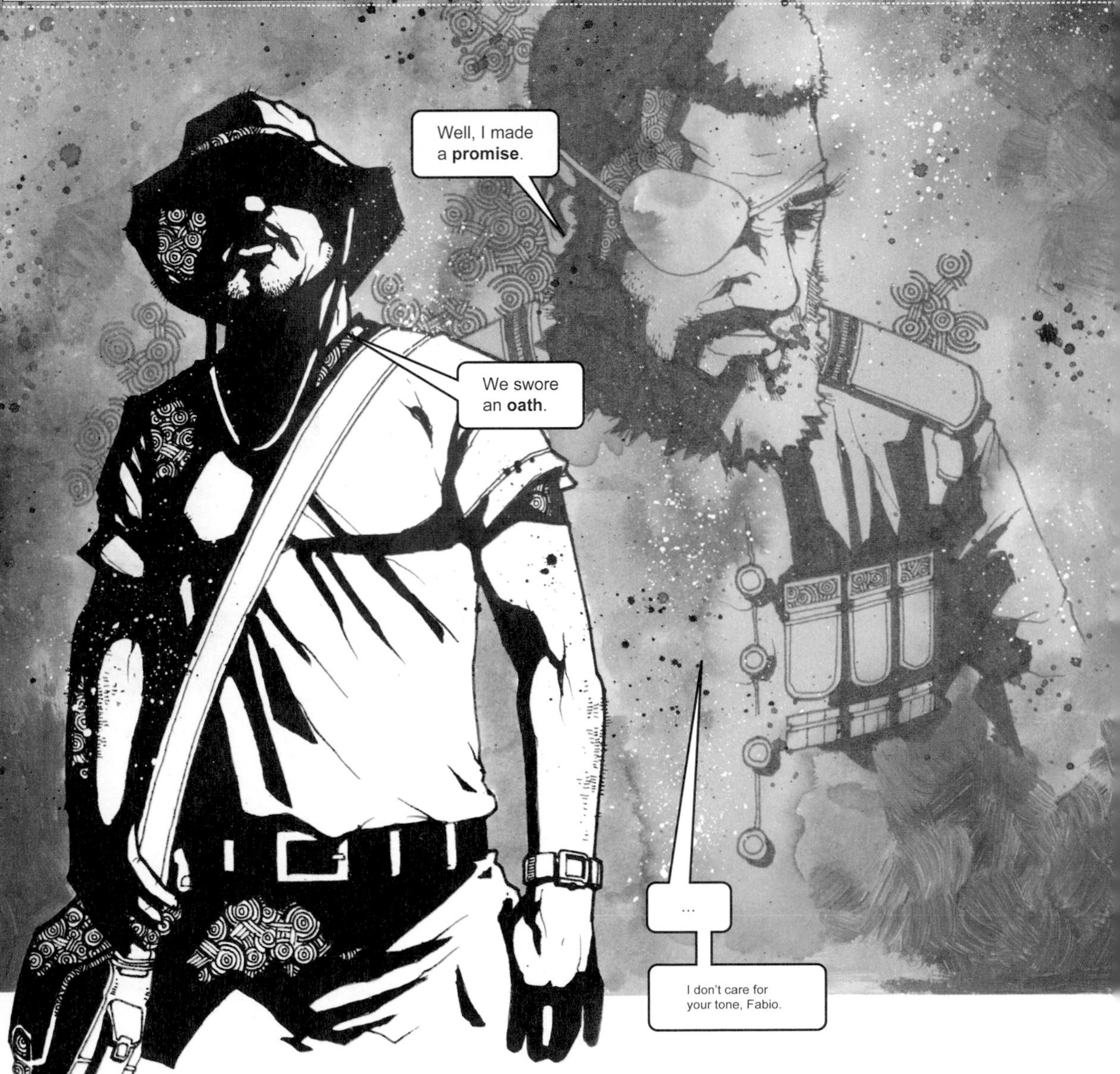
Well, I made a **promise**.
We swore an **oath**.
...
I don't care for your tone, Fabio.

In attendance:

(NC) - Brigadier General Nicholas Chase
(EM) - Colonel Emmanuel Mfede
(FR) - Colonel Fabio Rossi
(MK) - Colonel Manon Karembeu
(UT) - Lt. Colonel Ulf Tarnat

The following conversation was transcribed from the secret recordings of Ulf Tarnat, which were discovered among his personal items in the months following his death.

This is that conversation in full:

FR: Tough. You're walking around with your eyes closed, Nicholas.

NC: And who determines that? You?

UT: Hold on. We haven't been in the same room together in 3 years, so let's calm down. We still all want the same thing, right?

MK: Do we want the same thing? Have we ever? It is becoming fairly obvious that the General has always expected complete loyalty from us, but is unwilling to submit to the same expectations.

NC: A hierarchy exists…

FR: [Interrupts] That's not what…

NC: [Interrupts] A hierarchy exists in all military endeavors. I decide how we best serve the mission and I expect orders to be followed. Are we pretending that this is some kind of revelation?

EM: We are well aware of protocol, sir. They don't believe that's the problem.

NC: Then, for God's sake, someone end the preamble and speak your mind.

FR: Crispus is dangerous, Nicky.

NC: Again, you said this before and I still don't agree with it. Like his father, he is difficult but remains a man of vision.

MK: Oh, it's obvious he has plans for himself if you're paying attention.

UT: Did you know that he reinstituted the Praetorian Guard?

NC: I did. And he did it with my approval.

MK: Yes, but did he consult you about it before or after the fact? I'm betting it was the latter.

NC: It is a personal vanity. In this room, do we really have the audacity to condemn a man for that?

MK: This goes beyond vanity.

NC: Enough. Do any of you have any proof that he doesn't support the plan? I'm beginning to think that this is about your children, Fabio.

EM: Nicholas, please…

FR: I don't care if you name yourself Augustus, sir. I simply want the threat to our mission eliminated. He has to go.

NC: Absolutely not. Until he shows some outward sign of betrayal, he remains my choice. And I want to be clear… again… I lead this mission. The final choice is mine.

MK: Oh, I see. This is about emotional attachment. If you don't think you can do it, I will be happy to take care of the problem.

NC: Not another word from you, Manon.

EM: Nicholas, please, listen to reason on this.

NC: You too, Emmanuel?

EM: I have broader concerns… I have no idea whether or not Crispus is a threat. How could I, or anyone including you, know what the totality of his plans are. He is obviously ambitious, but so are we. The difference is we know we are right.

NC: It is unfair to portray his ignorance as an indictment of bad faith.

FR: We are at war with a world of ignorance. Who but us knows where all this leads?

NC: And who led us to this? Who was it that manufactured this entire thing? Was it you, or was it me?

MK: This is becoming difficult for me to take seriously anymore.

UT: Manon, don't antagonize…

MK: [Interrupts] No, it needs to be said. Wake up – all of you. There is no hope of us succeeding any longer. This was never going to work.

FR: You underestimate some of…

MK: [Interrupts] Please. Look at us, bickering about a single life – a historical footnote that should already be dead. The man is irrelevant. The truth is, we remain slaves to our singular nature. We might as well carve up the world and each take a piece. It would be more honest than this… this… politicking.

UT: Maybe we all need to relax and realize the precarious situation we find ourselves in. I don't think anyone should say anything they might regret.

NC: I regret nothing.

FR: What?

NC: I said I regret nothing. I am confident in every choice I have made, just as I am confident in Constantine's son.

MK: Then perhaps we need to part ways.

EM: Don't say that, Manon.

NC: Oh, no. She can say whatever she wishes, but allow me to be clear. This mission goes forward under my command. Stepping away is the same as being cast out.

EM: Nicholas, you don't mean that.

FR: Oh, no… look at him – he means it.

NC: You were all handpicked by me. I chose you, not the other way around. I will never seek the approval of, or acquiesce to, any of you.

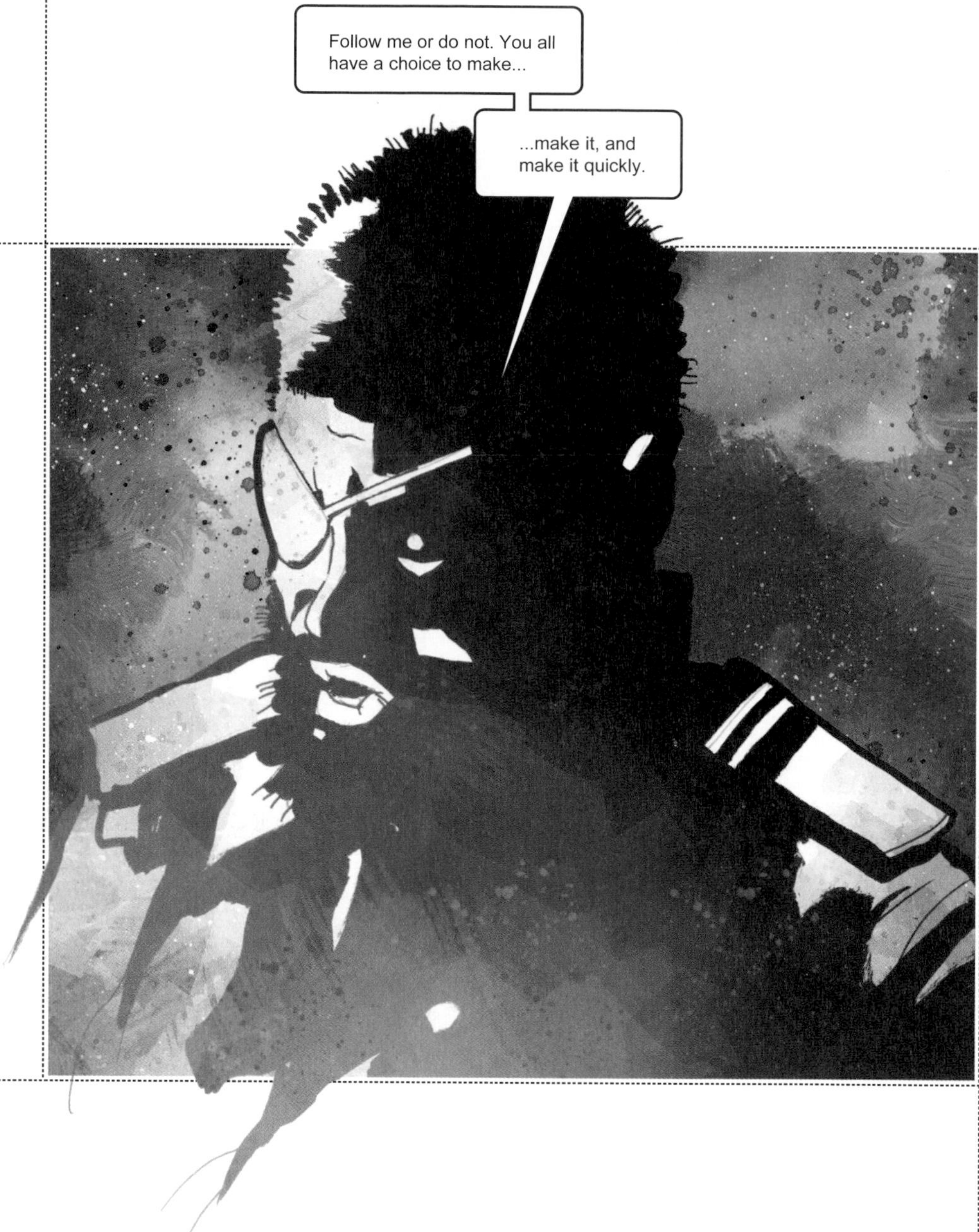
Follow me or do not. You all have a choice to make...
...make it, and make it quickly.

Rome.
That evening.

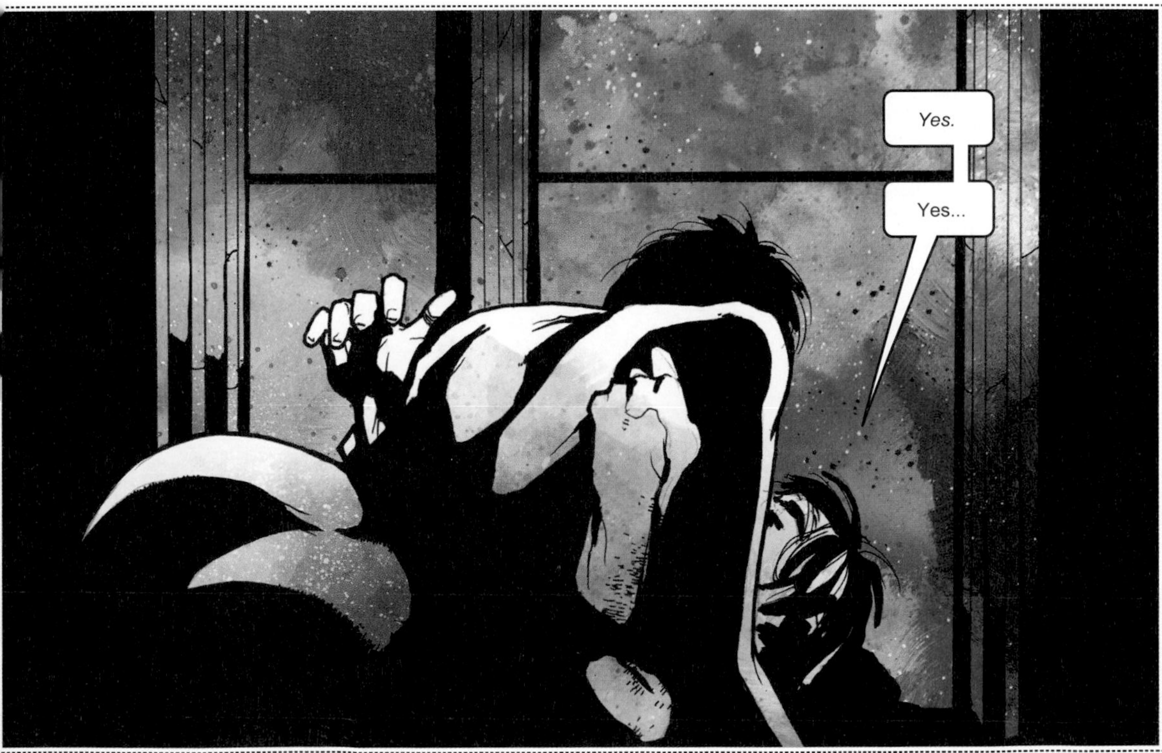
Yes.
Yes...

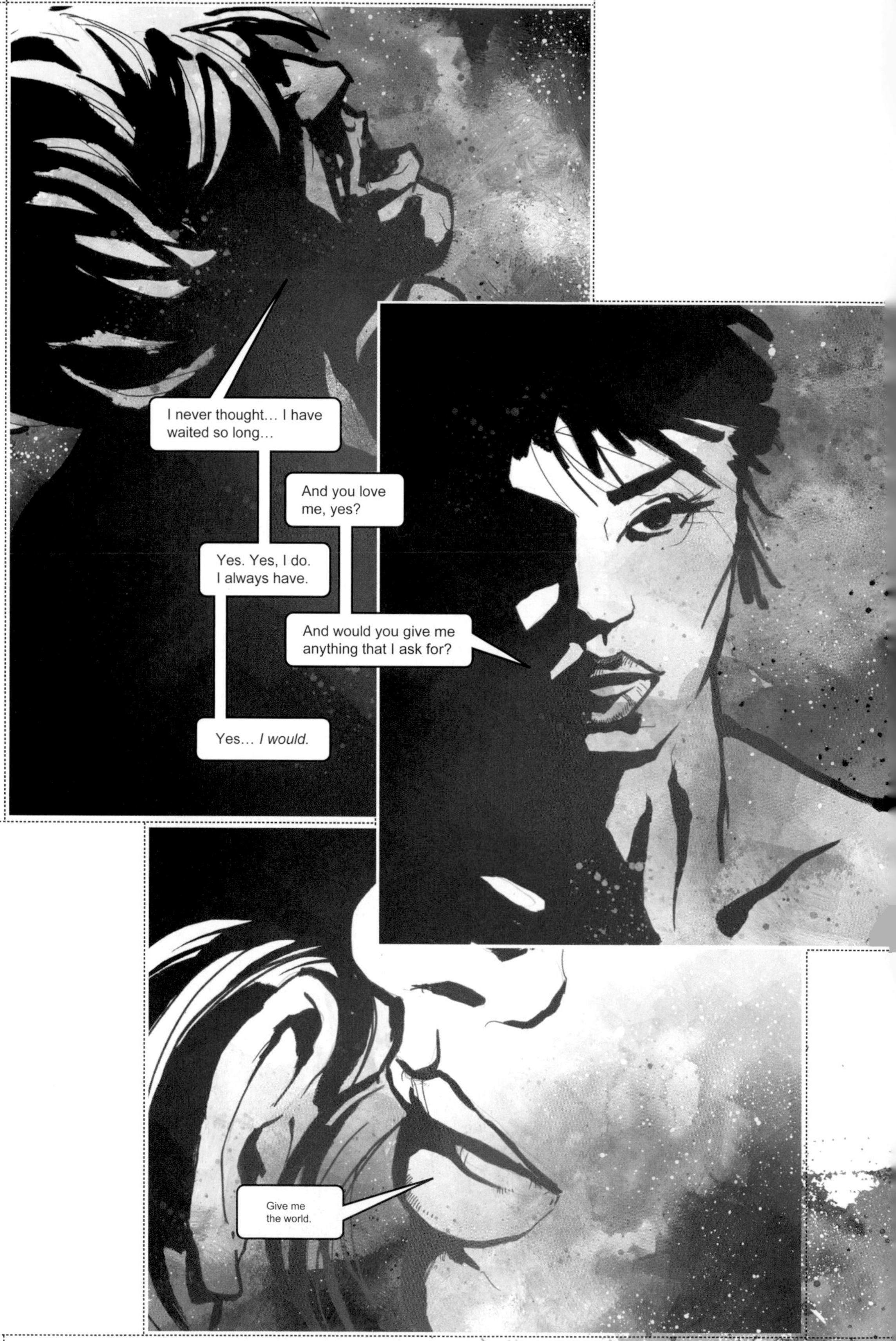
I never thought… I have waited so long…
And you love me, yes?
Yes. Yes, I do. I always have.
And would you give me anything that I ask for?
Yes… *I would.*
Give me the world.

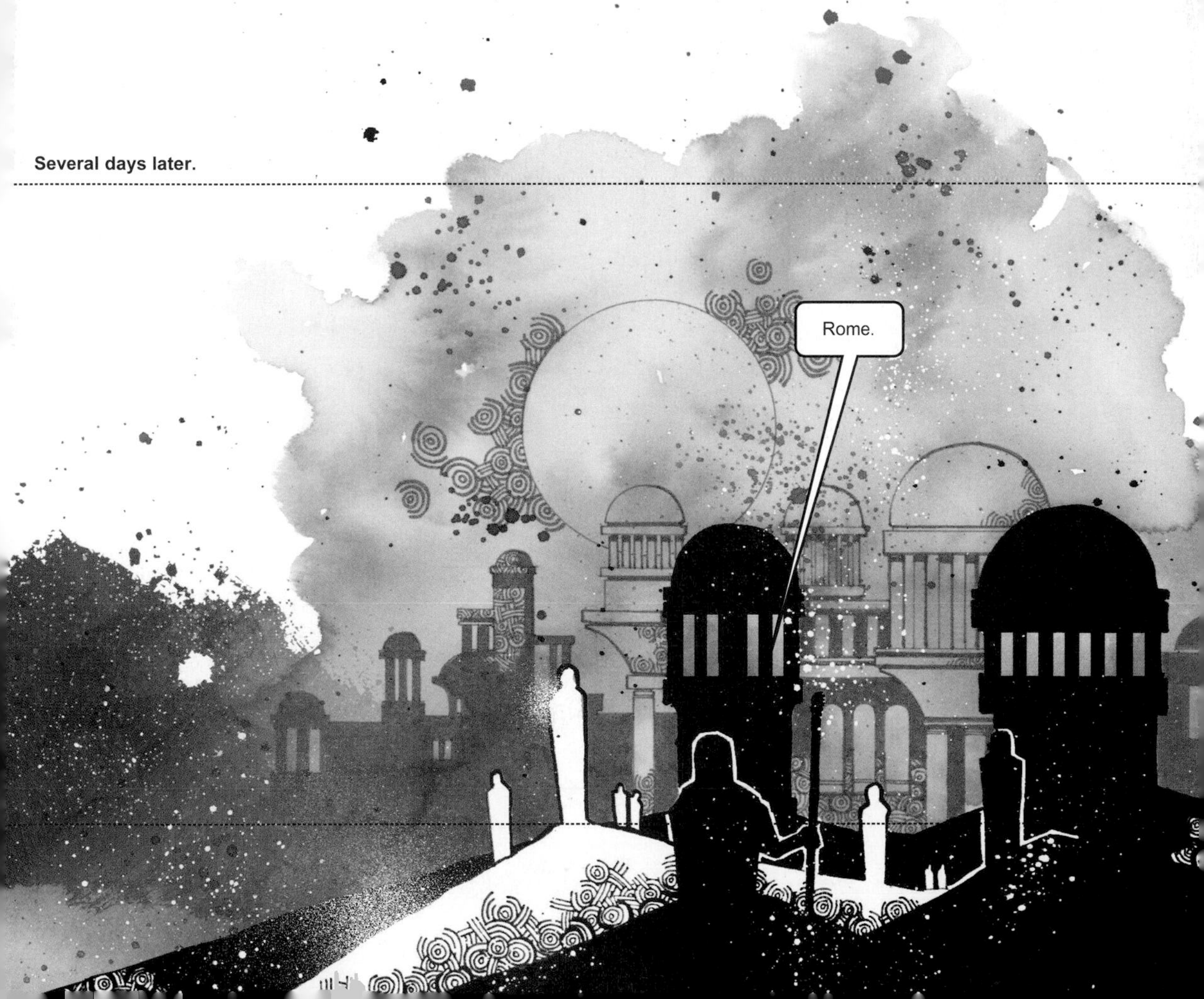
Several days later.
Rome.

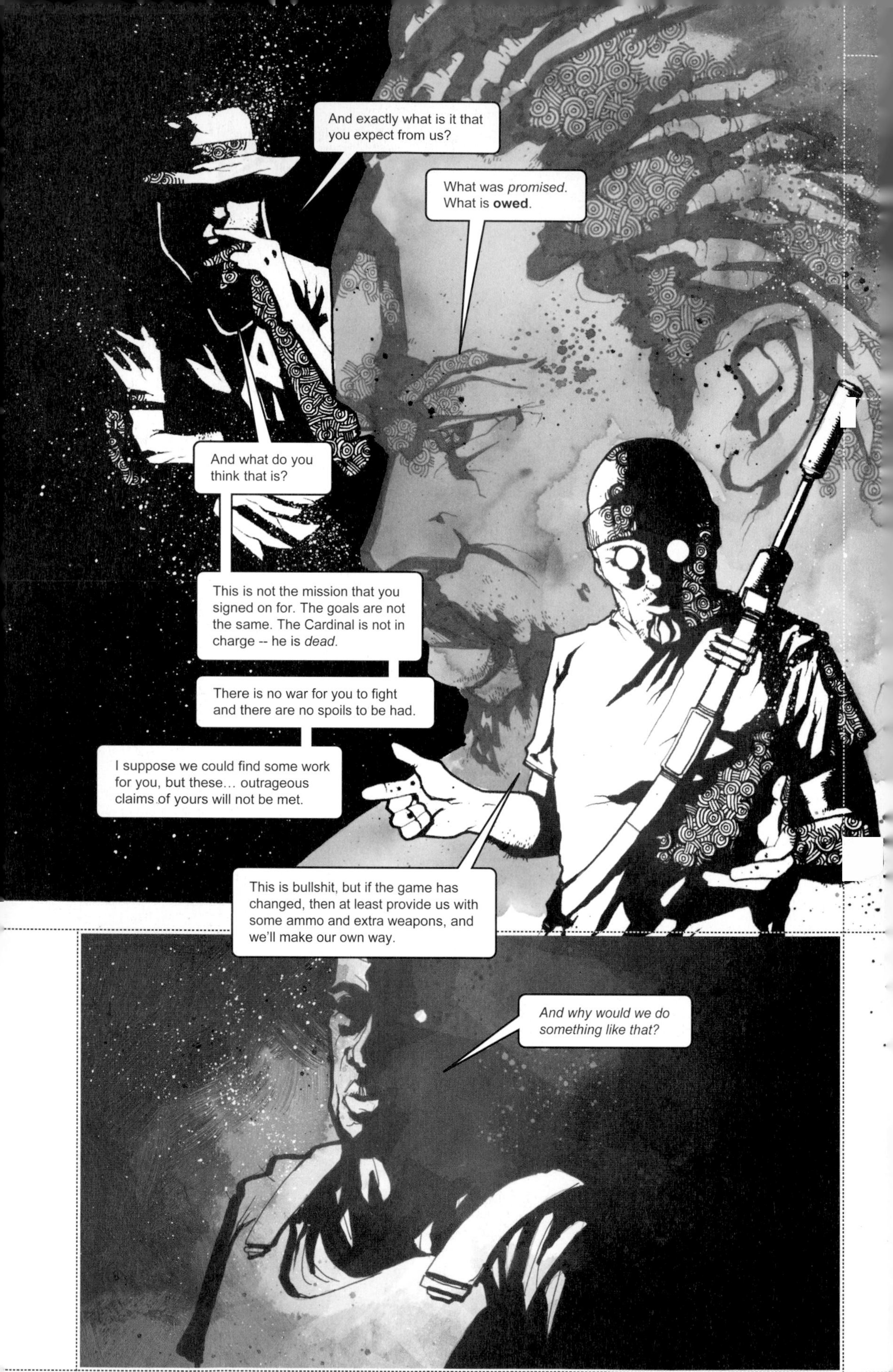

And exactly what is it that you expect from us?
What was *promised*. What is **owed**.
And what do you think that is?
This is not the mission that you signed on for. The goals are not the same. The Cardinal is not in charge -- he is *dead*.
There is no war for you to fight and there are no spoils to be had.
I suppose we could find some work for you, but these… outrageous claims of yours will not be met.
This is bullshit, but if the game has changed, then at least provide us with some ammo and extra weapons, and we'll make our own way.
And why would we do something like that?

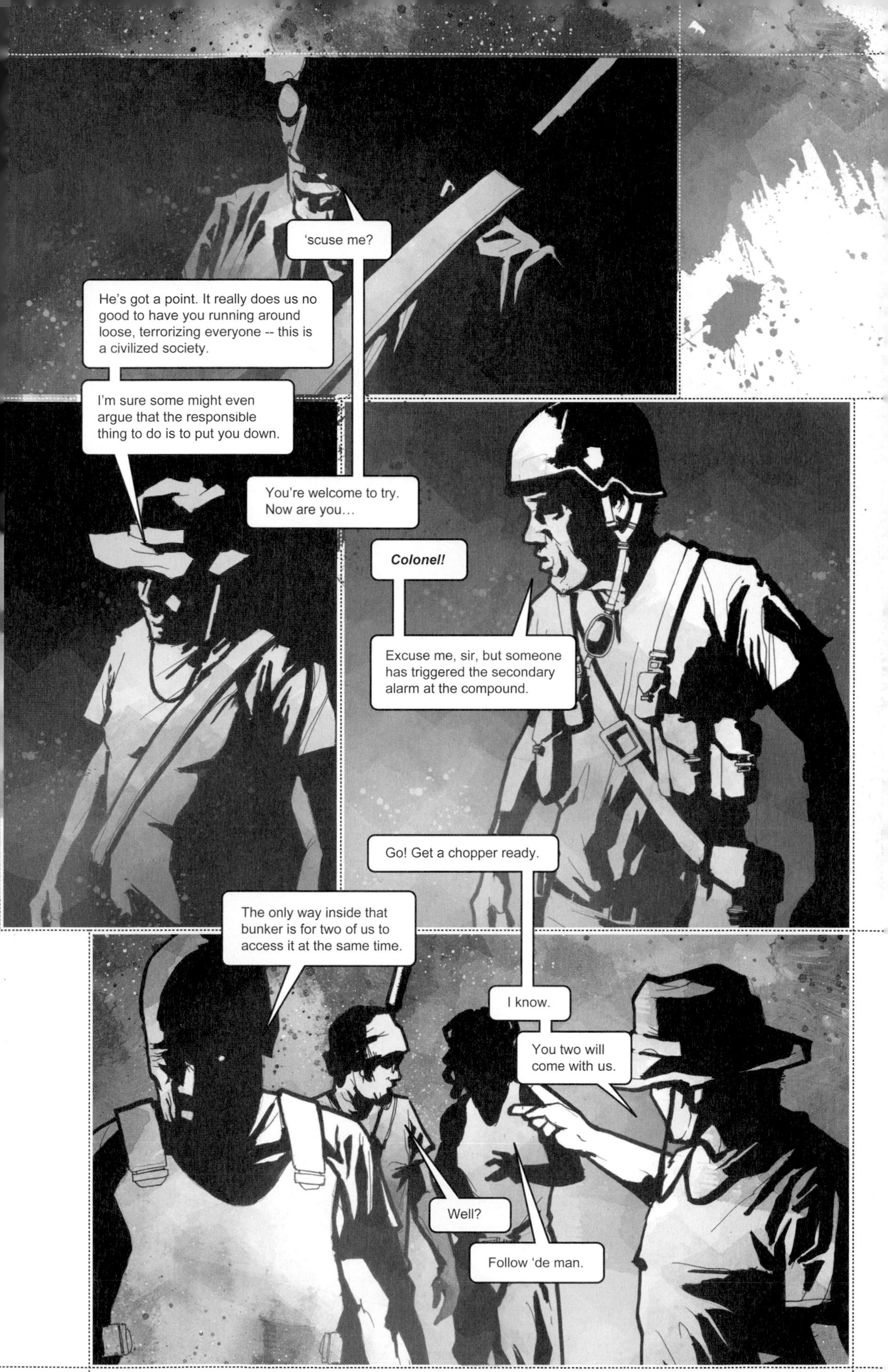
'scuse me?
He's got a point. It really does us no good to have you running around loose, terrorizing everyone -- this is a civilized society.
I'm sure some might even argue that the responsible thing to do is to put you down.
You're welcome to try. Now are you…
Colonel!
Excuse me, sir, but someone has triggered the secondary alarm at the compound.
Go! Get a chopper ready.
The only way inside that bunker is for two of us to access it at the same time.
I know.
You two will come with us.
Well?
Follow 'de man.

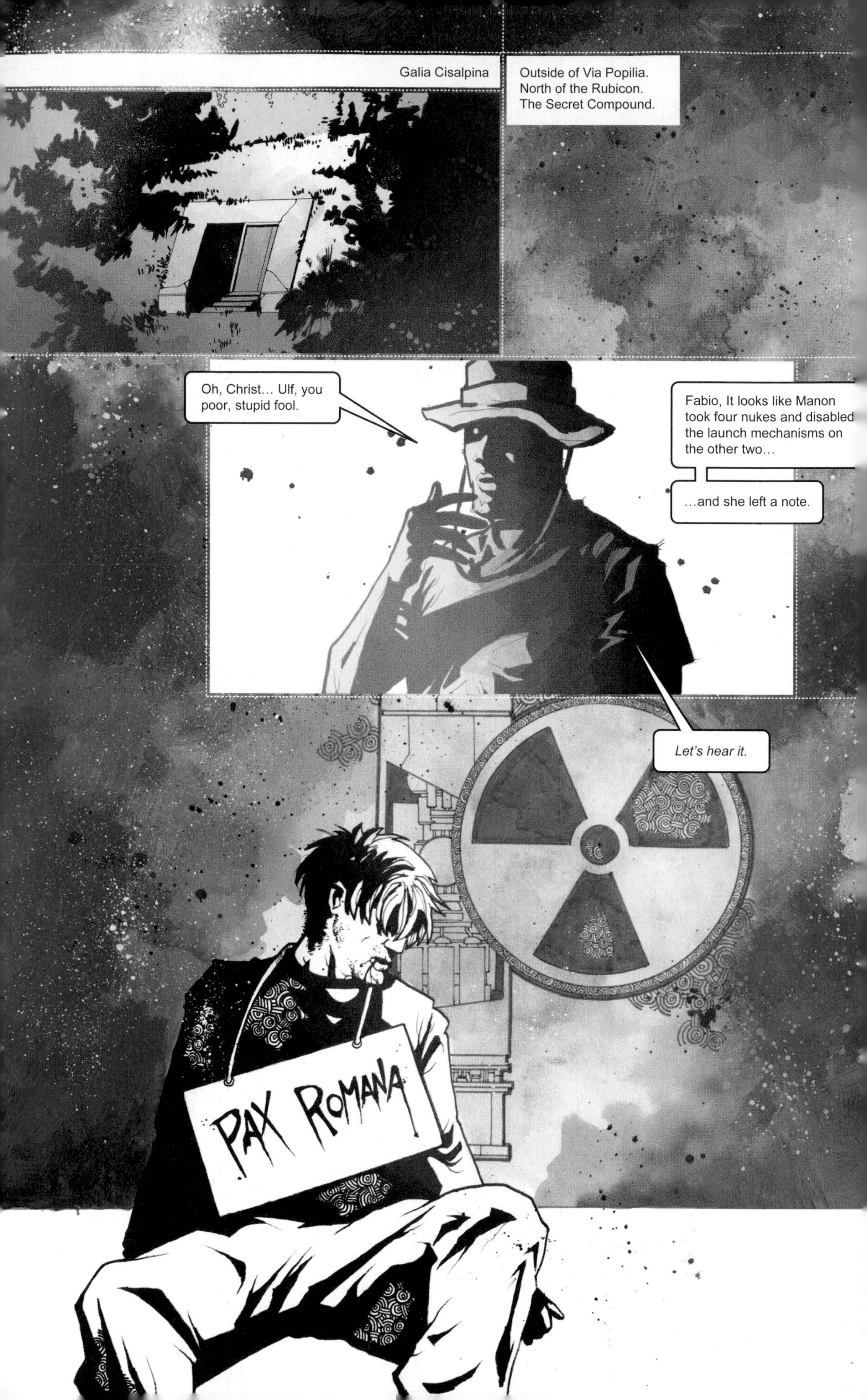
Galia Cisalpina
Outside of Via Popilia.
North of the Rubicon.
The Secret Compound.
Oh, Christ… Ulf, you poor, stupid fool.
Fabio, It looks like Manon took four nukes and disabled the launch mechanisms on the other two…
…and she left a note.
Let's hear it.
PAX ROMANA

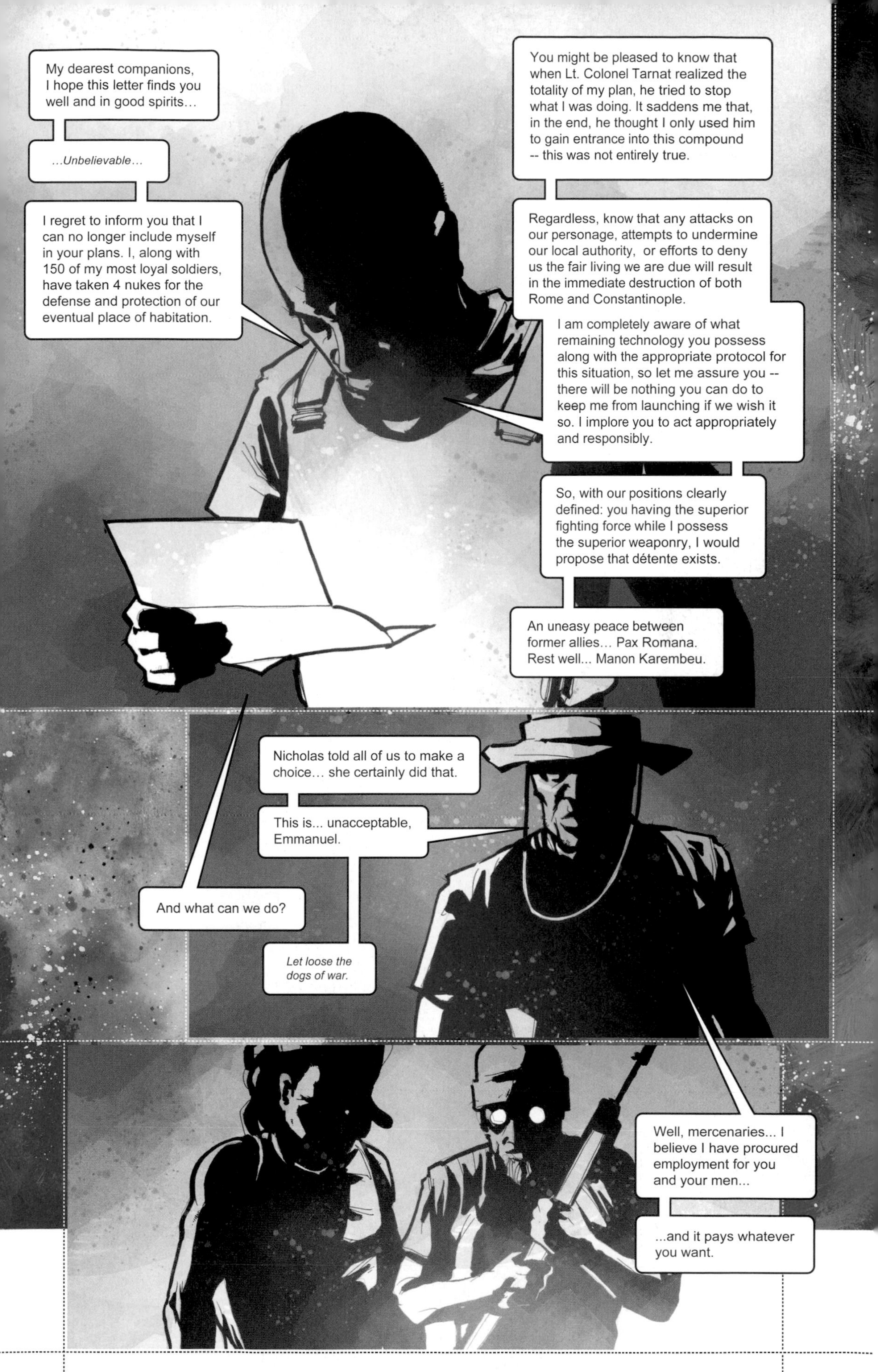

My dearest companions, I hope this letter finds you well and in good spirits…
…Unbelievable…
I regret to inform you that I can no longer include myself in your plans. I, along with 150 of my most loyal soldiers, have taken 4 nukes for the defense and protection of our eventual place of habitation.
You might be pleased to know that when Lt. Colonel Tarnat realized the totality of my plan, he tried to stop what I was doing. It saddens me that, in the end, he thought I only used him to gain entrance into this compound -- this was not entirely true.
Regardless, know that any attacks on our personage, attempts to undermine our local authority, or efforts to deny us the fair living we are due will result in the immediate destruction of both Rome and Constantinople.
I am completely aware of what remaining technology you possess along with the appropriate protocol for this situation, so let me assure you -- there will be nothing you can do to keep me from launching if we wish it so. I implore you to act appropriately and responsibly.
So, with our positions clearly defined: you having the superior fighting force while I possess the superior weaponry, I would propose that détente exists.
An uneasy peace between former allies… Pax Romana. Rest well... Manon Karembeu.
Nicholas told all of us to make a choice… she certainly did that.
This is... unacceptable, Emmanuel.
And what can we do?
Let loose the dogs of war.
Well, mercenaries... I believe I have procured employment for you and your men...
...and it pays whatever you want.

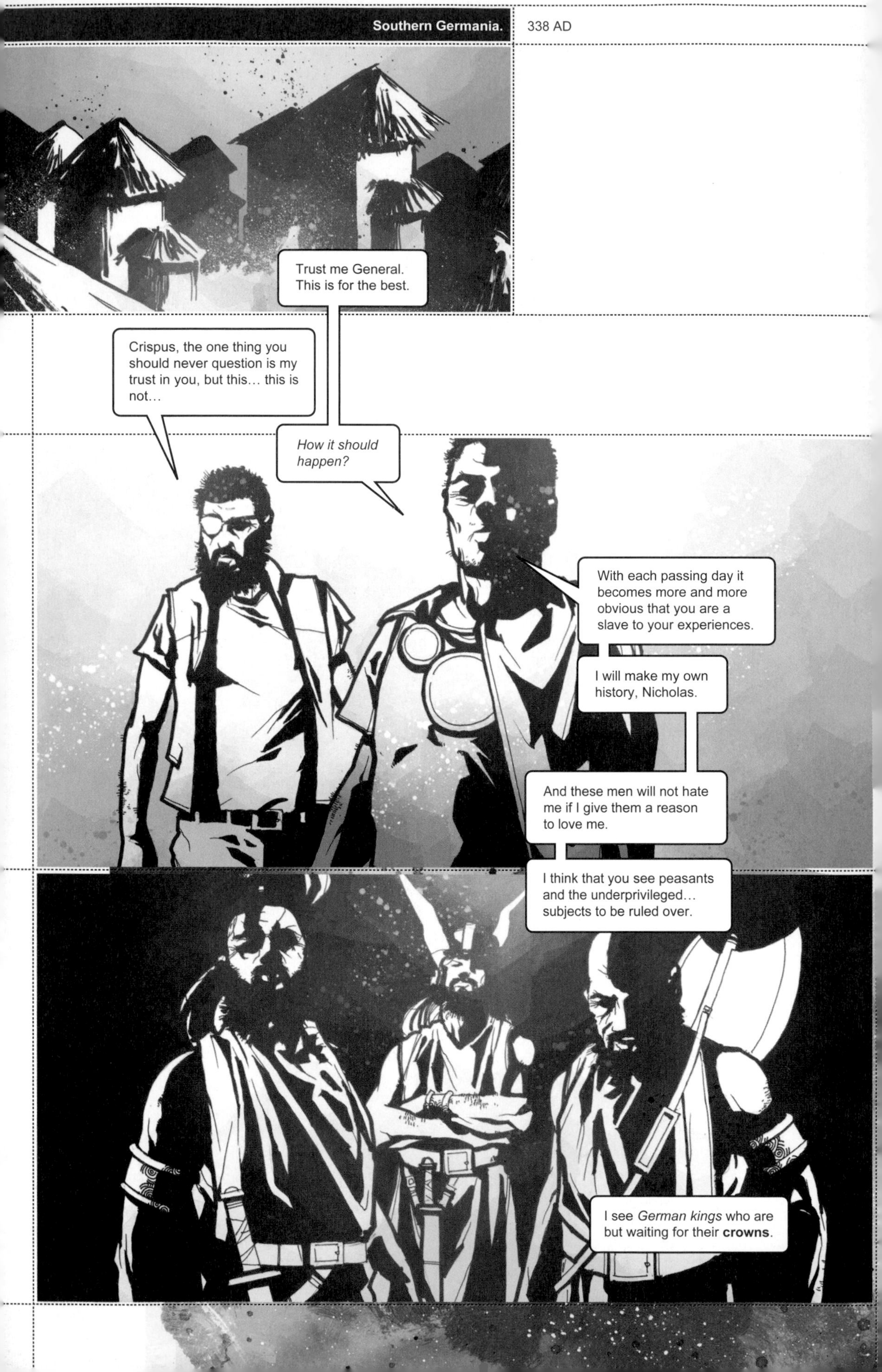
Southern Germania.
338 AD
Trust me General. This is for the best.
Crispus, the one thing you should never question is my trust in you, but this… this is not…
How it should happen?
With each passing day it becomes more and more obvious that you are a slave to your experiences.
I will make my own history, Nicholas.
And these men will not hate me if I give them a reason to love me.
I think that you see peasants and the underprivileged… subjects to be ruled over.
I see *German kings* who are but waiting for their **crowns**.

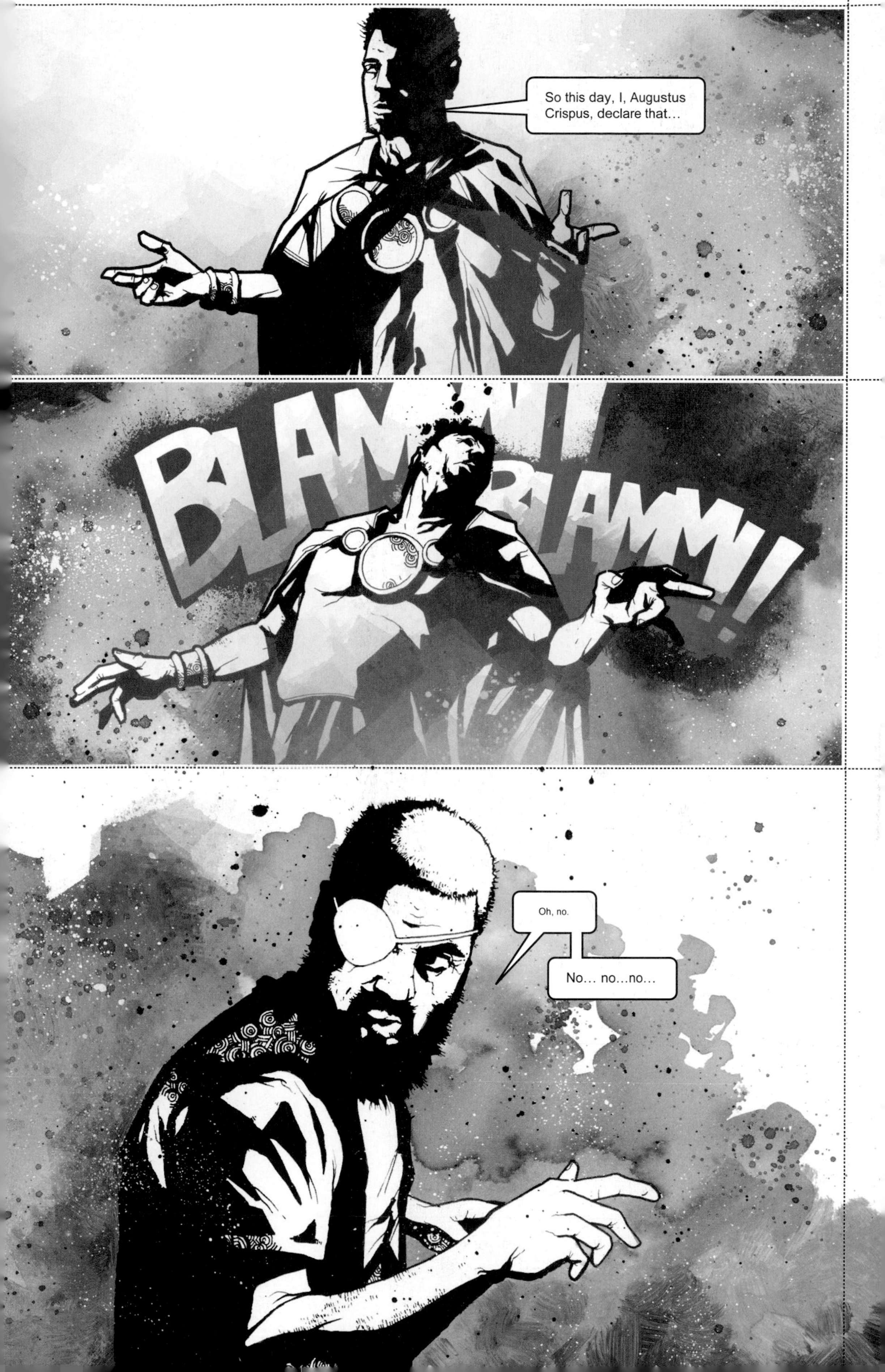
So this day, I, Augustus Crispus, declare that…
BLAM! BLAM!!
Oh, no.
No… no…no…

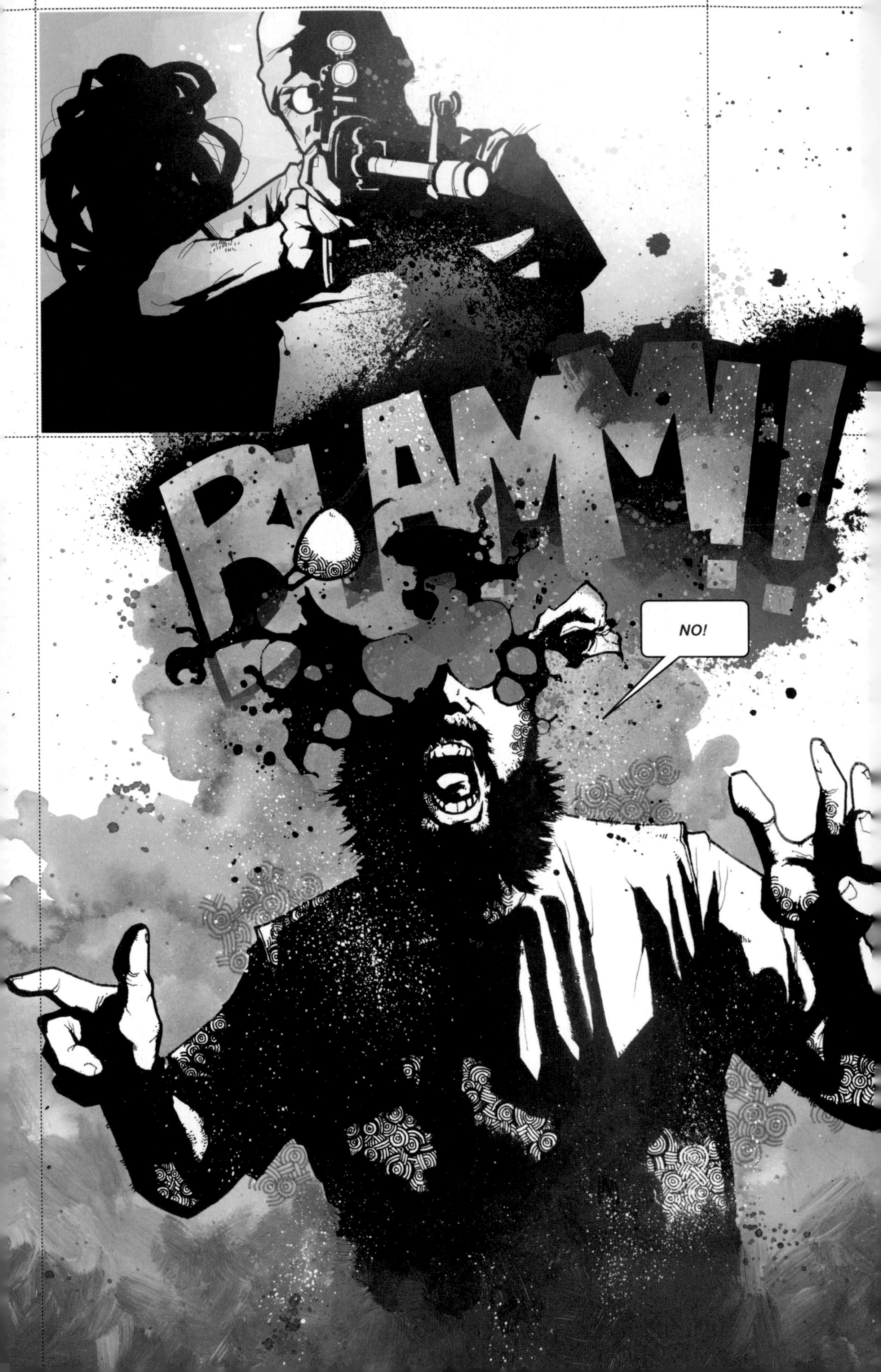
BLAMM!!
NO!

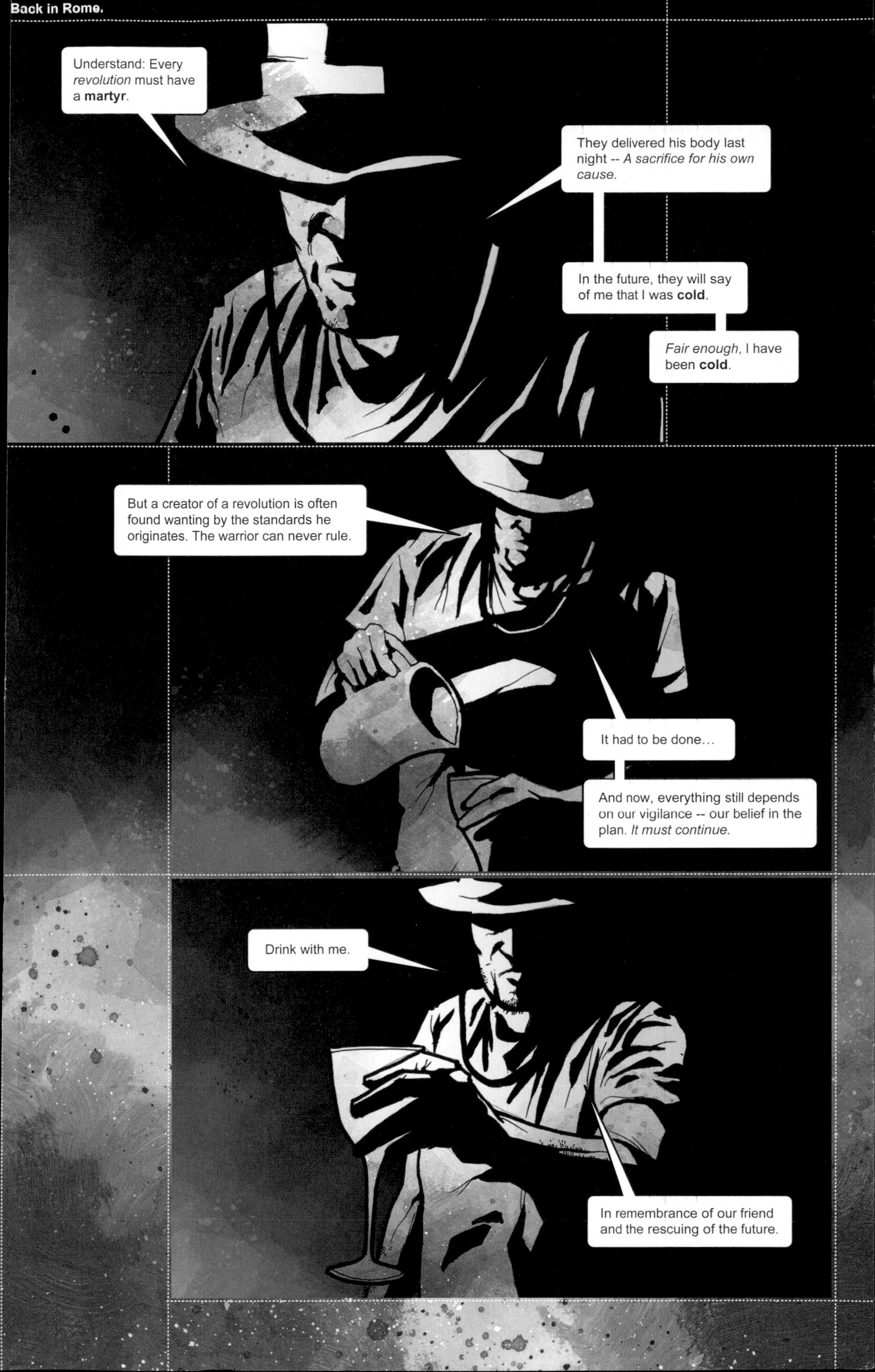

Back in Rome.
Understand: Every *revolution* must have a **martyr**.
They delivered his body last night -- *A sacrifice for his own cause.*
In the future, they will say of me that I was **cold**.
Fair enough, I have been **cold**.
But a creator of a revolution is often found wanting by the standards he originates. The warrior can never rule.
It had to be done…
And now, everything still depends on our vigilance -- our belief in the plan. *It must continue.*
Drink with me.
In remembrance of our friend and the rescuing of the future.

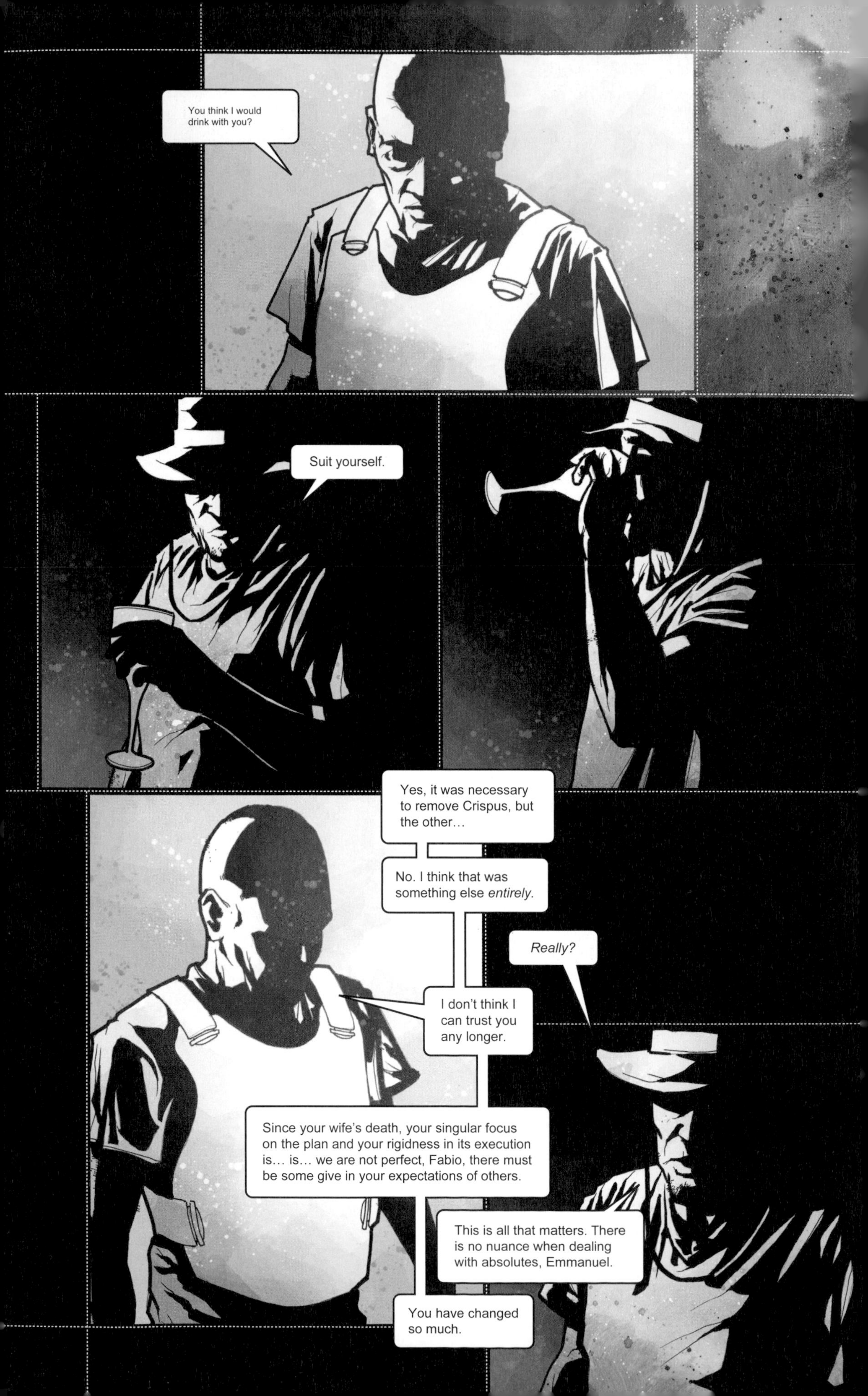
You think I would drink with you?
Suit yourself.
Yes, it was necessary to remove Crispus, but the other…
No. I think that was something else *entirely*.
Really?
I don't think I can trust you any longer.
Since your wife's death, your singular focus on the plan and your rigidness in its execution is… is… we are not perfect, Fabio, there must be some give in your expectations of others.
This is all that matters. There is no nuance when dealing with absolutes, Emmanuel.
You have changed so much.

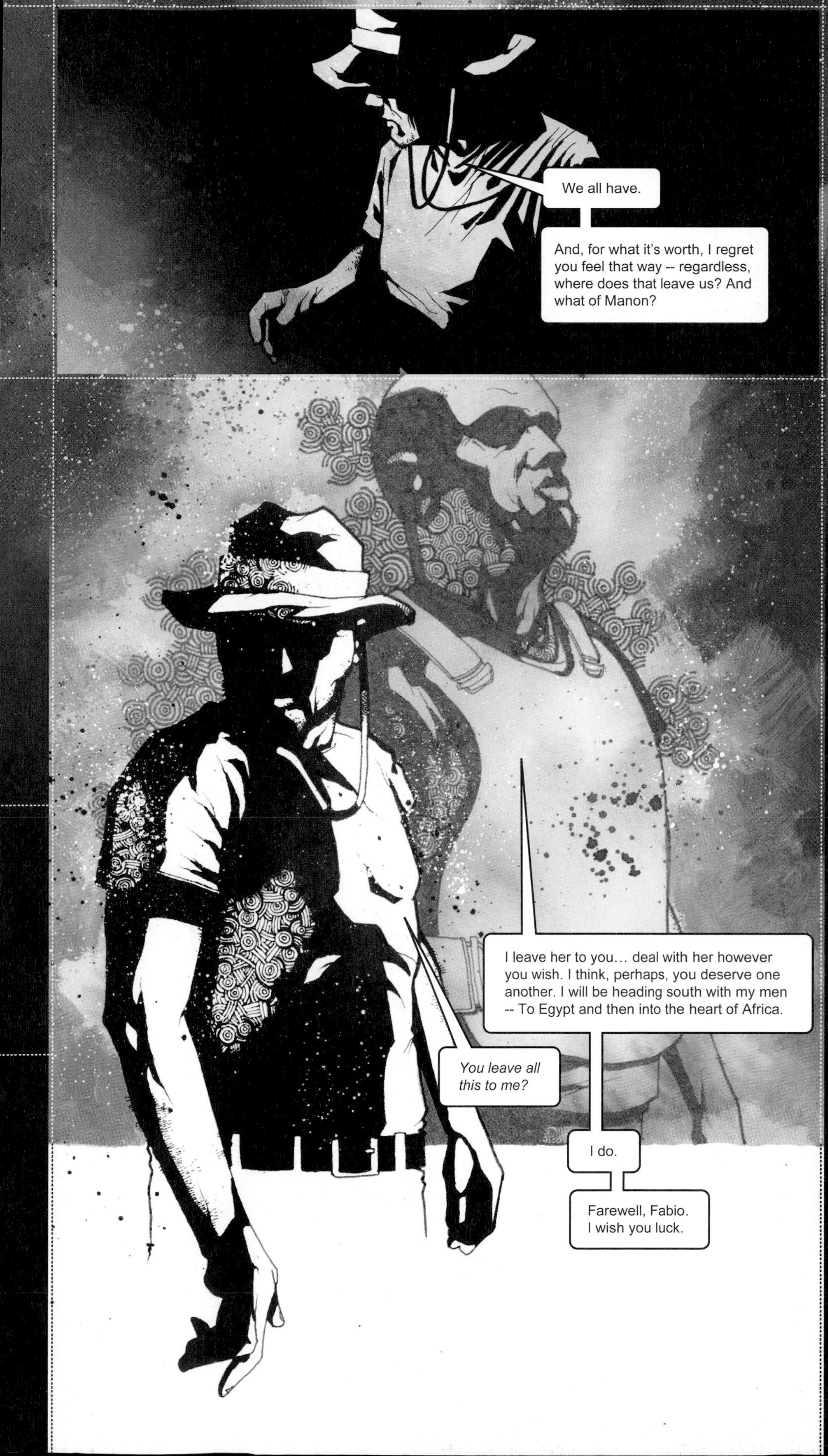
We all have.
And, for what it's worth, I regret you feel that way -- regardless, where does that leave us? And what of Manon?
I leave her to you… deal with her however you wish. I think, perhaps, you deserve one another. I will be heading south with my men -- To Egypt and then into the heart of Africa.
You leave all this to me?
I do.
Farewell, Fabio. I wish you luck.

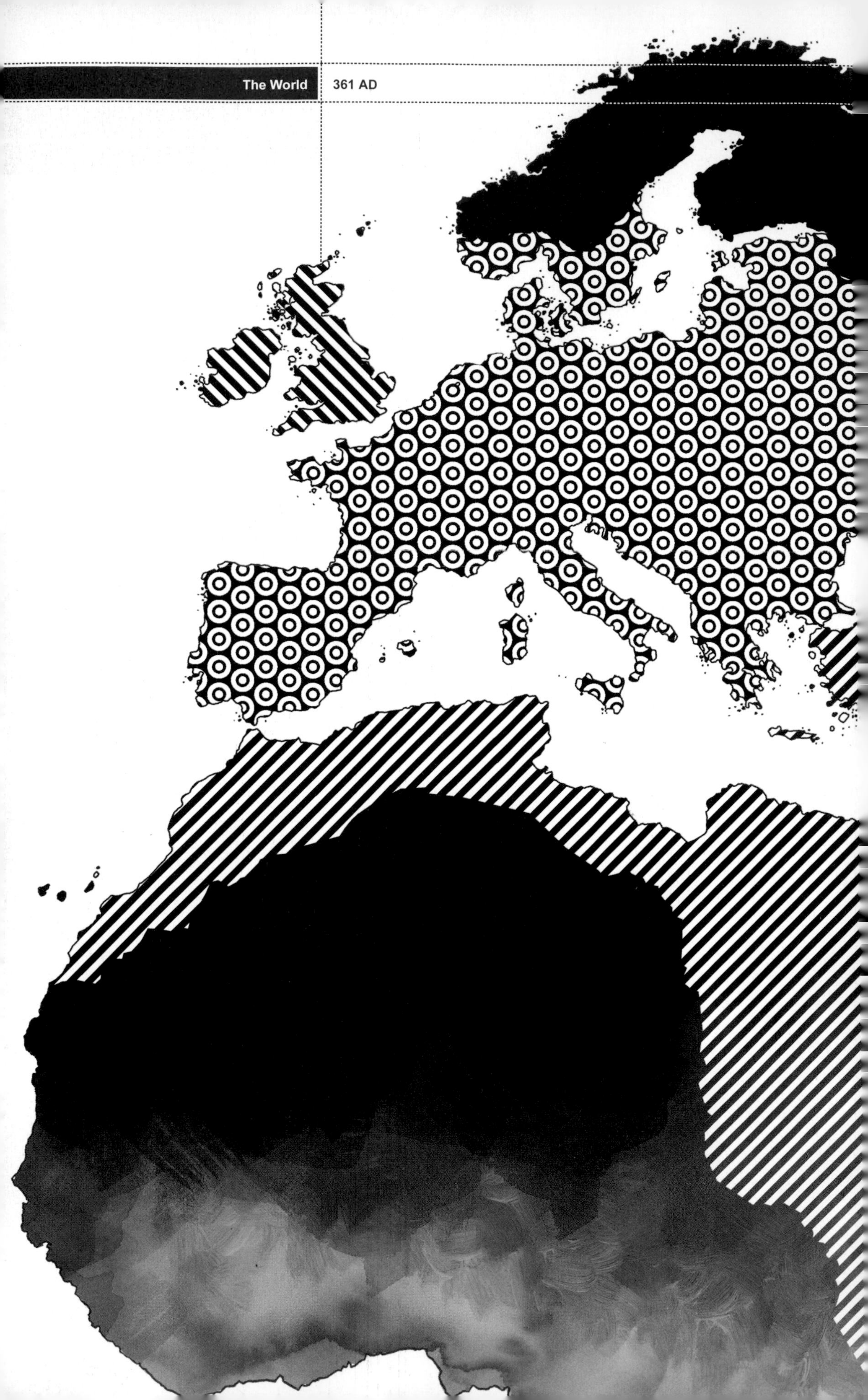

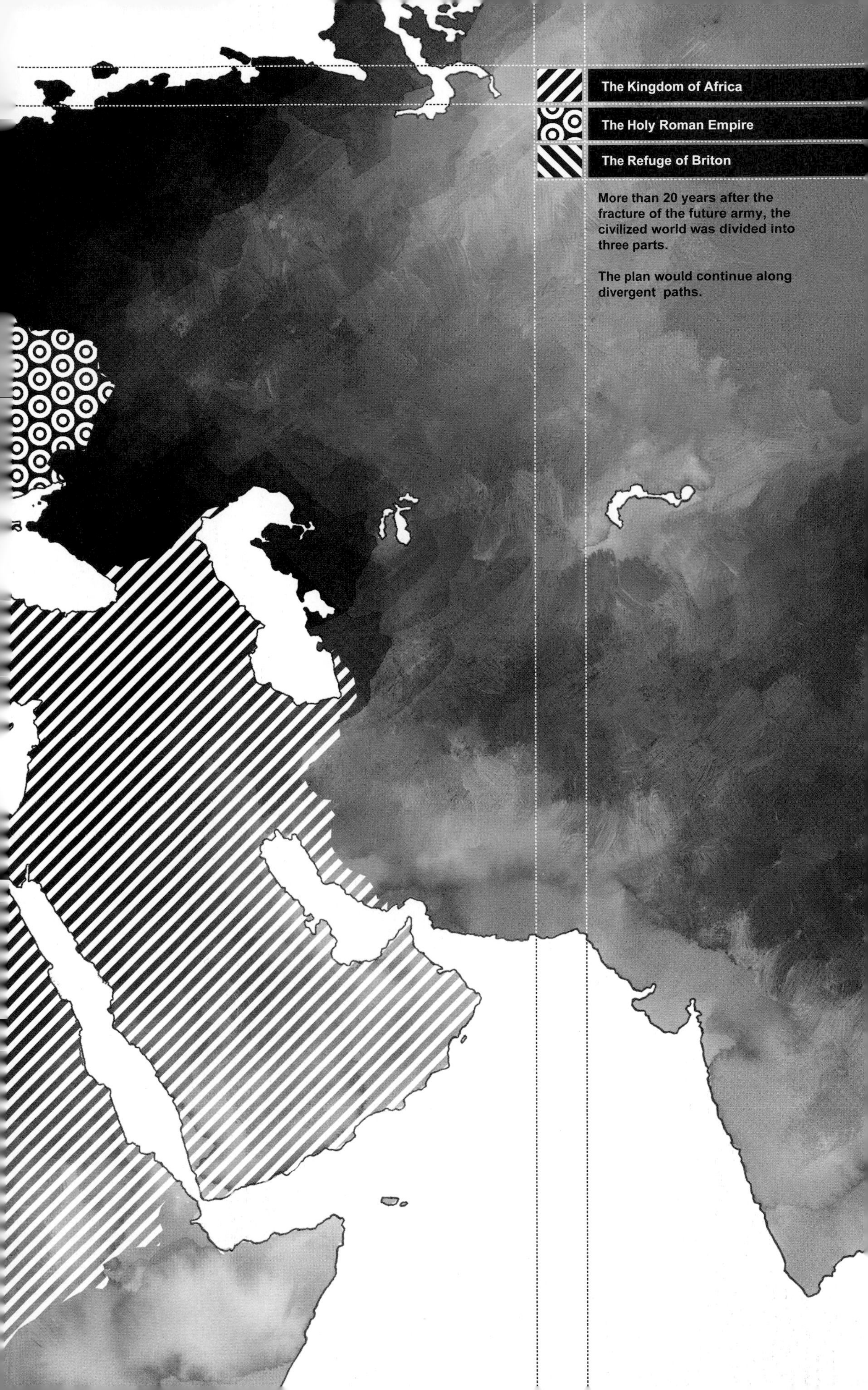
The Kingdom of Africa
The Holy Roman Empire
The Refuge of Briton

More than 20 years after the fracture of the future army, the civilized world was divided into three parts.

The plan would continue along divergent paths.

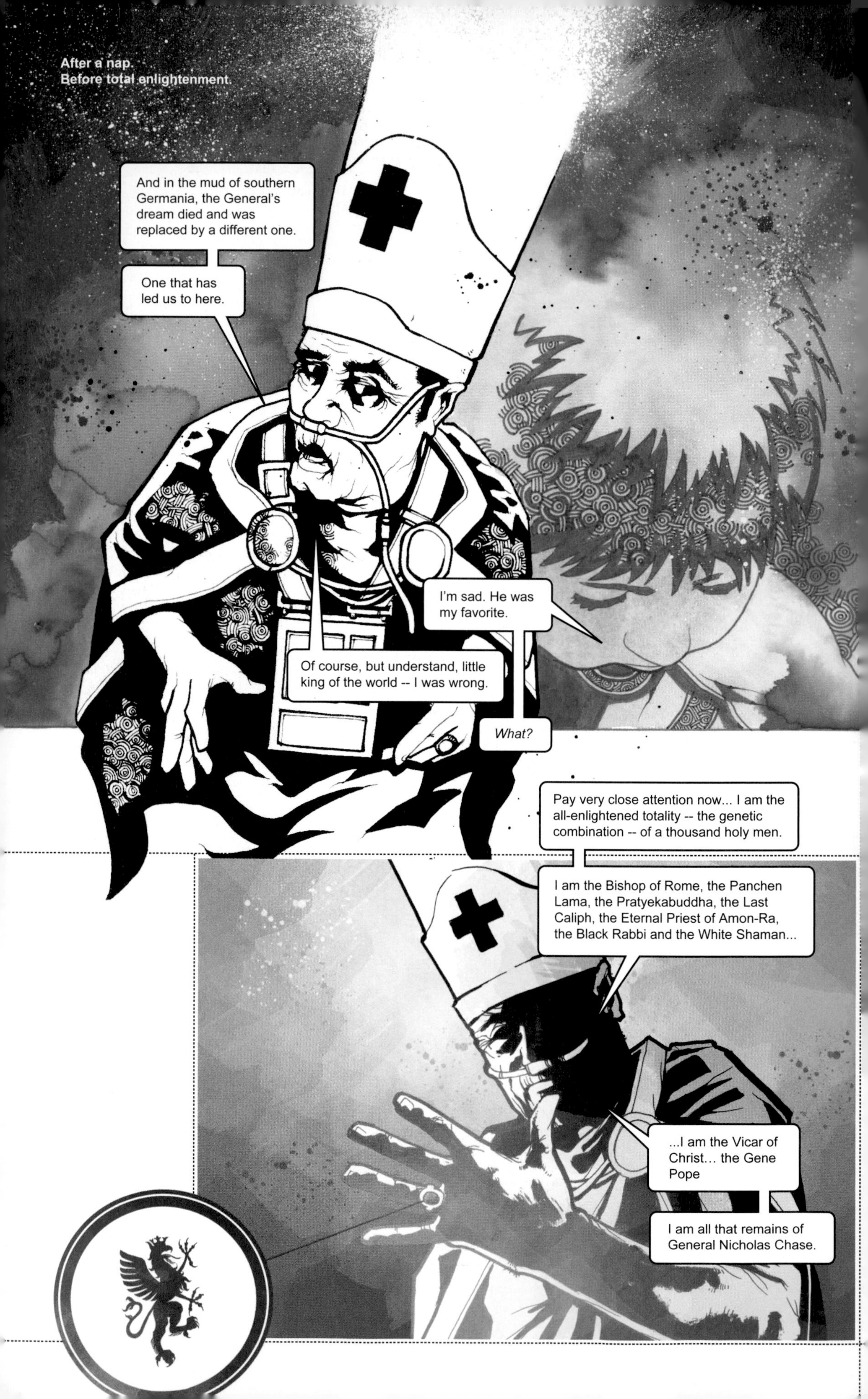
After a nap.
Before total enlightenment.
And in the mud of southern Germania, the General's dream died and was replaced by a different one.
One that has led us to here.
I'm sad. He was my favorite.
Of course, but understand, little king of the world -- I was wrong.
What?
Pay very close attention now... I am the all-enlightened totality -- the genetic combination -- of a thousand holy men.
I am the Bishop of Rome, the Panchen Lama, the Pratyekabuddha, the Last Caliph, the Eternal Priest of Amon-Ra, the Black Rabbi and the White Shaman...
...I am the Vicar of Christ… the Gene Pope
I am all that remains of General Nicholas Chase.

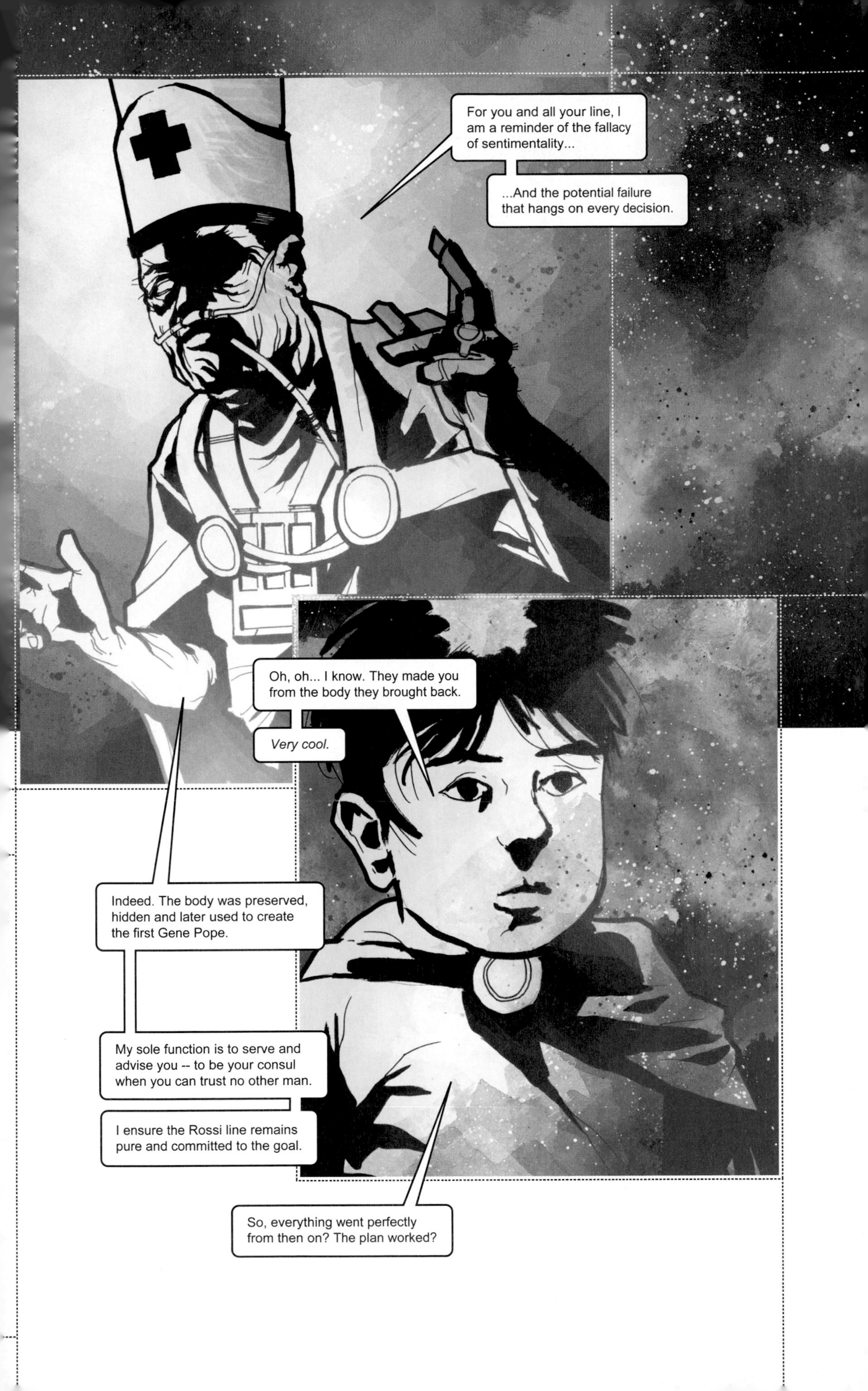
For you and all your line, I am a reminder of the fallacy of sentimentality...
...And the potential failure that hangs on every decision.
Oh, oh... I know. They made you from the body they brought back.
Very cool.
Indeed. The body was preserved, hidden and later used to create the first Gene Pope.
My sole function is to serve and advise you -- to be your consul when you can trust no other man.
I ensure the Rossi line remains pure and committed to the goal.
So, everything went perfectly from then on? The plan worked?

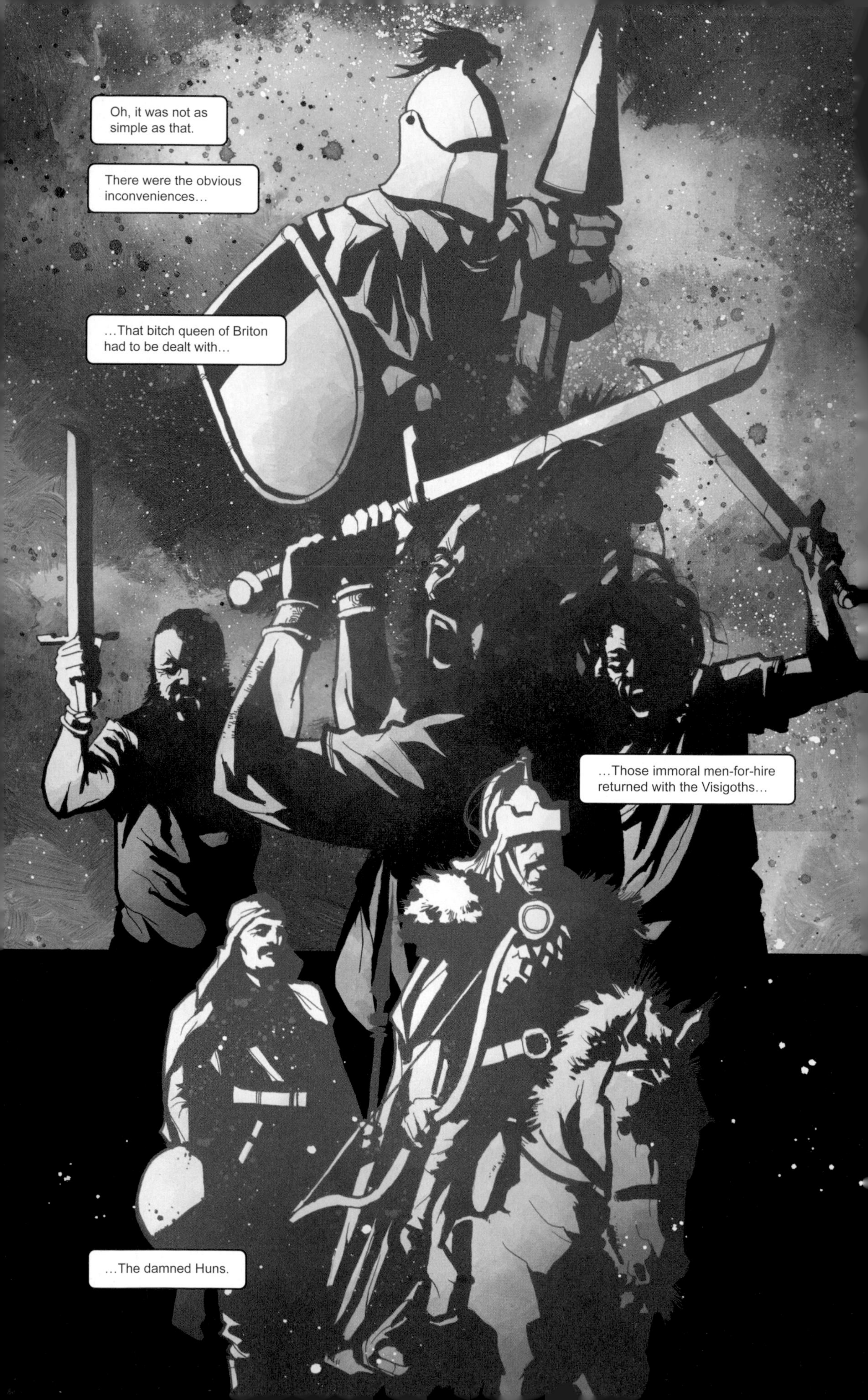
Oh, it was not as simple as that.
There were the obvious inconveniences...
...That bitch queen of Briton had to be dealt with...
...Those immoral men-for-hire returned with the Visigoths...
...The damned Huns.

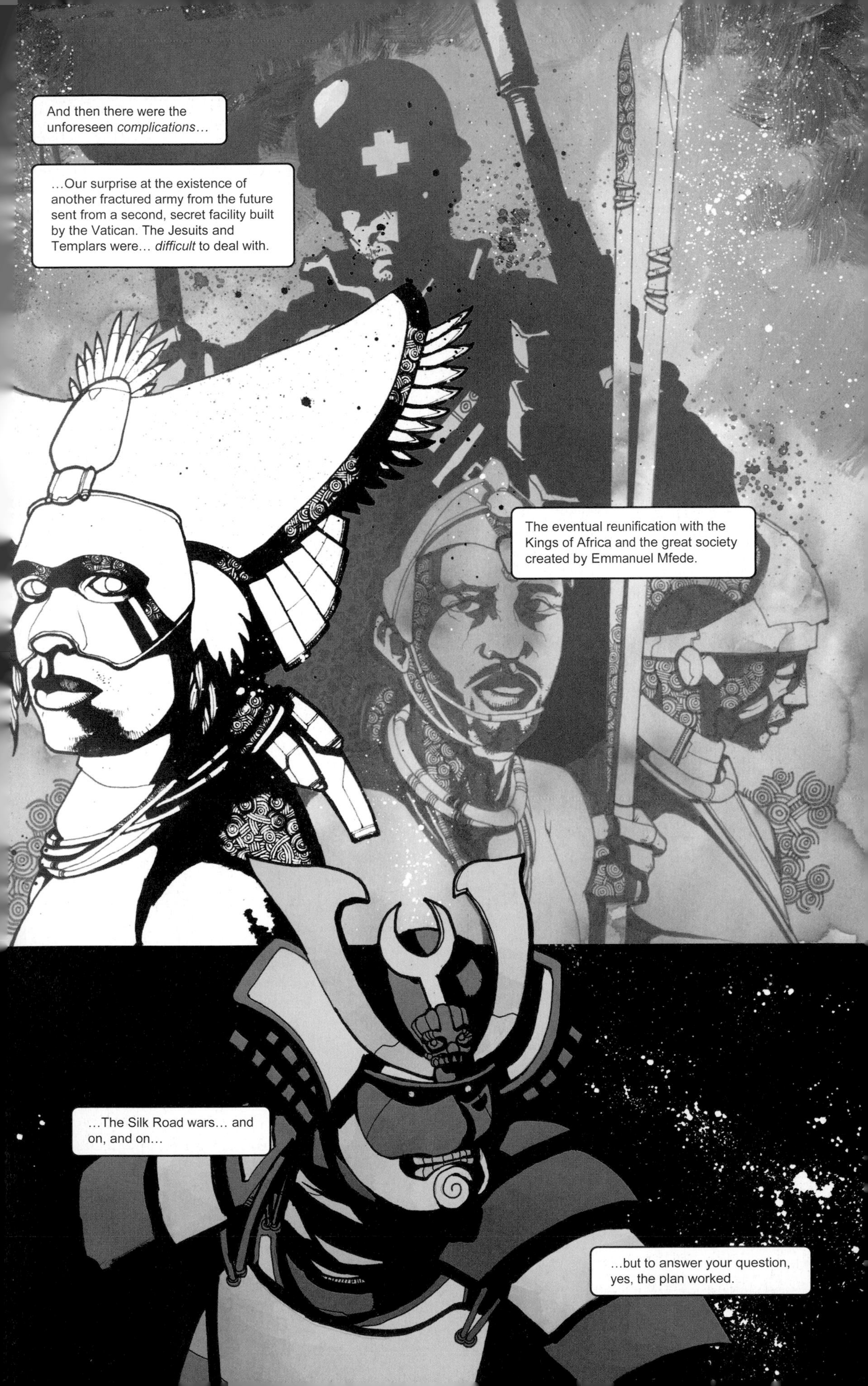
And then there were the unforeseen *complications*…
…Our surprise at the existence of another fractured army from the future sent from a second, secret facility built by the Vatican. The Jesuits and Templars were… *difficult* to deal with.
The eventual reunification with the Kings of Africa and the great society created by Emmanuel Mfede.
…The Silk Road wars… and on, and on…
…but to answer your question, yes, the plan worked.

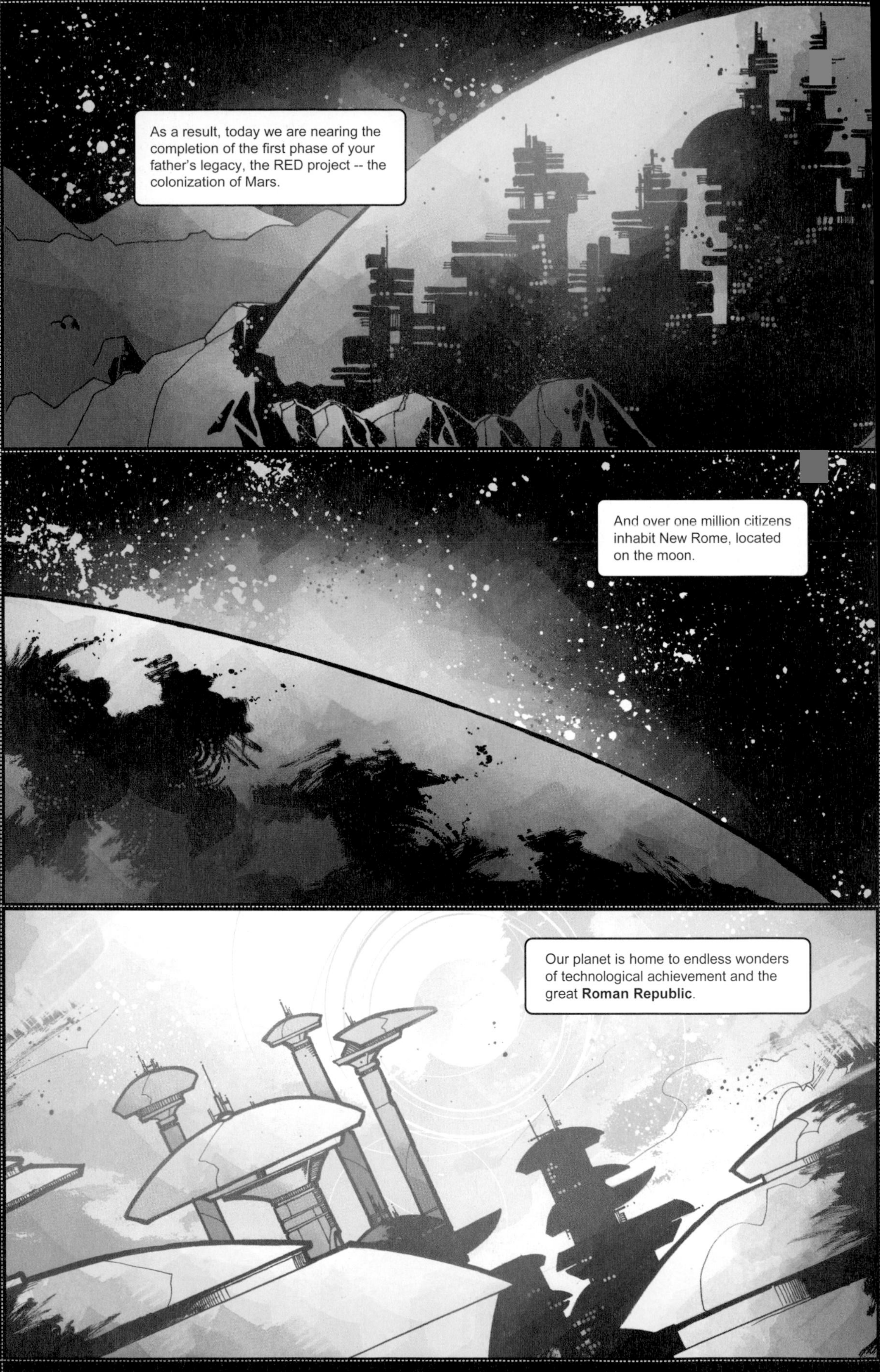
As a result, today we are nearing the completion of the first phase of your father's legacy, the RED project -- the colonization of Mars.
And over one million citizens inhabit New Rome, located on the moon.
Our planet is home to endless wonders of technological achievement and the great **Roman Republic**.

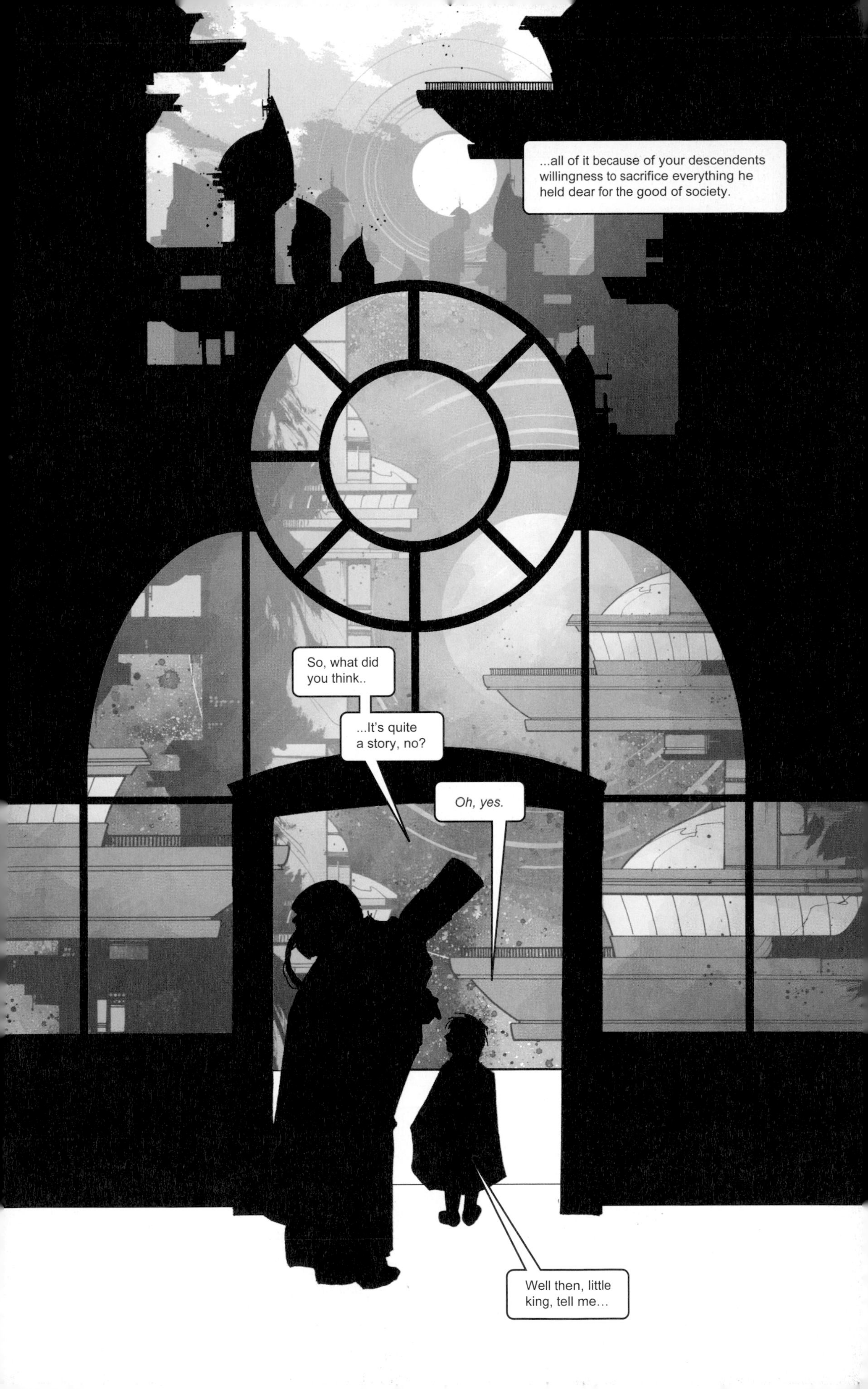
...all of it because of your descendents willingness to sacrifice everything he held dear for the good of society.
So, what did you think..
...It's quite a story, no?
Oh, yes.
Well then, little king, tell me...

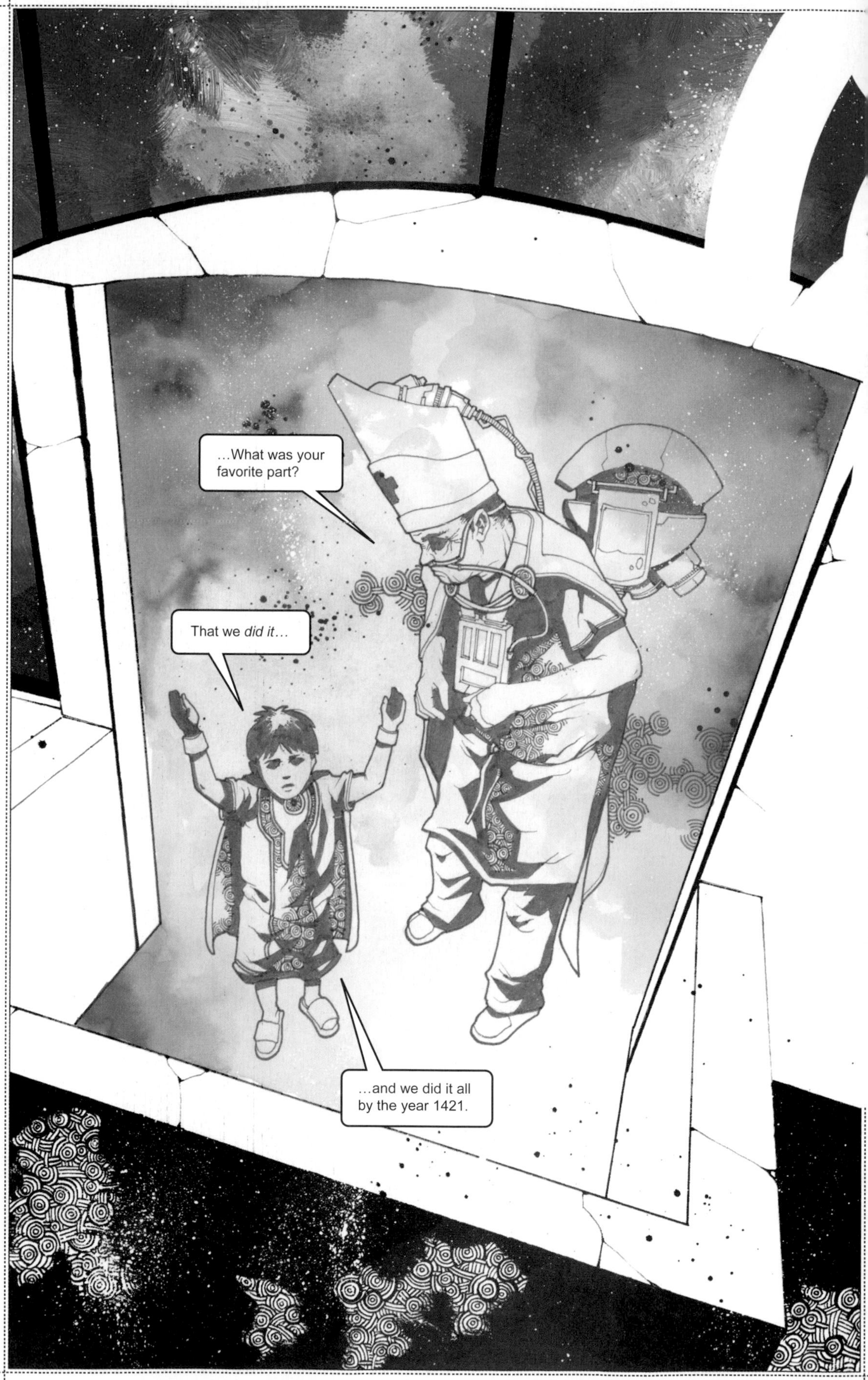
...What was your favorite part?
That we *did it*...
...and we did it all by the year 1421.

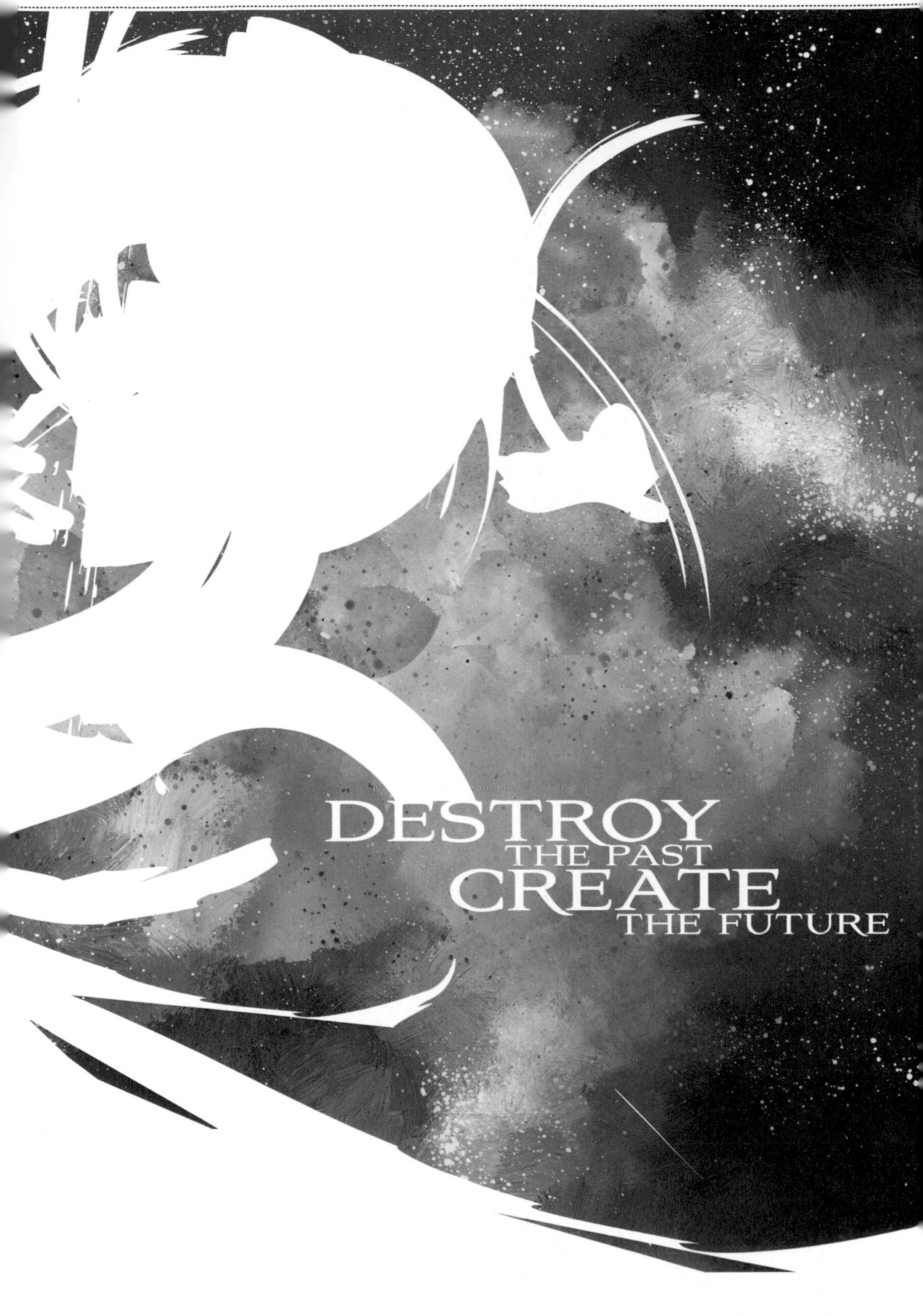
DESTROY
THE PAST
CREATE
THE FUTURE

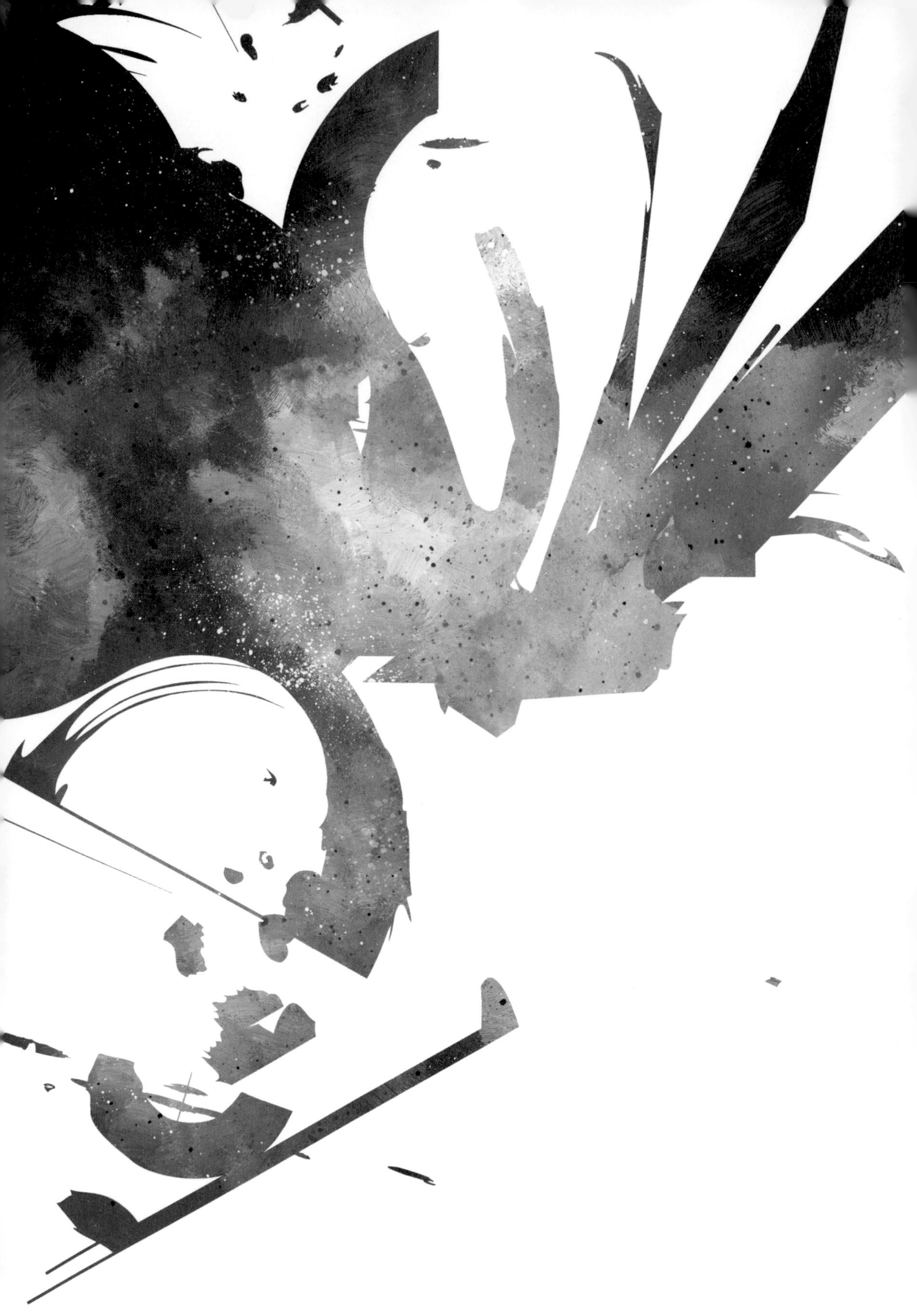

THE SECRET
VATICAN
ARCHIVES

THE HISTORY
OF ALL THINGS

THE KINGDOM OF AFRICA

THE HOLY ROMAN EMPIRE

THE REFUGE OF BRITON

337AD - 1108AD

*A timeline of Holy Rome
from the consolidation to
reestablishment.*

338 AD
The murder of Flavius and
General Nicholas Chase.
The final fracture of the
temporal army. Colonel
Emmanuel Mfede takes
control of Egypt and
establishes the Kingdom
of Africa. Colonel Fabio
Rossi's eldest son
Constantine III crowned
emperor of Holy Rome.

352 AD
Production of
gunpowder begins
in Briton.

378 AD
Lead by temporal
mercenaries, the
Visigoths begin attacks
into Roman territory.

379 AD
Visigoths defeated due to
a short-term alliance
between Holy Rome and
Briton. Failed
assassination attempt by
Queen Manon I leaves
Fabio Rossi a paraplegic.

337 AD
The crowning of Flavius.
The murder of Ulf Tarnat.
Colonel Manon Karembeu
steals four nuclear
weapons and establishes
the Refuge of Briton.

350 AD
The Kingdom army
crushes the Ethiopian
forces of King Ezana.
Full African
consolidation begins.

361 AD
African consolidation
completed.

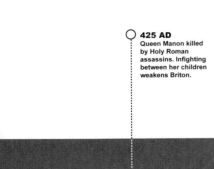

425 AD
Queen Manon killed
by Holy Roman
assassins. Infighting
between her children
weakens Briton.

400 AD
Secret envoys are
sent by Constantine
III to Teotihuacan
and Chang'an, in the
kingdom of Jin.

447 AD
Invading 400,000-strong
Hun army led by Attila
destroyed with a
nuclear weapon.

449 AD
Using the preserved
DNA of Nicholas
Chase, Fabio Rossi
oversees the creation
of the first and
second generation
Gene Popes.

Series ONE	GENE POPE	5
Series TWO	GENE POPE	12
Series THREE	GENE POPE	19
Series FOUR	GENE POPE	8
Series FIVE	GENE POPE	1
Series SIX	GENE POPE	17
Series SEVEN	GENE POPE	21

The first two series of Gene Popes were basic models combining a minimal number of genetic imprints. As successive models increased in complexity and the number of imprints grew exponentially, a product failure was imminent. That failure occurred with the Series-5 models and as a result only one of that model was ever created.

The total number of each model is listed above.

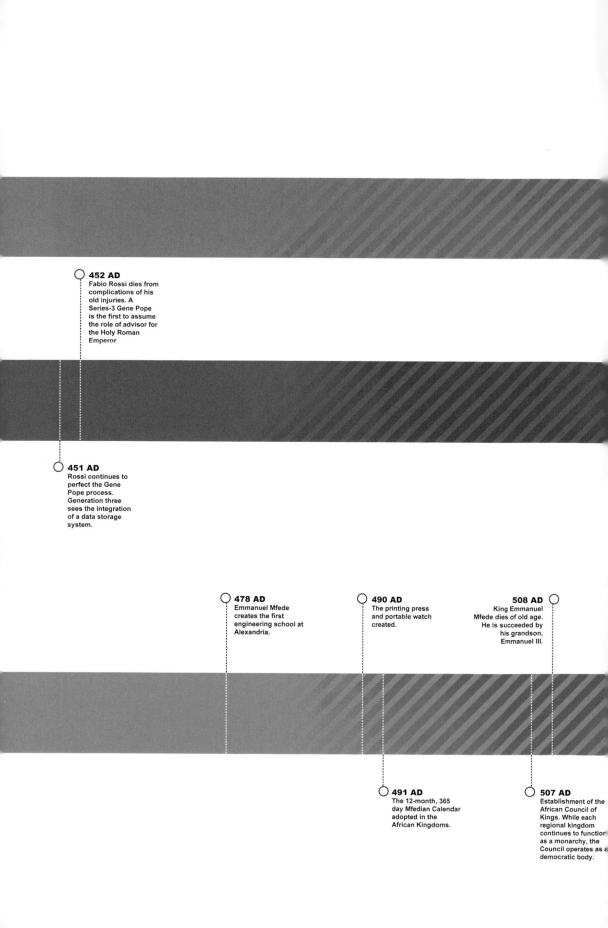

452 AD
Fabio Rossi dies from complications of his old injuries. A Series-3 Gene Pope is the first to assume the role of advisor for the Holy Roman Emperor

451 AD
Rossi continues to perfect the Gene Pope process. Generation three sees the integration of a data storage system.

478 AD
Emmanuel Mfede creates the first engineering school at Alexandria.

490 AD
The printing press and portable watch created.

508 AD
King Emmanuel Mfede dies of old age. He is succeeded by his grandson, Emmanuel III.

491 AD
The 12-month, 365 day Mfedian Calendar adopted in the African Kingdoms.

507 AD
Establishment of the African Council of Kings. While each regional kingdom continues to function as a monarchy, the Council operates as a democratic body.

572 AD
The Civil War of
Briton begins.

578 AD
A second temporal
army arrives in
ancient times.
Launched at the
same time as the
original mission
under Bishop Pelle
and General Chase,
this group was sent
to a later date – An
insurance policy to
ensure the will of the
church was enacted.

577 AD
Ulf II emerges as King
of Briton and begins
a reunification
campaign with the
intent of rejoining
Holy Rome.

579 AD
The second temporal
army, who now called
themselves Templars,
murdered Ulf II and
took control of Briton.

520 AD
Operating under
normalized
diplomatic status in
Alexandria, the Gene
Pope helps to reignite
the pagan worship of
Egyptian mythology.
Declares himself the
Eternal Priest of
Amon-Ra.

540 AD
Sewage processing,
water treatment and
citywide plumbing
successfully
implemented in both
Constantinople and
Rome.

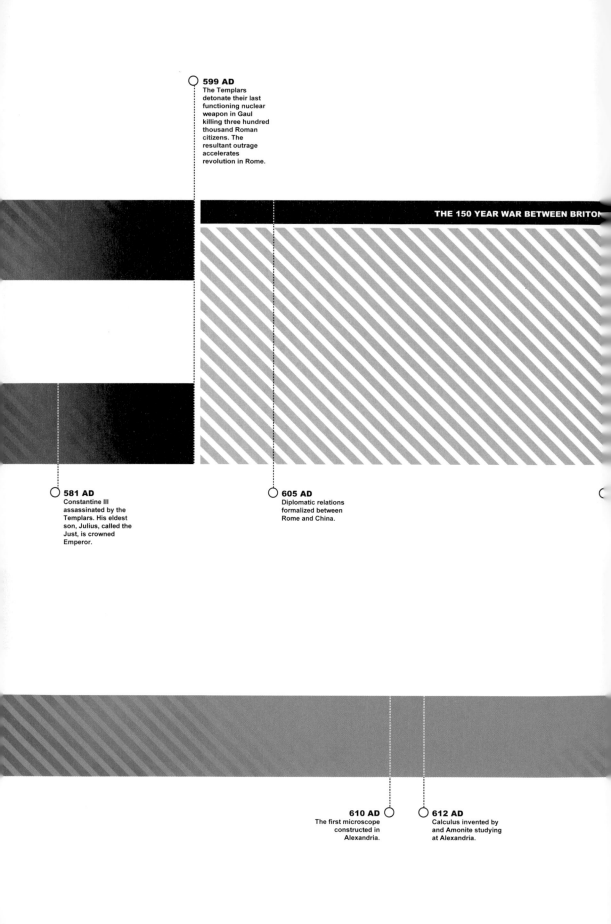

599 AD
The Templars
detonate their last
functioning nuclear
weapon in Gaul
killing three hundred
thousand Roman
citizens. The
resultant outrage
accelerates
revolution in Rome.

THE 150 YEAR WAR BETWEEN BRITO

581 AD
Constantine III
assassinated by the
Templars. His eldest
son, Julius, called the
Just, is crowned
Emperor.

605 AD
Diplomatic relations
formalized between
Rome and China.

610 AD
The first microscope
constructed in
Alexandria.

612 AD
Calculus invented by
and Amonite studying
at Alexandria.

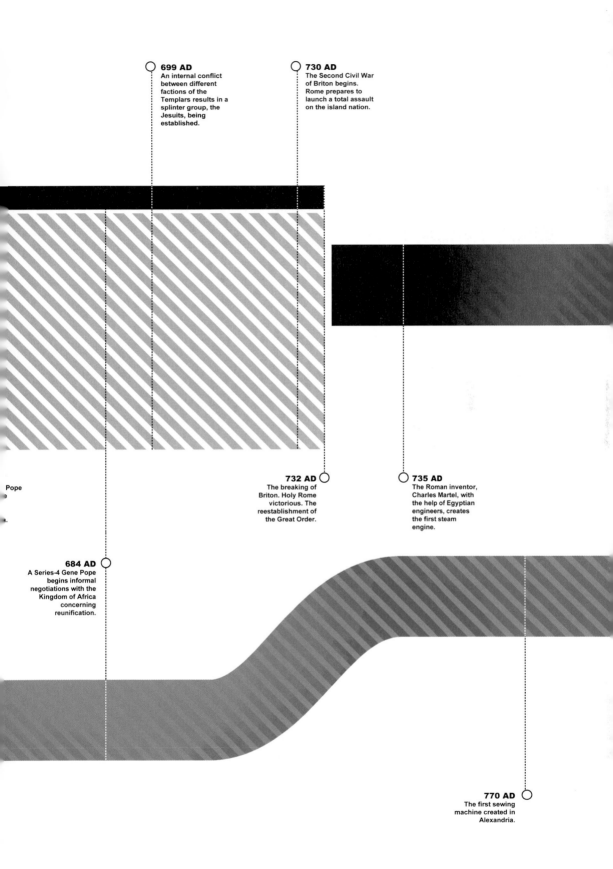

699 AD
An internal conflict between different factions of the Templars results in a splinter group, the Jesuits, being established.

730 AD
The Second Civil War of Briton begins. Rome prepares to launch a total assault on the island nation.

Pope
e

.

732 AD
The breaking of Briton. Holy Rome victorious. The reestablishment of the Great Order.

735 AD
The Roman inventor, Charles Martel, with the help of Egyptian engineers, creates the first steam engine.

684 AD
A Series-4 Gene Pope begins informal negotiations with the Kingdom of Africa concerning reunification.

770 AD
The first sewing machine created in Alexandria.

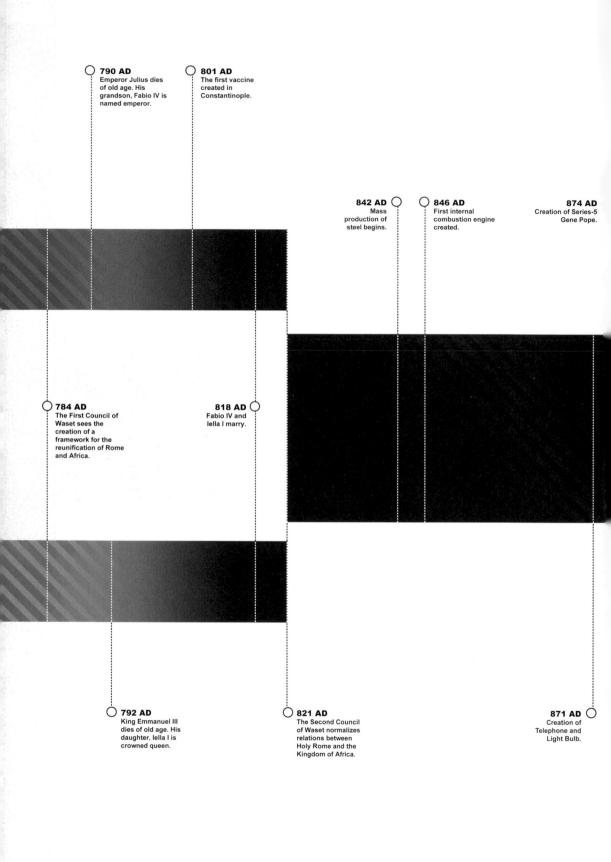

790 AD
Emperor Julius dies of old age. His grandson, Fabio IV is named emperor.

801 AD
The first vaccine created in Constantinople.

842 AD
Mass production of steel begins.

846 AD
First internal combustion engine created.

874 AD
Creation of Series-5 Gene Pope.

784 AD
The First Council of Waset sees the creation of a framework for the reunification of Rome and Africa.

818 AD
Fabio IV and Iella I marry.

792 AD
King Emmanuel III dies of old age. His daughter, Iella I is crowned queen.

821 AD
The Second Council of Waset normalizes relations between Holy Rome and the Kingdom of Africa.

871 AD
Creation of Telephone and Light Bulb.

913 AD
Constans the
Apostate falls under
the tutelage of the
Gene Pope.

Together they plan to
take control of Holy
Rome.

1014 AD
Assassination
attempt by
Constans the
Apostate on
Constantine VI
fails.

1105 AD
Reestablishment
of Democratic Rome.

Creation of Series-6
Gene Popes.

954 AD
The Great Schism.

Fabio IV and Iella I
are both murdered.

Constans murders
all his siblings
except Constantine
VI and takes
control.

Constantine VI
escapes to Africa.

982 AD
Constantine VI
establishes a Roman
government in exile.

1095 AD
The assassination
of Constans the
Apostate.

Constantine VI
regains control of
Holy Rome.

Production of
Gene Popes is
halted.

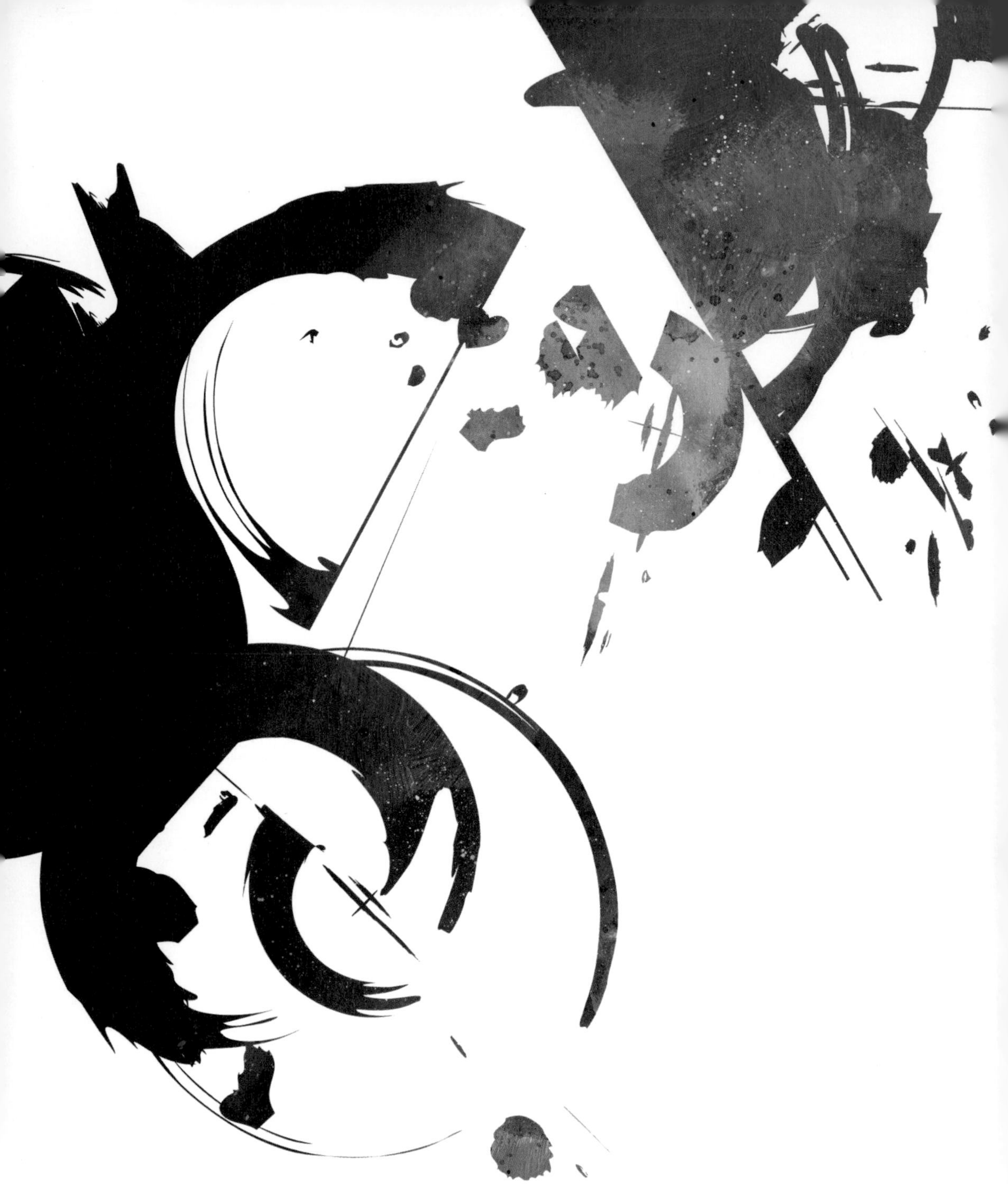

Jonathan Hickman is the visionary talent behind such works as the Eisner-nominated **NIGHTLY NEWS**, **TRANSHUMAN** and **RED MASS FOR MARS**. He also plies his trade at MARVEL working on books like **FANTASTIC FOUR** and **SECRET WARRIORS**.

His twin brother, Marc, writes literary reviews for the Des Moines Register and thinks my being compared to Alan Moore is the craziest thing he's ever heard. Marc, it's time to stop calling the house, asking for Mr. Moore's ballsack, laughing hysterically, and then hanging up. **Seriously.** *You're creeping out the kids.*

Jonathan lives in South Carolina surrounded by immediate family and in-laws, which he plans on leaving unless they start showering him with the love and affection he deserves.

This includes his wife.

You can visit his website: *www.pronea.com*, or email him at: *jonathan@pronea.com*.